Journey
to the Center
of the Theater

JOURNEY TO THE CENTER OF THE THEATER

by Walter Kerr

Alfred A. Knopf   *New York*   1979

THIS IS A BORZOI BOOK
PUBLISHED BY ALFRED A. KNOPF, INC.

Library of Congress Cataloging in Publication Data

Kerr, Walter [Date]   Journey to the center of the theater.

Includes index.
1. Theater—New York (City)—Reviews.   I. Title.
PN2277.N5K38   1979   792.9   78-20545
ISBN : 0-394-50360-0

Manufactured in the United States of America

FIRST EDITION

----

for my brother

Contents

Contents

Contents

Introduction:
Stages of a Journey

We may have to rewrite the parable. The Prodigal Son comes home bringing the fatted calf with him.

That is what happened to the Broadway theater during the years 1971–78. More specifically, that is the way the vast audience that had once inhabited Broadway behaved: it wandered away from what had always been home, it found what it had been looking for, and it retraced its footsteps bringing its new treasure with it.

Because the pieces that make up this book, all of which originally appeared in *The New York Times,* do not chart the strange journey chronologically but simply reflect sights along the way, it may be best to provide a quick outline of the grand tour:

The departure. In September of 1971 I went to the first opening of the Broadway season. I stood outside a theater on Forty-fifth Street, looked left toward Broadway itself and right toward Eighth Avenue, and said to myself, unoriginally but out loud, "My God, it's a ghost town." Here was the one-time center of the American theatrical world. And there was no one on the street.

There were seven playhouses on that single block between Broadway and Eighth. A few of them still had leftover entertainments—hanging on, but barely—from the year before. The block itself was sandwiched between two main arteries that ought to have had pedestrian traffic on them, turning in toward the still-lighted marquees. It was not exactly a cowpath, as Alexander Woollcott had once testily reminded Edna Ferber when she'd blamed traffic for her late appearance at a play in which he was performing.

But it might as well have been a cowpath now. Not only was the street deserted, the evening air was empty of promise. No sense that this was a beginning of things, with a buzz and a rush to follow in a few weeks' or a few months' time. The stillness seemed permanent, without any sort of underground creative rumbling that promised shortly to force its fresh impulse through cracks in the pavement. You could put your ear to the ground and hear only the subway.

As a creative center, as *the* producing center at which the writing, rehearsing, and performing that sustained the American theater were done, Broadway had virtually ceased to exist. Its energies were spent, a requiescat was in order. The official requiescat was delivered by a representative of the Shuberts, the organization that controls the largest number of midtown New York theaters, at a despairing Congress of the Theater at Princeton a year or so later. The Shuberts' spokesman, who had been counting empty seats and then empty playhouses all along, announced that he saw no future in the commercial theater as we had known it. Its audience had fled.

The search. It was commonly supposed at the time that the mass audience for theater—a cross section of young and old, intellectuals and expense-account revelers, adventurers and traditionalists—had abandoned its former home for good, drawn away by the lure of films or the laziness of television. Theater as a medium had outlived its attractiveness, deserved the desertion that would probably prove final.

As we now know—thanks to the ready help of hindsight—that wasn't the way of it. The audience didn't vanish into the woodwork, never to be pried loose again. It did not in the least lose its taste for theater. What happened was that the great cross section came apart, the mass audience splintered into its component parts, and each of the newly separated fragments went in search of its own theater, its own impulse. So far from abandoning theater, each fragmented group was determined to *create* theater, to relocate its heartbeat, on its own. In short order we had not one but eight or ten Prodigal Sons, all exhibiting a most exemplary industry.

The young, still unselfconsciously obeying the injunction to "do your own thing," produced the theater of *Your Own Thing, Hair, Godspell, Grease.* The adventurous looked into The Living Theater, The Open Theater, The Performing Garage, seeking rebirth in ritual, in mime, in improvisation. The classicists hurried to any off-Broadway arena that would offer them the riches Broadway had always neglected: perhaps *Iphigenia in Aulis* would yield an ancient secret that could be profitably used. Meantime, musical buffs wondered if the legendary Kern and Gershwin scores of sixty years ago were worth reinvestigating, and hied themselves deep into the countryside—at the Goodspeed Opera House in Connecticut—to find out.

A regional audience developed, one that didn't mind giving up visits to a tired New York so long as it could erect, and draw energy from, a Long Wharf in its own New Haven, an Arena Stage in Washington, a Mark Taper in Los Angeles. Institutional theaters—like Joseph Papp's Public or an off-off-Broadway workshop called the Manhattan Theater Club—catered to an audience that still liked to have a home to go to, a *center* of sorts: variety in a single building seemed a good way to test and taste the possible future.

With so much impromptu activity stirring on all sides, one altogether new theater, one truly new audience, leapt into being. Plays written and performed by blacks, hitherto unheard of, brought thousands of black patrons into the professional theater for the first time. And there was even an audience fragment left over—left behind, if you will—for Broadway; if most Broadway playgoers had scattered to the productive winds, enough were on hand to keep a new Neil Simon comedy or a revival of *No, No, Nanette* running.

Each of the splinters that had abandoned Broadway did so in high hope of finding or making something better, of putting a spade to drama's roots or a finger to its pulse. Though there were dropouts and even disasters along the way, each made real discoveries.

The return. Suddenly, in the summer of '74, Broadway box offices took in one million dollars more than they had the previous year. In the *summer*? Here, if ever, are the dog days, the doldrums, with no new shows opening, no rave reviews to spur attendance, no new stars to attract fans, nothing. Nonetheless, a surprising number of people had unexpectedly decided they wanted to see a show. Was something afoot?

It was. It stayed afoot into the season that followed. By December, unbelievably, there was talk of a theater shortage. The following summer grosses jumped another million. After that the arithmetic went crazy; each succeeding season set a new record. In the spring of 1978 *Variety* announced that box-office treasurers had "wrapped" more money than in any of the eleven preceding years. One hundred and forty million dollars, as it happened.

The audience had come back. Precisely what prompted it—at this odd moment—to turn around and come together again on Forty-fifth Street must remain as mysterious to us as the behavior of termites, of which more in a moment. Economics had something to do with it. Experimental houses have never been able to support themselves unaided; and subsidies, unequally apportioned to begin with, could not go on forever. A surprising alternative had presented itself, however. For instance, Joseph Papp had discovered that he could move the best work developed at the Public—*That Championship Season, For Colored Girls, A Chorus Line*—out of the smallish houses in which they'd been born and into the larger houses of Broadway, profitably. Indeed, in each instance the profit was double. Broadway was given a new hit to spell out in light bulbs above the marquee, improving the looks of the night sky; and a percentage of the new money earned was funneled directly back downtown to help the seedbed with its next crop. Sweet.

But I don't think any motive is exclusively economic. There was another: pride. Pride of discovery, pride of accomplishment. If hundreds of thousands of people were now hurrying into midtown to see what the Public had wrought, wouldn't it be as interested in what the Long Wharf, the Manhattan Theater Club, the Goodspeed, the Hudson Guild Theater, or a half-dozen others had been brewing? In a trice—if you don't mind calling two or three years a trice—each of these groups, and others still, had arrived bag and baggage on Broadway, toting an *Annie* from Goodspeed and an *Ain't Misbehavin'* from the Manhattan Theater Club, winning a Pulitzer Prize with the Long Wharf's *Shadow Box* and a Critics Circle prize with the Hudson Guild Theater's *Da*, grinning broadly while *Grease*—transported uptown from Second Avenue— threatened to occupy its new Broadway fortress forever.

The audience hadn't come back to see what Broadway was doing, it had come back to show Broadway what *it* had been doing during the years of the diaspora. It had come back to display its trophies and, in its exuberance, it transformed Broadway into a trophy case. I have just run my finger down the alphabetical theater listings in the daily newspaper, counting. There are, as I write, twenty-seven entertainments on the boards, all doing well. Only seven of the lot were created on and directly for Broadway. If we set aside two revivals and one British importation, we're left with seventeen productions—far and away the lion's share—acquired in the course of the audience's journeyings, and brought home alive.

The return of the audience with so much loot has radically altered Broadway's character, perhaps permanently. Broadway has not recovered its full creative powers, it is no longer the country's producing center. It has instead now become the country's exhibition center, a merry fair, a bazaar, a meeting place in which all comers can show off their choicest wares and then drop in to see what other people's look like.

It is this last point that interests me most—the reassembly in a single spot that breeds interchange. Happy as I am that Broadway is rich once more, delighted as I am to see the midtown cross streets lighted up like Christmas trees, I am most encouraged by the thought that many audiences are fusing into a single audience again. Why? For all our good luck, we're not awash in masterpieces yet. We want them, still need them. And if, by any stretch of the imagination, we behave in the least like termites, we may just possibly get them out of the bustling reunion.

This termite business comes to me from a small book of charmingly provocative essays, Lewis Thomas's *Lives of a Cell*. I pass on an observation:

"Termites are even more extraordinary in the way they seem to accumulate intelligence as they gather together. Two or three termites in a chamber will begin to pick up pellets and move them from place to place, but nothing comes of it; nothing is built. As more join in, they seem to reach a critical mass, a quorum, and the thinking begins. They place pellets atop pellets, then throw up columns and beautiful, curving, symmetrical arches, and the crystalline architecture of vaulted chambers is created. It is not known how they communicate with each other, how the chains of termites building one column know when to turn toward the crew on the adjacent column, or how, when the time comes, they manage the flawless joining of the arches. The stimuli that set them off at the outset, building collectively instead of shifting things about, may be pheromones released when they reach committee size. They react as if alarmed. They become agitated, excited, and then they begin working, like artists."

Shall we gather?

I

DOWN
THE LONG YEARS

1

The Manhunt

Guess which playwright grossed *more than* $3,050,000 in a single theater during a single recent year (and didn't get a nickel in royalties out of it, just to give you too strong a hint)? Guess which playwright, not content with draining the economy dry in that single situation, was also responsible during the same period for maintaining—exclusively or nearly exclusively—at least thirteen other playhouses devoted to festivals of his work (playhouses in Anniston, Alabama; Burlington, Vermont; Odessa, Texas; Lakewood, Ohio; Ashland, Oregon; Louisville, Kentucky; Washington, D.C.; Cedar City, Utah; San Diego, California; and, among others, New York, New York)?

Guessing game is over because you've got it. Shakespeare. So long as summer is with us, and sometimes deep into the fall, Shakespeare is performed out-of-doors in parks, indoors in amphitheaters especially built to accommodate his plays, in school auditoriums, in public libraries, in any adequate space that can be usurped for the duplicating and reduplicating of one four-hundred-year-old strand of what may safely be called culture.

But summer's not the whole of it, and neither, of course, is this continent. Shakespeare's popularity here is not simply a matter of box lunches on the lawn and agreeable two-day motor trips to some of our quainter towns; neither is it an attempt to appropriate for ourselves, by sheer volume of production, a playwright who belongs first to Great Britain and then to the world. The moment the leaves have fallen and the festival coffee stands shut up, the very same Shakespearean plays that have bayed at a summer moon will slip onto the wintertime schedule of every repertory company across the land—I have an impression that all university theaters in this country are required to produce *A Midsummer Night's Dream* at least once each semester—and if Joseph Papp particularly likes one or another of his Central Park mountings he'll pop it straight onto Broadway for a run, sometimes a long one.

Abroad, the Stratford company in England will send one or another of its seasonal tidbits down to the Royal Shakespeare Company's London base at the Aldwych, and if the Aldwych no longer borrows as much from Stratford as it once did, it's no doubt because the RSC's former director, Peter Hall, is now busily in charge of the brand-new British National Theater, whose original repertory included a four-hour Albert Finney *Hamlet*. As if that weren't enough, there's a serious move afoot in London to raise £1.5 million to build, independently, a full-scale reconstruction of Shakespeare's Globe near the site on which Shakespeare himself once performed and on which the cannon used in *Henry VIII* managed to set fire to the thatched roof, burning the whole octagon down. No end in sight here.

Further abroad, you can pick up Shakespeare in almost any country you care to reach by plane, train, or ship, problems of translation notwithstanding. The most affecting, perhaps the *only* truly affecting, handling of Ophelia's mad scenes I ever saw appeared in a French production staged by Jean-Louis Barrault; the most maddening experience I've ever loyally endured to the bitter end was a Russian film version of *Othello* with the original English dubbed onto the soundtrack (lip-sync forsooth, no dubber ever came near matching up Russian histrionics with that quietly sturdy iambic line); and no one was the least bit surprised to find Shakespearean directorial style heavily influenced for a five- to ten-year period by a critic who was neither British nor American but Polish (Jan Kott, who turned the whole canon into a replay of Samuel Beckett's *Endgame*). If England finally saw the day when the sun set on its empire, it has yet to see the day when the sun sets on Shakespeare.

Now to an obvious question that is almost never asked: why? You can say, right off, that Shakespeare's dominance of not only the English-speaking scene but of the world scene as well is due, plainly and simply, to the fact that he is the world's greatest playwright. You can say it and get an argument. What of Sophocles, Euripides, Molière? Pretty good men, all—and there are others. Surely *Oedipus* can be put up against *Hamlet* with a good chance of winning, or at least earning a draw. Is *Lear* absolutely a better play than *The Bacchae*? Which comedy of Shakespeare's can be most confidently pitted against, say, *The School for Wives*? Yet there are no Euripidean festivals in the Great Lakes region, no full seasons of Molière in Manchester.

Simplify the claim a bit and say that Shakespeare is the greatest dramatist ever to have written *in English*, a safe enough proposition.

Then what's he doing using up so much stage time, and so much critical energy, in Germany, Poland, France, Russia, where have you? Translation is a sticky business and those who must come to him through it certainly aren't hearing the English that presumably makes him great. Compound the claim somewhat to see if we can arrive at a formula that will explain away everything and say that he is not only the greatest playwright in English but *also* the man who produced the greatest number of playable plays. Volume does count. It's one reason we are able to maintain so many festivals over so many years: there are enough texts to allow for rotation. *As You Like It* can be skipped for four or five years at a time, there's always *Much Ado* to take up the slack, and, weather permitting, even *Cymbeline* and *Titus Andronicus* can be wedged in at intervals. The only other playwright who's had a continuing festival named after him on this continent is Bernard Shaw, and volume has something to do with that, too. Sheridan and Wilde, for instance, simply didn't produce enough material to keep seasonal wheels spinning.

Even so, the compounded answer doesn't quite do the trick. At least eighteen of Euripides' plays survive; and close to twenty of Molière's belong to the years of his maturity. Acknowledge these men as great, count the number of their plays available, and they should, it would seem, be in business alongside Shakespeare. They're not. Neither does anyone think of doing an Elizabethan (or Jacobean) festival, in order to pick up the accumulated work of Shakespeare's contemporaries, some of it marked by genius: Marlowe, Massinger, Jonson, Ford, Webster, and Beaumont and Fletcher *could* be packaged. We remain interested in one man, one man's work.

So interested that we are willing to sit through the same plays year after year (or so), suffering the boredom that is inevitable whenever productions are done badly, dedicated, chance-taking, looking, looking, looking. Of course some of this is lip service, culture-nibbling, doing what we were told was good for us when we were in high school (though I never knew anyone to read *Silas Marner* year after year just because he was told it was good for him in high school). Some of it is picnicking. Some of it is stargazing, sitting at adoring attention because Katharine Hepburn or Richard Burton or Albert Finney or Maggie Smith has chosen to drop by this year.

But when all allowances are made, there is still an ocean of interest—genuine interest, passionate interest, don't-bother-me interest—left over. No amount of false piety will explain away a single theater's grossing more than three million after twenty-five years of operation (Stratford, Ontario), let alone the mushrooming festivals and hundreds and hundreds of independently staged productions that crop up year after year in country after country. The massive, resolute, undeflectable audience that pursues Shakespeare through thick and thin is, I suggest, looking for something in particular, something that so excites them when they find it that they are prepared to survive incompetence, unintelligibility, bad roads, and *The Taming of the Shrew* along the way.

Looking for what? I know what *I'm* looking for, although, being a reviewer, I may be atypical; but I think not altogether. Let's see if we can get at it through one more process of elimination.

Shall we agree that audiences don't go to Shakespeare for the plots? In the first place, they know the plots, most of them all too well. It can be quite a chore sitting through a mediocre performance of the potion scene from *Romeo and Juliet* when you know absolutely everything that's going to happen after it—provided that damned girl ever does get through with the thing. (Allow for exceptions. The first time my wife saw *Troilus and Cressida* was at Stratford, England, in 1954, and in spite of a pretty but leaden performance by Laurence Harvey as Troilus, she was utterly fascinated because she actually didn't know how it was all going to end. Can happen—but never twice.) In addition, there isn't a plot that's not structurally troubled—*why* does Iago hate Othello so, is it Lear's fault or his daughters', is Macbeth really ambitious or merely his lady's pawn, what on earth gets into Leontes to make him a jealous madman on the instant?—or that could stand up, architecturally, to the *Oedipus*. And those stories that aren't troubled are either casual or downright cavalier, as Shakespeare himself genially indicated when he subtitled one of his comedies *What You Will*. A snap of the finger for the plots. Shakespeare borrowed his plots, mixed up his plots, dismissed his plots—though he was a master, of course, of making them lead to stageworthy scenes. But that's what they were to him: handy crowbars, chisels, wedges for prying the world open so that he could get inside it.

Neither do audiences really go for the language, though it be heresy to say so. Reams and reams of the language are lost at every performance, some because relatively few actors are up to reading it rapidly, clearly, and beautifully all at once, some because our attention isn't and shouldn't be on the words as words but on the suspenseful human secrets they're disclosing. If you want to know how truly beautiful *Othello* is *as language*, you'll do better sitting at home and reading it, reveling in it line by line. Again, the language as such, stunning as it is, can't be the *sine qua non* or the French, Germans, and Poles would be put off by their inability to hear it as we do and wouldn't be spending so much valuable theater time trying to catch, and very often succeeding in catching, the same elusive quarry we're after. The words, like the plots, are means of getting at something else.

What else? We're left with the interior lives of the characters. And I'm *not* going to propose that Shakespeare is great primarily because of his people, or that his knack for characterization is the one thing that triumphantly holds all else together. It's silly to isolate one facet of a man's talent and make it the sole, or the principal, badge of his genius. Greatness really comes all of a piece, stands indivisible, resides in the words that penetrate souls as much as in the souls that are penetrated, resides even in the *instinct* for choosing a plot that will set the subsequent processes into quick motion. (Shakespeare's greatness further includes an uncanny facility for making his materials *visible*, readily adapted to the physical stage; most good directors will tell you that the staging cues are all there, embedded in the movement of the text.)

I shall suggest, however, that there is something most peculiar about Shakespeare's methods of characterization, something unique about the *manner* in which his fretting shadows acquire life. His characters aren't stylized, as Molière's are. His characters aren't archetypal, as Sophocles' are. Neither are they psychological in the Euripidean sense, with rather schematized idiosyncrasies still not entirely free of the guiding hands of the gods. Shakespeare's men and women *are* free. They are almost free of him. More than any playwright who ever lived, I think, Shakespeare gave his imagined figures his blessing and their liberty, allowing them an individuality that need not be categorized and cannot be readily explained because it is *theirs*: willful, perverse, self-contradictory, electric, mercurial, evanescent, ineffable, inevitable, *there*. Could you prick them, they would bleed. But you cannot prick them any more than you can seize lightning bolts; once you've seen the flash, it's too late. They're alive not as analyzable ideas but as fleeting, crackling, ungraspable nerve ends, brain waves, emotions erupted from such depths that their sources can never be charted. In the very same moment they are present and have passed. Untrappable, unchallengeable.

To achieve the translucent substantiality that so undeniably exists onstage, Shakespeare, I think, surrendered more of himself, more of his own given life, to the thousand and one phantoms he created—handed it over intact, in all of its unpredictability—than any other man who spent his years making phantoms exult, cry, breathe, die. That is why we know so little about *him*. Because he had unconditionally and irrevocably transferred so much of himself to the creatures literally unleashed by his imagination, there was little left to know. A Greek could always argue with Aeschylus after coming from a performance of *The Eumenides*; because of the play's personal argument, he'd know he was dealing with a *person*. Euripides was so much a person in his plays that he could be exiled for what he wrote, as Molière could be censured. We have no such sense of Shakespeare. It's all dissolved into quicksilver, and the quicksilver is now on the stage.

Given the peculiar nature of what he accomplished, Shakespeare did make things difficult for actors—and for all the rest of us. We, actors and audiences alike, can only catch this world on the wing when we are made sufficiently airborne ourselves, lifted by a spurt of intuition that becomes a breeze and then a gale. The circuit is so live, so restless, so urgently self-charging, that it is hard to hook into, almost too hot to handle. Rarely do we make full contact. The experience of seeing an entire Shakespearean play fully realized in all its parts—and we know from experience that each of the parts is realizable—is so infrequent that we really give up expecting it, let alone demanding it. A few "perfect" productions in each man's lifetime, no more.

What we do expect, and for the most part get, is productions in which one or another passage, or one or another role, is suddenly touched with the life-giving finger that Shakespeare finally bestowed upon Prospero. These lucky strikes, in which an almost invisible small flame grows larger and larger until its illumination is literally stunning, come to different playgoers at different times. The accident of being at the right place at the right time, and all that. But each man can list his privately held hoard of treasures, and in all probability the sum total of one man's is approximately the same as another's.

I can readily list some of mine. I know that Romeo can be played with total, ebullient conviction because, more than twenty years ago, I saw Stephen Joyce play him, a puppy thunderstruck with joy and incapable of expressing it in anything less giddy than bubbling verse, at Joseph Papp's then new theater in Central Park. A winter or so later, in a school auditorium Mr. Papp had temporarily taken over, I learned that the Jaques of *As You Like It* need not be a surly misanthrope or a pontifical reciter of set pieces. He could be, as the young and already brilliant George C. Scott made him, an extraordinarily witty, extraordinarily funny gentleman-cynic, key to the entire play. Many years later, I saw Carole Shelley rediscover the root cynicism of the same play, though this time as Rosalind. In between, I had not only watched Irene Worth and Alec Guinness offer proof positive that the neglected and distrusted *All's Well That Ends Well* was superbly stageworthy, but, in the same production, that a character named Parolles—and how many of you have so much as stored that name in your memory banks?—

could, in his thieving bombast and his terrible humiliation, make you feel pity for him and shame for the human race. Douglas Campbell played the part, suddenly more vulnerable flesh and blood than a round dozen of Hamlets or Macbeths.

I have seen one production of *The Merchant of Venice* in which the casket scene proved the most delightfully sophisticated passage, a production of *Twelfth Night* in which Christopher Plummer made Sir Andrew Aguecheek the most complex and original figure on stage. I have heard—but only on records—John Gielgud deliver Hamlet's advice to the players not as though Shakespeare the playwright had been indulging himself in tangential shoptalk but as though Hamlet the man were driving his actors to a fever pitch toward a performance that might see murder at the end of it. When I saw Ophelia's mad scenes played affectingly, it wasn't because Ophelia, mad, touched any hearts; it was because the members of the court were so hideously embarrassed by the spectacle that they couldn't bear to look at the child. As they turned away, nearer nausea than patient grief, the values of the scene turned turtle, became honest in a fashion no one could quite have anticipated.

These are only a few of the important memories I keep firmly fixed in my head; you will have your own. But you see what they are: fragments, passages that succeeded where other passages did not, performances that sustained themselves over longish stretches but weren't properly matched by other performances.

Which brings me to what I think we're all doing as we go to the same plays again and again. We're trying to complete them, to add up perfect productions, in our heads. I may say to myself, "All right, I know what and who Jaques is now, I have met Sir Andrew Aguecheek live; will someone please do as much for me with Orlando or Malvolio tonight?" I may know that the casket scene is brimming over with sly humor, even if I don't hear its humor reproduced next time; next time will the trial scene work? I am satisfied that John Gielgud is right in giving Hamlet first-night nerves for the players' speech; what unexpected quality can I be made to hear in Macbeth's "Tomorrow and tomorrow and tomorrow"?

We know that the strange rustle of slippered feet, the heartbeat, the swift and untraceable flight of thought that are uniquely Shakespeare's exist, exist everywhere. We know because we've heard these things, parts of them, in the unlikeliest plays: in *Cymbeline* and *Titus Andronicus* and *A Winter's Tale*. Perhaps, if we go again tomorrow and tomorrow and tomorrow, we'll one day be able to assemble in our memories mosaics of our own, feel that we've successfully scoured all the nooks and crannies, and come away with at least a few more plays whole. No great effort to the continuing search; there are always surprises to keep us contented.

And no great hurry, either. For it is precisely the fluidity, the ambiguity, the contrariety, the unfettered independence and consequent spontaneity Shakespeare has given his people that permits them to pass from year to year, decade to decade, now century to century, without harm. Nothing impedes them; they can walk through ideological walls. Each age, as we know, rediscovers itself in Shakespeare, which means that the freedom the playwright gave to his creatures was authentic, with no fine print holding anything back. For himself, Shakespeare had only one thing to say, and he kept saying it over and over and over again: "What a piece of work is a man!"

And so we are still engaged, with him, in the greatest manhunt in history.

2

Molière, with Variations

When you've seen one *Tartuffe*, you've seen exactly one *Tartuffe*; you certainly haven't seen them all. I discovered this at a relatively tender age, having quickly come across variant playings of the famous under-the-table scene. A brief rundown, in case it's slipped your memory: the fraudulently pious Tartuffe has been trying and trying to seduce the wife of his benefactor, who simply will not believe the candid report his wife gives him; to prove that what she is saying is so, the lady orders her spouse to crawl beneath the table in the center of the room and wait till Tartuffe approaches her, whereupon he will hear lust rampant, deceit on the march. She does make a proviso: if matters should threaten to get out of hand, her husband is to pop out of his hiding place in time to preserve her virtue. A scene for actors and directors to dine upon, obviously.

It so happens that I first saw it done without a cloth draped over the table, which meant that we were not only able to watch the unctuous hypocrite's octopuslike pursuit of milady but could read the face of the hidden husband like a fever chart. Initial confidence in his devout friend's rectitude. Slight surprise at the sound of a few strongly worded endearments. Comfortable rationalization and dismissal of same. Fresh alarm. Shock. Humiliation at having been duped. Rage at having been wrong. Seething frustration at now having to remain under the table until the evidence is unmistakably complete. Impotent collapse and near-paralysis once it is complete, a psychic ennui that delays his appearance well beyond his desperate wife's endurance.

Grimaces? The gamut. An invitation to conscienceless mugging? Yes, it could have been that. More, it opened the way to the kind of irrelevant sight gagging that Molière doesn't really need. I've seen actors playing Orgon, the gullible husband headed for a cuckold's horns, grab a piece of fruit from the undraped table before diving under it. Thereafter he peeled, choked on, and tore to shreds the banana or orange he'd taken along for sustenance. I've also watched an Orgon doze off into slumber, so confident was he of a scoundrel's innocence, only to be thumped awake by the crack of Tartuffe's own palm, beating the tabletop in passion.

Excesses, no doubt. But everything depends on the actor. The reactions, made visible, are all legitimate; they are also legitimately funny if the performer is an honest man. And the business of letting us see him has one marked virtue: it keeps Orgon at the center of the play. Orgon is, after all, the core of the piece; certainly he is its motor and he may be its meaning. Orgon initiates all of the essential action, taking the conniver with his rosary beads into his home, betrothing him to a most unwilling daughter, deeding him his property with nary a thought for his family. The piece is *about* Orgon's credulity; in its original form, Tartuffe was not even exposed, we were simply left with Orgon's offering everything he possessed to the mealy-mouthed houseguest who'd bilked him. Molière, chief actor in his own company, played the part; that's where the meat was.

Yet the scene as scene plays best when the table is completely covered and Orgon concealed from view, a lesson I learned at the knee of the Comédie-Française long after I'd grown accustomed to cross-legged antics in plain view. Suddenly focus shifts and a wondrous comic tension asserts itself. Our attention is centered on Elmire, Orgon's wife, now, and we share first her bewilderment and then her increasing panic as Tartuffe's assaults become more violent and Orgon does not appear from the folds of cloth that enclose him. We've imagined all his first reactions; we are able to do that for ourselves. What in heaven's name is keeping him now? The longer the delay, the funnier the passage grows. We know the man to be obtuse. *How* obtuse? And what must Elmire do to rouse this mysteriously sluggish savior?

But notice something. If it is Elmire who is making the comedy here—coughing ever more loudly to attract his attention, turning odd word stresses into plain cries for help as she pries herself loose from yet another slimy embrace—we are once again preoccupied with Orgon, whether we can see him or not. Tricky. More complex. Richer.

Stephen Porter's 1977 production of the play for Circle in the Square did use the tablecloth, and Tammy Grimes, as Elmire, called down laughs sharp as thunderclaps in her baffled desperation, some-times circling the table like a lion tamer trying to draw one cat out of its lair, sometimes flat on her back as John Wood's Tartuffe grew recklessly ardent. Yet there was something wrong with the sequence, which is no doubt why so many echoes of past performances came clattering into my head as I watched. Its rhythm was subtly off, a matter of unpredictable spurts rather than an enveloping progression. Miss Grimes's coughs did not seem to come in quite the right places; and the spaces between them were long enough for us to lose the thread of what she was up to. Mr. Wood's passion flared in fits and starts, too, and I'm not sure it was at all wise to have him, during his inspection of the premises to make certain no one was overhearing, actually begin to lift the tablecloth. It was easy enough for Miss Grimes to halt him by bolting into his arms like a cannonball, but once we realized he'd thought of the spot as a possible hiding place, we expected him to return to it. He didn't, of course, and we had an unfinished gesture on our hands. And Orgon, concealed, did not really remain a comic presence for us; Stefan Gierasch, a fine naturalistic actor not overly skilled at stylization, had earlier made him too straight for us to revel in his discomfiture now.

So that's what happens, sometimes, even under as gifted a director of Molière as Stephen Porter is. At other times, in other productions and other plays, we're bowled over by performances and insights for which we're totally unprepared. Indeed, it's not often that we're offered revivals that represent the theater at its greatest, standing boldly under lights as though to proclaim what writing for the stage is all about; it's even less often that we get productions sympathetic enough to nurse every last nuance out of the boldness. But Mr. Porter, adapting as well as staging Molière's infrequently seen *Don Juan* for the Phoenix in 1972, elected to do it Molière's way—language, psychology, very little bumptious gagging—and the elegance, the intellectual power, and the deep comedy born of both were not less than hypnotic.

I had not thought so before, but surely Sganarelle is one of the great comic roles in the stage's strongbox, an investment in eternity that is going to keep paying off so long as the creative act itself survives. Sganarelle, derived from a stock figure in the vaudevilleish commedia dell'arte and here elaborated into a moon's-eye view of human instability, is the uselessly moralizing manservant of that great lover who loves no one, Don Juan.

He disapproves thoroughly of his master's bad habits, berates him soundly to all comers—excepting of course his master. Cringing, denying all he has said, lying with the suppleness of an articulate Siamese cat, and loyal to the brink of damnation, he continues to accommodate the libertine he is pleased to call his lord. He *will* go so far as to scold the man to his face, given the least opportunity—and take it all back with a toadying droop of an eyelid. His unforgettable last cry as Don Juan does go to Hell is the very shiver of comedy. "My wages!" is his first, and perhaps his final, concern, with tenderness for a damned soul sandwiched somewhere between.

John McMartin played him with the old commedia aching-rooster slouch—shoulders bent under the burden of his own duplicity, one foot trailing as though he might take off in the opposite direction instantly, ankles curling over as if his shoes had no edges to them—superbly. The slouch had become a moral one, the eyes were sleepy, wisps of hair bothered his face like cobwebs walked into, his protests rose and then expired on a roller coaster named Despair.

He may have been funniest in his fright—he felt so *silly*, he complained—over approaching the jeweled statue of a man Don Juan had killed in order to invite it to dinner (though he was rather interested to discover that it would come). But he was at his most revealing in a tirade that he himself was forced to interrupt. Attacking his master with the wrath of a Cotton Mather, he suddenly blurted out—nonstop, no change of rhythm—that Don Juan *had* to shut him up: he could not possibly keep the brimstone raining unless he met with some objection. A man who was all contradiction begged for contradiction: his very breath depended upon it.

Paul Hecht was an excellent foil for him—funny that the leading role should prove a foil for this tagalong figure, but that is how the play moves—and the butter-smooth propositions he made to whores and virgins, fathers and prophets, were one and all persuasive. Mr. Hecht understood that he was no mere rake but a philosopher: when he teased a saintly old man with the promise of a gold coin if he would only blaspheme, he was not buying excuses for his own conduct, he was teaching heaven what a bargain is. He believed not in his lust but in his intellectual honesty; the lust came as a consequence. Thought was as interesting as episode—it *was* episode—before Mr. Hecht and Mr. Porter had finished their night's work.

3

The *World* and Maggie Smith

Congreve's *The Way of the World* was both the most successful and the most curious of the three main-stage productions that opened the 1976 Stratford Festival in Canada, and Maggie Smith was the most successful and most curious creature in it. That figured. Miss Smith has more or less taken over the snake-charmer concession in that continuing sideshow we call the theater, and has, in the past ten years or so, laid waste more living rooms, chaise longues, leading men, ottomans, vanity tables, and handy bric-a-brac than any other enchantress in the business. She coils herself around things, and they disappear in small puffs of vapor, leaving only her violent red hair and her small, contrite mouth behind as a memento of the holocaust. Usually it's a comic holocaust; Miss Smith makes annihilation funny.

What didn't figure in the least was the way she'd chosen to play *The Way of the World*. She was Millamant, of course, haughtiest of the naughty, witty even before breakfast, so swift and lethal of tongue that one of the fops-about-town who appears early in Congreve's elaborate conceit announces that he wouldn't go near her "were she as Cleopatra." (Inasmuch as we could also see her as Cleopatra in Shakespeare's *Antony and Cleopatra* in the same busy repertory, we were in a position to appreciate the gentleman's apprehension.)

But let idle chaps prate. When Miss Smith came *on* as Millamant, in the palest of pale blues to let that hair set the world afire, she did indeed prattle away until someone pointed out that she wasn't giving echo fair play. (Echo had to wait till she'd stopped before it dared begin, and what echo could ever remember all that?) She prattled about the papers she used as hair curlers ("I never pin up my hair with prose"), she prattled about suitors ("I love to give pain"), she prattled about landscapes and lying and the unreliability of love. If everyone else talked in periods, coming to rounded, thumping stops, she let one line breed another indiscriminately, until you imagined language must have overpopulated the globe.

And yet. If there was one thing she was not, it was too mighty, too overwhelming, too *bright*. She'd almost hinted, right from the beginning, that she talked to keep her composure, that language was her last line of defense, that she was secretly more insecure than anyone onstage. Surrender syntax and all would be lost, and there was a constant danger that syntax might founder. Without slowing her pace, she managed to break sentences, retrace words, let lines trail to diminuendo (she was magnificent, and got a laugh that must have been heard all the way to Toronto, as she referred to a bumpkin as "this flower of knighthood," each word issuing more limply dismayed than the one just preceding it).

By the time she reached the celebrated marriage contract scene, in which she and her lover Mirabell state the conditions under which they will agree to domesticate themselves, she'd got a base to do something utterly unexpected. She was every bit as funny as she ought to have been for the most of it, enjoying herself enormously in a tragedy-queen near-faint as she reacted in shock ("Oh, name it not!") to her prospective husband's monstrous mention of childbearing. But, without a flick of those heavy-lidded eyes of hers, she altered tone utterly with one seemingly unremarkable request. Mirabell was told always to "knock at the door before you come in." With that—who'd have counted on it?—she was totally touching. During all of the imperiously outrageous terms this early apostle of freedom (1700) had been setting, terms bolder and in spots saner than those demanded today, she'd been most deeply concerned about one small, ordinary, unmistakably human need: the barest minimum of privacy.

I don't suppose many Millamants have made this line the heart of the entire, brilliantly epigrammatic passage. But then I don't suppose many Millamants have laid such an odd foundation: a woman who *could* become so flustered that, in a flurry of self-consciousness, she assiduously fanned someone else rather than herself. (She also *knew* that this bit of business was funny; but, you see, she had to do something to cover for herself.) An original, affecting, altogether superb reading of the role.

With Jessica Tandy shoring up the sidelines. Miss Tandy, scowling at a servant for bringing her cherry brandy in a container the size of an "acorn," played an aging, heavily enameled dowager ("I look like an old peeled wall") who controlled the purse strings of the plot. With her great frilled bonnet rising vertically from her head as though it were standing at attention, she rapped her dependents to order with a stout tongue and a sometimes candid, sometimes self-deluding appraisal of her own chances for coaxing a bit of romance back into her life. Jeremy Brett was less effective as Mirabell, nibbling so rapidly at his *mots* that he seemed an underfed squirrel. But Alan Scarfe, robust, resonant, falsely jolly, was most striking as a friend who was also the villain of the piece, which brings up one last anomaly buried deep in *The Way of the World*.

The play has always given producers trouble: too many minor characters, too many major characters, too many scenes described that might have been played, too many scenes played for a decent architectural balance. Director Robin Phillips hadn't cut any of this overload, which meant that we drifted off here and there, being in left field so often. But putting a first-rate company to the task of setting it all out firmly—from the opening tableau, which looked as though a high wind had hurled an entire bewigged century through a church door and up against the organ, to the final demure, candlelit dance—did finally display for us the play's subterranean complexity. There is a canker at its core. Though I don't know if a concordance has ever been provided for *The Way of the World*, it would surely show the word *hate* recurring at least as often as any other.

These worldly-wise, verbally felicitous fools ("One must have a wife to be untrue to and a mistress to blame") aren't happy with their wisdom *or* their felicity. Manner is a mask; behind it, energy, real delight, is running down. Perhaps that is why Miss Smith could be so irresistible and so right as she said "I could laugh inordinately" in tones that actually suggested ennui. The way of the world, so glittering, is wicked, as we know. A production that could make us laugh at the glitter while taking note of the dour truth was one to be tucked away carefully in the theater's memory bank.

4

Chekhov, the Play Doctor

Toward the very end of Chekhov's *The Wood Demon*, when three or four couples on a country estate are trying to rearrange the raggle-taggle patterns of their lives, there is a flash fire in a patch of woods nearby. The one most immediately concerned is Khruschov, impatient doctor to them all, passionate devotee of forestry, a chap in boots and peasant blouse who likes to help God create by planting birch trees and whose anger is unbounded when he contemplates the loss of so much as a sapling.

Coming to know him as we did through Ian McKellan's beautifully intemperate performance at the Brooklyn Academy of Music in 1974, we expected him to leap to his feet in fury and race off to help quench the flames. And he did do that, but very oddly indeed. He danced. He kicked his heels in joy before hurrying to the conflagration, as mysteriously elated as he was transparently anxious. Why?, another character wanted to know. Well, of course he'd try to help save the trees. But fires create an opportunity, too. "I'll plant new ones!" he cried gaily, quite beyond himself, as he ran.

We don't know that this doctor stands for Chekhov, and there's no need to force him into the role. But certainly he is doing just what Chekhov did with *The Wood Demon*. Eight years after he'd written the play, a relatively early and relatively light-hearted trial flight, Chekhov simply set creative fire to vast portions of it and planted in its stead *Uncle Vanya*. The later play is a distillation of the earlier—waste characters have been done away with, charming though they may have been, and the web in which the remaining ones writhe has been more judiciously spun—but it doesn't deny the earlier any more than it denies the exultation of tearing down to rebuild. A good man can find his pleasure in what is and in what yet may be.

It was fascinating to sit before this excellent youngish Actors

Company—born scarcely two years earlier in Britain, democratically organized and run—and watch past and future slip in and out like coins in a magician's hand. Whole stretches of *Vanya* were already in evidence: two stand-offish women deciding at last to trust each other, the disconsolate Vanya (née George) summoning up half-drunken courage to force himself upon the youthful wife of an aging, pontifical writer, the thunderclap that comes of the writer's arbitrary disposition of the family estates.

But there were other things here, too, and some I find myself rueful to have lost. The principal figure, for instance, is not Vanya-George at all—indeed Vanya-George kills himself before that forest can begin to burn—but the "wood demon" of the title, the restless, fanatical, self-deprecating, furiously demanding doctor. Mr. McKellan made a heroic misfit of him, quick to suspect that his enthusiasm was being mocked, determined to have his say and let the mockery rain, jumpy as a sparrow with a cat around, incapable of showing love without making it seem anger, sure that he was "narrow-minded, blind, second-rate" while insisting that all about him attend scrupulously to his outbursts.

He was in much too much of a hurry with his life to finish scratching an itch that bothered him, too certain he was a clod to give a woman a chance to return his ardor, too overwhelmed with emotion by the mere mention of forest lands to get to the end of a sentence without blowing his nose. The part was rich, funny, eccentrically touching, and if taming it to plot purposes made sense for *Vanya*, it was gratifying to see it at least once under full sail.

The experience was also helpful in reassessing Chekhov's attitude toward professed boredom. The virus of boredom does continue to infect the playwright's characters right down through the masterpieces, and actors are most often tempted to take ennui at its face value, playing it for pathos. Chekhov, at least in *The Wood Demon* and I suspect forever thereafter, indulged in no such nonsense. People who are constantly telling one another how severely bored they are are not precisely nuisances but they are perilously close to fools.

Let three men lie about on sofas in the afternoon heat, virtually competing to say which is the most depressed ("You don't know the meaning of the word boredom, old boy"), and you're probably going to hear laughter out front, proper laughter. Then let a woman drift through the sunroom to add, as though it were fresh news, that *she* is similarly afflicted and the laugh may well turn—as it did in Brooklyn— to a level-headed roar. There are pains in life, and they are real; there are also postures, and they should be pricked.

As if the point hadn't been made, an exuberant girl who feels herself on the brink of possible romance takes a very deep breath and explodes: "I'm so happy I'm almost bored with my happiness!" After that, there is very little chance of our sorrowing over the excuses folk make for their admittedly listless lives.

There is a groundwork of humor in Chekhov that remains firm no matter what complex structures may later be erected on it. We often lose sight of it, admiring the structures as we do. Seeing the rarely done *Wood Demon* thus became a beneficence: we were able to examine the groundwork in the open, when it was freshly laid, unburdened by the heavier masonry to come. In fact, it occurs to me that everyone who is going to play *Uncle Vanya* really ought to be required to play *The Wood Demon* first. That way we'd have it all, sly foundation and more imposing façade, a nudge in the ribs running right up through the building.

5

Andrei Serban's Chekhov

There were at least five images I shan't forget as long as I live in Andrei Serban's mounting of *The Cherry Orchard* for Joseph Papp's 1977 season at Lincoln Center, and I'm going to mention them to see what you can begin to make of the confidently daring, alternately vulgar and delicate, perverse, funny, deeply original, and visually stunning event that swept through the vast white-on-white reaches of the Vivian Beaumont stage like a circus-bred whirlwind bent on making the world clean.

One. In a bandbox of a ballroom, all filigree and flickering candle-flame, Madame Ranevskaya and her friends were swirling themselves to exhaustion on the tide of the music, though we knew that Chekhov's Madame Ranevskaya was desperately anxious to hear the results of the day's auction: had her home, had her beloved trees, been sold away from her? Swinging in a great arc from the door of the salon with her dancing partner, Madame happened to cross the path of her daughter, just now being lifted from the ground by her own companion on an upsurge of melody. In the split second that daughter passed mother, the daughter's birdlike hand darted downward to give Ranevskaya the quickest peck of a kiss and, in that same split second, to whisper the first rumor that the estate had been lost. Instantly the pulse of the dance—no more than an eighth note had been skipped—had carried the couples away again, gaily, indifferently. It was as though lightning had struck, struck with a kiss, pretending to be part of the festivities.

Two. Once the house had been stripped and all its inhabitants were ready to leave, one of the family suggested that they sit for a moment, just sit for a moment. There was immediate quiet, and agreement. The rooms they had known as children deserved a brief honoring. The furniture having gone, there was nowhere to sit but the floor. All found themselves places there, casually but carefully, unsuitably dressed for out of doors, lost in contemplation as they were in fact lost in space. Mr.

Serban, who has a genius for making sculptures of still-breathing people, had had them arrange themselves in a loosely crowded oblong, and I do not know whether he intended anything so specifically vivid as the vision it conveyed to me. I suddenly saw them distributed about a boxcar, perhaps on straw, on their way to execution.

Three. In the bustle of farewells and failed hopes and forgetting that crowded *The Cherry Orchard* even as its blood was being drained from it during its final scene, a single children's rocking horse, so old now that what must once have been giddily bright red paint had been scraped to the faintest of blushes, was carried high in the air against the vacant backdrop, bobbing gently and serenely as it went. We had seen portions of the horse before, when its dust coverings permitted, and knew it to be a relic of the household nursery. We saw it whole and bravely resolute, beyond time, as it vanished for good.

Four. Chekhov's Trofimov is an eternal student and revolutionary prophet who simply cannot find his galoshes. At the Beaumont a pair of galoshes came flying through the air like a couple of simultaneously wounded ravens *before* Trofimov had been able to complete his complaint over their inexplicable loss. They landed with a thump at his feet as he was getting out the last word. The effect was marvelously funny not only because of the spectacular parabola the boots made as they were so helpfully flung from the wings but because of all they told us about human beings living together. Someone in that house knew that Trofimov would lose his galoshes again, someone in that house could anticipate the precise timing and duration of his complaint, someone was *ready*.

Five. Irene Worth was the Madame Ranevskaya of the occasion, and I could delay us here with an accounting of a dozen or two swiftly telling gestures this unforgettable actress had devised by way of showing us the obtuseness, the sudden fierce *sense*, the self-indulgence, and the genuine dismay of an extraordinarily complex woman. She had to do it in snatches, for reasons I'll get to; but she did it. The single inspiration I'm going to cling to, because it was the boldest, was her last loving look at the house she was leaving. There was, by the way, no real house to leave; Mr. Serban, ingeniously abetted by designer Santo Loquasto, had given us only an enormous void, an infinity of plain canvas, a place in which eagles might have exercised their freedom. And so Miss Worth didn't look at it, she inhaled it, moving in a great running circle deep, deep into the unreachable horizon and then around and forward to encompass the curve of the forestage, not panting but sucking in breath as she flew, reaching out at last to grasp the hand of the companion waiting to take her away. But she didn't seize that hand. Instead, on impulse, she barely brushed it with her fingers and danced off again on another grand tour, eyes ablaze, lungs filled, heart broken, lips parted in what was very nearly an all-devouring smile. And then she did it one more triumphant, unbelievable time, a bareback rider on the rim of the world. When she left, she took it all with her.

Now if some of these instances had the smell of the circus about them, some of vaudeville, some of chamber music, some of a thumping brass band, some of Peter Brook and some of Robert Wilson and some of Samuel Beckett transformed into a high-wire mountebank, they had come by the aura consciously. There was a time, a few years earlier, when we'd been hearing a great deal about "total theater." All that it ever seemed to amount to, then, was a disjointed conjunction of mime, tumbling, unintelligible speech, and strobe lights. But here, I think, we had it—somewhat flawed because it embraced so much, but functioning as a visual, verbal, and emotional whole.

Circus? Chekhov's octogenarian Firs, cotton-haired caretaker of the estate, took time all by himself to do an elderly but jaunty jigstep across the backdrop, top hat bounding in the rhythm of the carriages he was used to. The children's aging governess, still doing her magic tricks to entertain them, topped her red-tasseled Harlequin's costume with a clown-white face. Members of the household felt free to plump pillows into place on the tops of their heads just as real people do in the privacy of their homes—it was all logical enough, once you saw it—and the sense that we were being visited by Madame Ranevskaya and Her Merry Minstrels was often strong.

The comedy ranged from the hilariously plausible to the frantically forced, as though to prove that when Chekhov *said* he wrote comedy he meant it, with no holds barred so long as the play proper got done, too. Meryl Streep, as the housemaid determined to have a young valet for herself, was given the slapstick concession, or a very large part of it. She had to work hard, too hard, to establish a level of gagging we're certainly not accustomed to in *The Cherry Orchard*, and some of her extravagances—crashing to the floor in a faint after a single kiss—fell as flat as she did. But, incontestably, she won. By the time she was tripping herself up in the petticoats that were slithering about her ankles or tackling her valet with the expertise of a right guard, she was wonderfully funny. So, too, was Max Wright in the small, often overlooked, role of an accident-prone clerk, a role Chekhov had written with bumbling sight gags in mind. Mr. Wright's efforts, during a melancholy mood, to disentangle a pistol from his belt, trousers, and the guitar strap that seemed determined to enshroud him forever were masterly.

In the meantime, and in the center ring, had we lost *The Cherry Orchard*? No, we had not. We'd lost a conventional production of *The Cherry Orchard*, to be sure. But we didn't need that; we've had many and can have more any time we care to. For the moment we had a *Cherry Orchard* placed in a larger, airier, freer and at the same time more ominous landscape. When Miss Worth began to speak of the spring blooms of her childhood, the scrim that served as a backdrop began to glow and to rise simultaneously, revealing row upon row of feathered May trees, not quite released from the winter's cold but iridescent with oncoming life. The vision was exquisite, and, under the formalized lighting that Jennifer Tipton had arranged, we understood what we were looking at. At sunshine the color of snow. At a moth-scape. Death and life at once. Equally evocative, once the play moved to an open field for a lazy late afternoon, was the contrasted silhouetting of newly come telegraph lines towering carelessly over field hands laboriously dragging an ancient giant plow.

There was one symbolic superimposition that seemed to me thunderingly wrong. The radical student Trofimov was played utterly straight, with very little attention given to *his* delusions and pomposities. To back up the young man's function as revolutionary prophet, the skyline changed once again, this time to overwhelm us with factory chimneys beneath a soot-stained red sky. But this literalized intuition of a wholly industrialized world seemed to me worse than obvious; it was out of tone, gratuitous, more than Chekhov foresaw, more than he meant, more than he wrote.

And a kind of loss must be acknowledged. If scrims were rising and dazzling vistas beginning to swim in new light while Miss Worth was speaking, the speech itself, the rhythmic continuity of the role, was bound to be interrupted. All of the performances *were* so interrupted, challenging the actors to make their effects in fits and starts, separated vignettes, and to depend upon an overall styling to make a satisfying mosaic of the pieces. The thoroughly admirable company, working with a gracefully colloquial adaptation by Jean-Claude van Itallie, was quite up to the dare. Miss Worth sat at the lip of the apron and commanded the universe itself to be still while she ever so slowly tore a letter from her lover into two equal halves; the severing of the last shred of paper had the force of a guillotine, resolutely faced. George Voscovek, Raul Julia, Marybeth Hurt, Priscilla Smith, and a half-dozen others established themselves on the wing, vanishing, returning, asserting their brief right to center stage, yielding ground again.

The mosaic was made, *The Cherry Orchard* survived and expanded, the theater itself was both refashioned and renewed. I don't think I had ever before seen anything quite like this production on a stage and—arguing a point here, surrendering an old preference there—I left the theater exhilarated.

6

Bernard Shaw Unbound

One of our problems with contemporary dramatists is that we know too damned much about them. We only half see their plays; the other half of our decidedly divided attention is firmly focused on *them*. For instance, when the American Shakespeare Festival Theater in Connecticut revived Tennessee Williams's *Cat on a Hot Tin Roof*, it was blazingly clear from the reviews that people weren't so much asking what Williams had to say about his characters as they were asking what the characters had to say about Williams. Our knowledge of a playwright's private life, personal philosophy, and quondam whims can stand square in the way of his work.

I became more convinced of this than ever when I spent three days strolling the graciously landscaped streets of Niagara-on-the-Lake in southern Ontario, slipping into seminar sessions of its 1974 Shaw Festival by day and then making for the handsome cedar-lined playhouse come evening, watching *Too True to Be Good, The Devil's Disciple,* and *The Admirable Bashville* go by.

Shaw, of course, was a man given to thrusting his *persona* upon us—all but driving that wagging finger and those spiked eyebrows down our throats—and if, during his lifetime, we were wildly distracted from his characters and what may possibly be called his plots by our efforts to relate them directly to what he'd said in a preface, newspaper interview, or newsreel appearance just beforehand, the fault was elaborately his. He seemed to want us to think of George Bernard as the work of art, and all his stage children as mere inexpensive reproductions.

Fortunately, now that he is dead—I don't mean that it is fortunate for us that he is dead, though it may be for the best of his plays—we can begin to shake ourselves free of that voice from the wings, that superawareness of a sassy, stern Superman scanning the text for us, and just listen to the text. It does wonders for *The Devil's Disciple,* let me tell you.

The Devil's Disciple, much to my astonishment, is becoming a better play all the time, year by year, Shavian silence by Shavian silence. How, you may ask, can a play become *better,* since after all it remains the same old collection of funny and sober lines, funny and shameless characters, funny and impertinently contrived situations? Well, more or less this way. I've been seeing *The Devil's Disciple*—that antic in which the outrageous Dick Dudgeon detests his moralistic mother, proposes that all present say grace before a family will is read, and substitutes himself on a 1777 gallows for a chap whose wife interests him—off and on for many years, but I had never before seen it when there wasn't a serious dislocation between the rococo period plotting of the play and Shaw's eagerness to speak his own highly iconoclastic mind.

The plotting, as one of Niagara's seminar speakers matter-of-factly pointed out, is the plotting of "sentimental melodrama," the very kind of antiquated theater Shaw most detested, a species he hoped eventually to wipe from the face of the earth. The play's first act centers on the reading of a will, a device sacrosanct to all scribblers who owed the least debt to Scribe. The plum that the second act pulls out is hoarier and more sure-fire still, the plum of mistaken identity: Dick Dudgeon is mistaken for the village minister, as unlikely an error as British soldiery e'er made. And where is the heartthrob? The one kiss Dick Dudgeon ever gets from the minister's wife who interests him so much is the kiss she gives him as he goes to his death in her husband's place. Oh, the late nineteenth century surely lived it up in the theater!

No doubt the reason a matinee idol like Richard Mansfield was able to play *The Devil's Disciple* while Shaw was still unpopular in America was its apparent familiarity, its sweet willingness to play the audience's game: a nobly reserved love story, a hero with a noose about his neck for much of Act Three. And what was Shaw doing fiddling about with such flamboyant nonsense? Many things, I suppose. He wanted important actors to star for him, he wanted a large audience, he even—as he so honorably insisted—liked money. And while he was stirring the ancient pot-au-feu, he could add his own seasoning. After all, deep inside the attractive balderdash he could point out that the righteous might be intolerable frauds, the scoundrels virtuous by their own (and his) standards, the half-Puritan, half-slushy *mores* of the day as unreasonable as they were insincere. You could say that he was boring from within while taking great care not to be boring.

But always when we saw the play—until this very moment—the

two elements, melodrama and mockery, didn't mix. They either bumped or side-stepped each other awkwardly. You see, just so long as we *remembered* romantic melodrama, we expected quite different things from it; and knowing Shaw as well, as overpoweringly, as we did, we kept waiting for his voice to interrupt the alien proceedings.

In time, we came to tolerate the plot, and even to hurry through it, waiting for "Gentleman Johnny" Burgoyne to appear, that truly Shavian savior of the last act of all. The commander of the British forces invading a New Hampshire rebel colony would now speak as silkily and as sacrilegiously as Shaw himself, firing epigrams to the right of him and preposterous common sense to the left (he assures Dudgeon that hanging would be infinitely preferable to a firing squad, considering the marksmanship of his men), and we could all settle back and purr to a rhythm that wasn't an anachronism. The fact of the matter is that stars no longer chose to play Dick Dudgeon but began to reserve for themselves the fat lines, the elegant and caustic playfulness, of To-the-Rescue Johnny.

Until, as I say, this very moment. At Niagara it was all changed. Director Brian Murray had, with the help of an extremely able company uninhibited by mixed traditions, reassessed the situation. We don't really remember sentimental melodrama anymore, do we? Haven't had it around in thirty or forty years. Very well, then. No need to be self-conscious about it, no need for apologies. *Play* it. Take it at its own value, honor the specifically theatrical pleasures that always were in it, mean it gesture by gesture.

Consider the passage—it might have been pure fudge—in which Alan Scarfe, a Dick Dudgeon craggy as a chip from the Grand Canyon bound loosely in leather, propped his boots on a farmhouse table and stared across it at the woman he wasn't free to love, whatever he might feel. The woman, whatever she might feel, had tried hard to hate him and was losing ground rather steadily. In a moment the soldiers would come to mistake him for her wanted husband, and there was going to be a very tense, very quiet, once very stagy few seconds in which she would have to decide whether to speak the truth or no. Life and death in the balance, to say nothing of love.

Mr. Scarfe and Domini Blythe played the entire sequence with such emotionally charged reserve, with so many small overtones circling about them, with such dramatic *patience* that the scene worked as it might have worked if it had been written by a man who believed in it. It is, in the end, a good situation, if you like situations at all, and it has now lost its feel of belonging to a theatrical form recently banished. Director Murray hurried nothing, evaded nothing, insulted nothing. He let the play stand as though it were of no fashion, old or new, as though it were *sui generis*. Lo and behold, it began to manufacture its own blood, assert its identity as this play and no other.

But of course it's not just a matter of having lost our self-consciousness about dated plotting (there was a time when Shakespeare's plotting seemed dated, too; somehow or other we got beyond it). We are also now able to see the play past Shaw. Shaw, decent fellow, has at last removed himself; we are not listening for him to say anything new; we are not fearful of being scolded tomorrow for having missed the point. Freed of Teacher's immediate presence, we are at much greater liberty to hear him here, there, and everywhere, onstage; he is *in* his handiwork now, he's been assimilated. And so *all* of it seems Shavian, the melodrama part and parcel of the meaning and the fun. Shaw's was an eclectic imagination (it's quite a jump, recall, from *Widowers' Houses* to *Saint Joan*) and there's no reason why this play shouldn't be as much his, as much like him, as any other. We've lost our narrow expectations of him (our expectation that he will always be writing *Major Barbara* and going on about munitions) and at last made him Shaw Unlimited. Aging is helping, and the play is wine.

7

Saint Joan Outfoxed

Actresses almost always seem a little bit stunned after they've finished playing Shaw's *Saint Joan*, and it's not because they're emotionally or physically drained by the fine work they've done. Something else. There they stand, perspiring in their chain mail under the hot stage lights, chins up, cropped heads tossed back, expectant quivers still playing about their lips—but puzzlement and an odd worry lurking deep in their eyes. No, it's more than worry. It's certainty. They know—now, at the end of things—that they've been disappointing in the part, that the personal miracle hasn't come off.

Do you want to know why? To avoid future shock, actresses attend: Shaw's Joan isn't a good part. It's thought to be a plum, I know; that's why stars and near-stars are always so eager to plunge into its swaggerings, its defiances, its piteous crumplings in the Inquisitor's court. But the fact of the matter is that Shaw barely roughed the girl in, whisked her offstage when anything of importance to him was going on, and—rather plainly, I think—felt uncomfortable as a writer with the lyricism and the historical pageantry of the Maid. Joan's voices, Joan's bells, Joan's larks in the sunshine and lambs in the fields weren't Shaw's cup of ink, and he is eager to get past the rhetoric that *must* be given to a chronicle play's heroine ("I shall dare, dare, and dare again, in God's name! Art for or against me?") and on into the argument that's playing tricks in his head. That argument will steal the show from any actress, riposte by riposte, scene by scene.

Actresses do make good tries, and in 1977 Lynn Redgrave at Circle in the Square was no exception. Miss Redgrave tried to take the play by storming it, right off, which may have been as good an attack as any; at least she got to make an impression before the wily men of the play began undercutting her right and left. Miss Redgrave came on as the "wench" she is sometimes called, in what seemed seven-league boots and with the thunder of horses' hooves. She may have been a spiritual innocent; she was no innocent in the wiles of the world. With a mocking little curtsy and a crooked half-smile, she presented her case for being taken to the Dauphin confidently and headlong, measuring her effect out of the corner of her eyes.

A minx who knew how to keep her tongue in her cheek, she could afford to bide her time; they'd come round, *everyone* would come round if she set her jaw boldly enough and waited till her questioners had worn each other out. When the military man to whom she was appealing blurted out "Well, I am damned!" and Joan replied "No, squire; God is very merciful," she didn't read the line the way Shaw's stage directions suggest *("with muffled sweetness")*. Nonsense, that was a sly joke she'd just got off, she *knew* it was a joke, and who'd have pretended to be so naïve as not to notice? Miss Redgrave did not exactly make her Joan an upstart; but she made her reasonably bright.

She was brisk and businesslike, too, in her early scenes with the Dauphin, plucking him from his attempted concealment with a wry lift of her eyebrows and a near-leer that defied him to fool *her*. In a soberer moment, listening to her friend Dunois's caution that "God has to be fair to your enemy, too, don't forget that," she was touchingly reflective. But by this time the play's trap had been sprung and the actress was in process of losing control of the piece to what must always be called her nonsupporting company. The men of Church and State, the thinkers and deceivers ever, the cool and analytical cerebralists had arrived and Shaw had blessed them; blessed them with his own quick-wittedness because they were capable of swapping concepts, toying with and trading and upending *ideas*.

Once a suave British nobleman, a churlish British chaplain, and a quietly determined French bishop had sat down in a tent to analyze Joan's role as a "Protest-ant" threatening the universal rule of the Church and as a "Nation-alist" threatening the local rule of the barons, the evening's real content had asserted itself and—from an actress' point of view—the jig was up. In the play, we never hear Joan make these debating points; nor do we see her act them out. That's all courteously done for her by three brilliant voices that instantly prove more powerful, theatrically speaking, than the heavenly voices she reports hearing. Indeed, the next time we see Joan she is petulantly swirling about Rheims Cathedral in something close to a childish tantrum. Joan has lost the worldly battle without ever having fought it. Lost the play, too.

In most productions she has the climactic scene in the bishop's court snatched away from her as well—by the Inquisitor. Obviously

Shaw decided that if God could play fair with the enemy, he could, too; he therefore gives the evening's very best speech to the subtle man who is going to condemn Joan, letting him make the most plausible case conceivable for the Church's relentless pursuit of heresy. If *this* theft didn't come off in John Clark's production at Circle in the Square, it was only because Inquisitor Paul Sparer wasn't subtle enough. Mr. Sparer had chosen to be mealy-mouthed from the outset, intoning ritualized positions that no longer carried the impact of fresh thought, wringing his hands with a piety that seemed as false as Tartuffe's.

The speech was damaged: when Mr. Sparer proclaimed the Inquisition's "essential rightness and mercy," we were certainly not supposed to nod assent; but we *were* supposed to understand what he meant when he used the terms. The actor denied us the insight. Instead of firmly believing in his own propositions, he seemed insincere through and through—which meant that Joan had nothing solid to contend with, no real dramatic opponent. Oddly, the failure of the Inquisitor's passage to do its own work did not hand the scene over—this time—to Joan. Miss Redgrave's Joan had been a rock-sturdy, knowing, impetuous Joan in its beginnings. But it had nothing to challenge now, and so could only go limp. Miss Redgrave's appearance—eyes sunken in anguish, face contorted by self-doubt—was affecting; and her wounded animal's cry after she had signed the recantation was chilling. But whatever faggots were being gathered for her in the courtyard below, the real fire of the play—the intellectual fire—had gone out.

Miss Redgrave need not have been too discouraged, however. It's all happened to fine actresses before, and—temptation being strong—it's going to happen again. Shaw's play is called *Saint Joan*, but *Saint Joan* is the battle Joan can't win. Shaw's got it sewed up for his spokesmen.

8

Shaw: When Cheerfulness
First Broke In

There are two sneaky, subliminal, and even inadvertent jokes in Shaw's *The Philanderer*, the second best of which is displayed all over the place at the opening of Act Two. Act Two takes place in the library of an Ibsen Club, circa 1893, and displayed all over the place—most notably on the sedate bookshelves—are signs requesting, if not demanding, SILENCE. Fat chance. In a play by Bernard Shaw? The act runs for forty minutes and the signs keep glaring at us the whole time that Shaw's characters (Shaw, Shaw, Shaw, and Shaw) rattle on without a moment's interruption. Pleasantly waggish.

The best of the unstated jokes, though, is on Shaw himself. With his second play, *The Philanderer*, he had hit upon his true vein and didn't know it.

You see, he'd begun his work for the theater as an ardent Ibsenite, prophet of the new realistic-sociological dispensation, a man determined to impose Ibsen's moral concerns and Ibsen's dramatic method upon the too carefree and irresponsible London theater. Of his first three plays, two were attempts to reshape British drama to the Norwegian's temper: *Widowers' Houses*, an attack on slum conditions and the exorbitant rents charged the poor, and *Mrs. Warren's Profession*, an exposure of the "respectable" folk who profited by prostitution (with a few hints of incest thrown in). St. John Ervine called the latter play "hard, almost bitter" and "as moral as Savonarola."

And right smack between the two, Shaw stood Ibsen and all Ibsenites on their respective heads. His leading character in *The Philanderer* (himself, of course, described in the piece as "a famous Ibsenite philosopher") is having a perfectly terrible time with the forces he's unleashed. Having urged the world's put-upon Noras to escape their dolls' houses and become "advanced women," he discovers that what they are advancing on is *him*, passionately. With two of them tugging at him simultaneously, one so tigerishly that he is forced to reverse melodrama's customary procedure and cry out, "Unhand me, Julia! If you don't let me go, I'll scream for help!," he rather rues the day he philosophized about anything.

As every other character in the play rues the day he helped found an Ibsen Club, though practically every character we meet belongs to it. The club permits women to join, naturally enough, though only if the membership committee votes them sufficiently "unwomanly." (Men must be "unmanly" as well; no macho here, and how is it we've lagged so far behind Shaw in arriving at unisex?) If some male members are unhappy, it's because they can't get into the club's smoking room: the women have taken it over entirely. (That's why the men are now in the library, unsilent.) One muttonchopped old chap finds some consolation in the new situation: he knows that if he wants to be alone he can go to his home, whereas if he wants to be with his family he can come to the club.

But mostly the new freedoms are causing a high degree of fretfulness. Old Muttonchops, incensed at the "unwomanly" behavior of a knickerbockered daughter, insists, with some thunder, that if she can't be womanly she can at least behave like a gentleman. (Surprisingly, there was applause during the 1976 Roundabout revival when he completed his dressing down with a stentorian "I am speaking not as your daddy but as your commanding officer!") Meantime, a doctor is in deep distress over the news that a disease he has discovered doesn't exist in the least, an inflamed inamorata is attempting suicide by trying to leap through an unsuitable window, and the philanderer himself is praying for nothing but peace.

What Shaw is doing here is exactly what he would do in his most ebulliently contentious, perversely funny later plays—taking the other side of his own argument. He couldn't resist doing it, not in his maturity (and here we see that he'd had the itch in his very beginnings). Shaw was a debater who could not bear the ineptitude of the opponent offering him rebuttal: he could, ever so maliciously, think of better counterarguments himself. And so he simply refused to share the platform with anyone: he would gleefully attack his own positions, thank you, and let fair play win. (In the later plays if he wished to attack munitions makers, he gave the longest, most carefully reasoned, most impertinent speeches to the munitions maker just as—in wishing to give Joan of Arc new status—he'd offered the longest and most adroit passage to her Inquisitor.)

This wasn't and isn't light-mindedness. It's not even exactly broad-mindedness. It is, rather, a restlessness of mind, a quickness to question the very logic he has espoused, a handy wit for besting himself (both ways), a capacity for seeing six sides of an issue and enjoying all six. The wit never did consist in simply making a jest, though he learned, line by line, to become funnier and funnier; it consisted in a habit of thought that held all habits of thought to be suspect, subject to upending. Turn the matter over and over and over and take delight in watching it spin.

Looking at the Roundabout Theater's sleek and amiable resurrection of a foolishly neglected play, we could see that Shaw already had in his hands the clue to what would become his career. *He* couldn't see it because *The Philanderer* failed to find a producer at the time. No one, apparently, could quite grasp what the unpredictable man was up to. And so he turned tail, or turtle, with *Mrs. Warren's Profession*, going back to the Ibsen mold he'd just been reducing, with a schoolboy's enthusiasm, to mincemeat. It wasn't his mold but—characteristically—he continued to admire it, and so he gave himself over to what he called "didactic realism" once again.

As it happens, *Mrs. Warren* wasn't produced, either, though for reasons of censorship (those hints of incest, mark you) rather than indifference, forcing him on to a luckier, more sportive stroke, *Arms and the Man*. After that, with its romantic nonsense shot full of holes though the bullets were only chocolate, he was on his way.

9

Nora, Nora

The difficulty with Ibsen today is that we must try to take two separate things seriously, the playwright's ideas and the playwright's playwriting. The ideas, of course, present no particular problem. One had only to listen to Claire Bloom's last long speech in the sleek 1971 off-Broadway revival of *A Doll's House* or to glance at the brief excerpts from Ibsen's "Notes for a Modern Tragedy" that had been included in the program to know that the ideas were sound, advanced, on target. "A woman cannot be herself in modern society," the notes read. "It is an exclusively male society, with laws made by men and with prosecutors and judges who assess female conduct from a male standpoint." Kate Millett sounds old-fashioned beside that.

But how, how, how do you take the playwriting seriously? From what vantage point, what perch or roost or perspective in time, can you attend, without doubling up, to the spectacle of a woman so determined to keep a secret from her husband that she promptly spills it, virtually within his hearing, to the very first acquaintance who walks in the door? Add to that the fact that she hasn't seen the acquaintance in years, and doesn't even recognize her when they do meet, and you've got a rather peculiar secret-keeper on your hands.

Peculiar things are going to keep happening, peculiar and predictable. Ibsen did work by notebook, which means that he jotted down most logically all the little twists and turns of motivation he was going to need and then clipped them together to make a scene whether they precisely flowed or not. If they didn't flow, he forced them ("Tell me, is it true you didn't love your husband?").

The terrible danger in this shuffled-note method is that you are going to hear the papers rustling, the clips suddenly slipping on. You can't *help* hearing them. And so you know, infallibly, that the moment the child-wife Nora exclaims, "Oh, God, it's good to be alive and happy!" a doorbell will ring and a furtive fellow will slip in who's going to

bring down her doll's house in ruins. Just as you know, with a certainty
close to hilarity, that when Nora's fatuous lord and master, Torvald,
exclaims, "I often wish you were threatened with some impending
disaster so that I could risk everything!" disaster is not only impending
but here. Torvald has but to go to the mailbox ("I'm going to see if
there's any mail"), slit open the first letter to hand, and the fat is in the
fire.

The underpinnings are all transparent, line by line and blow by
blow, and we must struggle to induce in ourselves a state of mind that
holds humor at bay in honor of the social proposition being so implausi-
bly illustrated. It's a real battle, one that is often lost; Ibsen believed in
his mechanics as well as in his creed, and we cannot. The effort isn't
exacerbating, especially; we needn't come away exhausted from it. It is
possible to look at the foolishness and feel fond, if not doting, as we wait
for the message that is going to come of it all. But it's nip and tuck the
whole way, and the thin ice of the situation poses treacherous problems
for actors.

It's not only a matter of how the good lady doing Nora is going to
try to stitch together the two parts of the role, the giddy, fawning
creature who is willing to leap up and down like a puppy dog snatching
at proffered bones for two acts and the serene, stern woman who lays
down the new law in Act Three, having matured wonderfully during
intermission. It's also a matter of how everyone onstage—pompous
husband, long-lost confidante, sniveling blackmailer, dying Dr. Rank
who is willing to offer Nora his love with his next-to-last breath—is
going to get us past the transparent rigging and into the ringing
preachment. Do they try to steal home, eliding all that is awkward as
quietly as possible? Do they rush it, pouncing upon line two before we
have quite noticed line one? Do they stylize it, lifting themselves into
daguerreotype postures that plainly have little to do with reality?

Miss Bloom's company tried a frontal attack, with a bit of the
daguerreotype thrown in. Donald Madden, a Torvald who might well
have seen Dr. Rank about hypertension, glided across the highly lacquered floor (this Nora had such difficulty getting money out of her
husband that you felt he wouldn't even allow the lady carpeting) to
exchange his wife's swift kisses for quickly palmed coins as though they
were Pierre and Pierrot giving a summer-park performance in a high
wind. Robert Gerringer, the forger who had come to accuse Nora of
forgery (motives do get piggybacked in this odd way), kept his mouth
open and working so that no matter who was talking his teeth would
show. All worked at a high pitch and in some fever, as though a
Racinian *tirade* might spin off into space at any moment.

Even so, there were some genuine successes within the near-stylization. Roy Shuman's Dr. Rank, for instance, was meaningfully mannered: head thrown back, hands always on the point of clapping, eyes darting this way and that as he bluntly, briskly mocked himself and his approaching death. The effect was perfect, that of a man already halfway to the horizon waving farewell with his thumb to his nose. And Patricia Elliott, as the friend so quickly privy to Nora's secrets, spoke vast amounts of exposition exquisitely, then zeroed in fiercely upon the play's point as she gripped her shawl severely and remembered that she'd found happiness only in her work.

But what of Nora? Claire Bloom had made, I think, an admirable choice, though a choice with a canker to it. Most Noras won't sacrifice the opportunity to charm, to be birdlike and winsome and if possible adorable, during the first two acts. And you can't entirely blame them. Nora is, as written in these acts, a ninny underneath, a girl who really can't feel any sympathy for creditors because, after all, they're "strangers," a girl who—though her secret debt is much on her mind—hasn't the faintest notion of how much of it she's paid off. She subsists, it would seem, on macaroons. But actresses who go for charm and a pretty mindlessness are stuck with the last act. How does one turn an enchanting child into a dominating adult, especially when the transition is missing?

Miss Bloom tried to create the transition from the beginning, surely an intelligent thing to do. Even as her Nora was nestling her pretty head against her husband's waistcoat while she seduced him with quick flattery into giving her old friend a job, there was a strain about the eyes, an indication of an intelligence withheld, that added initial dimension to the role. Where most Noras seem to have an instinct for being playful, fluttering as to the cocoon born, Miss Bloom's playfulness was plainly put on, a cool trick she had learned, a device that did not wholly engage her.

She was constantly listening to herself make the sounds a pompous husband expected, aware of their insincerity and worried about the gulf between what she was doing and what she might be feeling. Faintly alienated from the outset, she had given us a base for the play's ending. The reserve that we felt in her was the conscience that might have been awakened at any time but was not in fact awakened until it was time to make that speech and slam that door.

The catch to doing it this way, because the part *is* split in the writing, was a curious sense of heartlessness that overtook Nora en route. Being to a degree disengaged, she seemed not only indifferent to her children and extremely obtuse about her friend Kristine's personal problems but horrendously cold-blooded about the devoted Dr. Rank. He announced his impending death and she scarcely looked up from her sewing. He made a gesture of love toward her, a gesture that had to be disinterested because he would never see her again, and she recoiled as though he had proposed, perhaps, another forgery. Clipping the butterfly's wings left us with something of a dragonfly.

Miss Bloom worked honorably, looked well, arrived at her last scene logically, and didn't seem anyone you'd care to trust your heart with (I'm not thinking of Torvald, who is an oaf, but, say, of Dr. Rank, who is not). Miss Bloom had cooled Nora to make way for the ultimate avalanche; the move did take away anything that was ever very appealing about her.

How subtle differences can be! At the Vivian Beaumont four years later, Liv Ullmann's Nora proved the most enchanting I have ever spent less than enough time with; it was also the most honest. Miss Ullmann's success was not simply a personal one, a matter of teasing just enough fronds of loose hair about her face to make her seem softly, saintedly alluring. That would have been easy enough to do, since, as a presence, Miss Ullmann is patently, consciencelessly, adorable. But she seemed to devote nothing of her wiles to making herself winning; her energies were entirely devoted to showing how winning *Nora* could be—when she wanted to be.

Which brings us face to face with a new and wholly unexpected complexity. The actress could play Torvald Helmer's "little squirrel," all right, enslaving him precisely as she enslaved us: crooking her head like a five-year-old to cajole an extra banknote out of him, popping those macaroons into her mouth while slyly pretending not to be the quickest little liar on the block, looking her husband straight in the eye upon demand though not before she had let one wistful finger linger between her lips for a moment. To Torvald she could only seem a natural child, never a carefully considered one. To us she was something else altogether.

For Miss Ullmann, working under director Tormod Skagestad, had found an original and moving means of anticipating her third act in her first. She was an entirely knowing woman from the outset, delighted that she had learned how to be "very, very subtle" in handling her lord and master, aware that his "masculine pride" was too delicate a thing ever to be damaged, happy not so much in her role as in her marvelous skill at playing it. She *enjoyed* being captivating, and in virtually total control: the question, if there was one, was *how* she wanted to run the world, from inside or outside. If anyone needed to slam that door and go in search of a genuine identity, it was poor, obtuse Torvald, inhabitant of a dreamhouse.

But there was, as there needed to be, a soberer undertone to this.

Lovely in mauve as she rocked in her chair, she was also lonely there, for she had no true partner. Her reflective eyes told us again and again what it was to be beguiling in a vacuum, how little human reward there was in being a permanent performer. And nowhere did she convey her sense of the instability of an *acted* life more than in that everlastingly ticklish moment when blackmailer Krostag was to appear at the door. She read the line that proclaimed her happiness, the happiness that was to be so fortuitously shattered a bare moment later. But she read it not quite as though she were knocking on wood, hoping to draw off the fates. She read it as though being alive and happy in the way that she was alive and happy was at least half a fraud, which meant that the fates were going to make themselves felt no matter what. The knock on the door was exactly what she'd expected. Ibsen's thorny melodramatic juxtaposition had been made inevitable. As simple as that. And as right.

Oddly, the actress was less impressive in her last act, during her ultimate reckoning with Torvald. I think I know why. Suddenly she had dropped her smile, which had always been more than a butterfly's smile. As though ridding herself of everything that could be construed as conventionally feminine, she abandoned not only the graceful moues she had reserved for a pampered husband but also the very knowing smiles that had so often fleetingly told us the truth. Half of her seemed to disappear, needlessly. A free woman is not condemned to being a humorless woman, certainly not this one. With Torvald rationalizing so fiercely, might not an unbidden smile have restored to us the whole woman we'd already come to know?

But Miss Ullmann came wonderfully close to healing the open wound in Ibsen's play.

10

Inside *The Playboy*

W ell, there's wonders hidden in the heart of man" mused Philip Bosco admiringly, in the 1971 Lincoln Center production of *The Playboy of the Western World*, immediately upon learning that a certain young chap had up and split the skull of his tyrannical father. And, it seemed, there were wonders hidden in the heart of the Vivian Beaumont as well. For in spite of the fact that director John Hirsch had laid a visually coarse hand on John Millington Synge's play, an unexpected boon had befallen us all. For the first time in its history, the Beaumont had—by accident or design or a little bit of both—assembled a tight, right company for a play it meant to produce.

David Birney for Christy Mahon, the woebegone lad who had risen up to clout his da. Stephen Elliott for the roaring da, his white hairs matted into the bloody crown of a halved rooster. Mr. Bosco for practically any of the sly and tipsy hangers-on, Sydney Walker for practically any other. You could begin to hear the play lifting its wild lyrical voice.

But what of Pegeen Mike, daughter of the pubkeeper and instant adorer of the boy who has done such a handsomely bloody deed? And the Widow Quin, who can offer the same boy a hut to keep him warm and a pint of grog to keep him warmer? Botch these two parts and the men, the good men, will get you nowhere. It was at this point that luck, or one of the gentler gods, entered the scene.

For the Widow Quin, cool as could be as she bartered a red cow for a possible husband, Frances Sternhagen had been found. She couldn't have been hard to find; she'd been around, doing Pinter and other things beautifully, for years. But someone had invited her to lift her golden chin here as she clinched bargains with an arrogant smile, to shoot her two hands forward futilely in an effort to clutch the great prize of a fellow who was surely going to escape her. And from the Canadian theater Martha Henry had been summoned to put a dishrag to the pub bar, to use her apron as a window curtain, to devour the disheveled boy who'd fallen into her lap with the high ardent ferocity of a timberland wolf.

The performing was seamless, or very nearly. The leaps of voice fit, the river-tumble of images raced along at sustained pitch. Miss Henry set the pace for it all, spacing out and slapping down her flattened vowel sounds as though she held the evening's gavel in her hand and meant to use it. Mr. Birney, fingers clutching his battered cap in spasms of joy as he discovered he was a hero to folk slowly dying of routine and yearning for a single "gallant" act, used his shyness as a barely uncocked valve, forcing his intense happiness out through the narrowest of emotional openings, bleating his new-found ecstasy because it was more than he could abide.

Believing himself abandoned and forced to the road again, he read Synge's mournful apostrophe to the world's gypsies with a heartbreaking music that made you rush to the bookshelf the minute you got home. At home, I found it: "It's well you know it's a lonesome thing to be passing small towns with the lights shining sideways when the night is down, or going in strange places with a dog noising before you and a dog noising behind, or drawn to the cities where you'd hear a voice kissing and talking deep love in every shadow of the ditch, and you passing on with an empty, hungry stomach failing from your heart."

Mr. Birney made that a highly personal matter. And when Stephen Elliott, only half dead in spite of all that had been done to him, made his first return from the grave to describe, in fury, the lout of a boy who claimed to have killed him, the rhythmic howl of his rancor became hilarious. All present linked the language together as though they were themselves so many racy metaphors walking the byways arm in arm.

The actors, then, were right enough, perceptive enough, well enough spoken to sing the play forward and let it display itself for all that it is. *The Playboy of the Western World,* one of the six or eight finest plays of the twentieth century, is a great many things. It is more than its language, though its language might nearly have been enough. Inside its language there is a bizarre but utterly authentic insight moving and twisting so deviously that you can scarcely put a name to it though you know in your bones it is there.

The play can be explained step by step. People who have no romance in their lives will accept any romance, including parricide. People brought face to face with an actual killing, however, will recoil from it, aware now that "there is a great gap between a gallant story and a dirty deed." But those two pieties do *not* explain the play; neither do they end it. It ends in submission, victory, and pain (as all great tragedies do; how curious that this should be a farce!). The father, slain a second time, returns a second time. But Christy now is master, the father servant. And Pegeen Mike loses her love.

What we are following, and know that we are following, is a story with the inner power of a myth. We are not following the *myth*, mind you. That is the mistake so many of us make when we prattle on about myth today, imagining it to be in the forefront of the audience's mind or imagining that a writer can make a myth just because he wants to. Myths can't be invented, only discovered. They are discovered *inside* things, sometimes familiar things, often inside stories that are first interesting simply as stories. Here we are tracking down the narrative, almost detective-story style, watching people behave, charting their motives, checking their responses, laughing at what is outrageous about them while agreeing that it is so. We are aghast at the story and we give assent to the story. Why? Because, somewhere dark down at the heart of the farce, we intuit dimly that father-killing concerns all of us, that satisfaction in father-killing incriminates all of us, that we not only have to deal with such ambiguities, we *are* the ambiguities.

Look. The mythic tease and torment of the killing/overthrow of the father is as old as drama; more, it is as old as dreams. It appears in the *Oedipus*. But in the *Oedipus*, and in everything else I can think of including *Lear*, it is held to be wrong, regarded as an evil to be punished. Except in *The Playboy of the Western World*. In *The Playboy* it is held to be in some sense salutary, even necessary. Furthermore, the father agrees to his toppling.

That is something fresh and original and *also* true that this play contains, contains easily, contains without pushing, contains as entertainment and as part of the record of what men can observe about themselves and their shifting, preposterous fates. *The Playboy* is a funny play, it is a beautiful play, and it is an inevitable play all at once.

II

JUST YESTERDAY

1

Royalty

In some curious way, the timing was right. Nineteen seventy-six was just about the year we ought to have been looking at *The Royal Family* again. George S. Kaufman and Edna Ferber wrote *The Royal Family*, presumably a satirical pinking of the Drew-Barrymore theatrical dynasty, in 1927, and there was a real feeling of 1927 all over again as the curtain went up on the armor-and-deep-rose of Oliver Smith's setting. But I don't mean that we were simply being taken back to 1927, when an ingenue came down a curving staircase like a swallow returning to Capistrano and the bad boy of the celebrated clan simply bolted over the balustrade to get at his fencing partner. Of course we were watching a period piece: we'd have known that from the Ina Claire coiffure that Rosemary Harris floated so serenely beneath, a sort of seawave marcel, if seawaves were ever blond. But something else was also happening. It was 1927 *now*.

How? What created the sensation? Why did the play keep reminding me so constantly of *A Chorus Line*, which it resembled not in the least? Let's see if I can get at it. Late in the evening, impresario Sam Levene, having removed his cape and black fedora but done nothing to dim the fire in his eyes, was attempting to persuade Miss Harris (who was approximately Ethel Barrymore) not to marry the South American millionaire who could take her away from the insecurities, the overwrought nerves, and the compulsive emotional posturing of her profession. Mr. Levene, a father figure composed of bits and pieces of Svengali, David Belasco, and an Old Testament prophet, had a new play in hand for her. And, he enthused, this was the very moment to do it, for this was the very moment when theater in America was leaping to life, when the mantle that had once draped itself so augustly about London and Paris was passing to New York, when an institution was unmistakably coming into its own.

Mr. Levene read the speech with passion, whatever sly self-interest may have been embedded in it, and you suddenly took it straight, sitting up to remember that those had been years when O'Neill, Sherwood, Howard, Anderson, Barry, Rice, Kingsley, Behrman, and, oh, half a dozen others (including all those lovely people who wrote comedies like *The Royal Family*) made Broadway bright, busy, and on its way to heaven knows what. The fact that heaven knows what included a depression and a talking Hollywood, both of which would take huge bites out of the theater's headlong rush to glory, was unanticipated then. For the moment, glory was possible and a considerable array of creative people, together with hordes of ardent playgoers, cared. Nineteen twenty-seven, year of caring, year of belief.

The next thought that struck me was that in 1976 we'd begun to care again, in the 1927 way, with some confidence, going to the theater on our own, bright-eyed and bushy-tailed, instead of being dragged there kicking and screaming (as had been the case so short a time before). If this weren't so, audiences wouldn't have multiplied so phenomenally the previous two seasons. If it weren't so, we wouldn't be so surprisingly interested in revivals, in our own special heritage. And, if it weren't so, we wouldn't be so avid for evenings like *The Royal Family* and *A Chorus Line*, evenings *about* the theater. I said earlier that these two entertainments were markedly different. They are. *The Royal Family* romanticizes the theater; *A Chorus Line* humanizes it. But they both love it, and there, at last, is the connection.

The open declaration of love in *The Royal Family* was handed to Eva Le Gallienne, who was in any case the bright special star of the occasion. She, too, was busy persuading both her daughter and granddaughter to cling to the stage, forsaking all others except for time out to have children who would in turn become performers (one of her own had been most considerate, choosing to be born during a layoff in Holy Week). In the course of her cajoling, she let her still-lustrous eyes stray toward the balcony as she remembered, step by step and breath by breath, what it was like to enter a stage door, to make one's way around the rigging and the canvas that turn false life true, to stir dust with a step across a deserted platform in a deserted auditorium, to inhale the world that is a dark nothingness at noon and a radiant, self-made universe at eight. The speech was, at root, both familiar and sentimental. But Miss Le Gallienne had a right to it, hard-earned; and she read it, spacing her memories forcefully and believing every resonant word, as though bells were ringing: call bells, victory bells, New Year's bells, '27 or '76. The truth behind the trite was unearthed; you knew that the lady could not tell a lie. She was superb.

It would have been a mistake, by the way, to go to *Royal Family* expecting outrageously funny farce. It wasn't that now, if ever it had been. Certainly there were laughs, many of them: Miss Harris preparing to read a telegram from mad brother Tony (John Barrymore, no secret) but first taking care to see that she was positioned at center stage; daughter Mary Layne defending the stage against an amorous stockbroker by challenging her pursuer to name just two eighteenth-century stockbrokers; Miss Harris, again, sprawled so gracefully on a sofa that it seemed to have melted into place about her, replying to her brother's fierce insistence that he must flee the apartment for Europe by reminding him that the *Aquitania*, after all, could not be backed to the door. But the confection wasn't really satire, and the most nearly impaled figure (Tony) proved the least well written of the lot. It was essentially a thing of sentiment, and director Ellis Rabb had been meticulously careful to keep it that way, letting Miss Le Gallienne drift alone into an empty drawing room while her brood battled and cooed in the next room, moving gently to the rhythm of a nostalgic phonograph record, giving her the stage space and the stage time to recall precisely and proudly how her husband had first taken four curtain calls on the closing night of a play and then, but only then, died in the wings.

Mr. Rabb may have been a little too meticulous. He had stretched the piece out to very nearly three hours, and since the Kaufman-Ferber valentine contained certain repetitions to begin with—*two* born-in-a-trunk actresses were forced to contend with marriage proposals in much the same way, matriarch Le Gallienne came close to playing two death scenes—the gentle pace palled now and again. But the play's deep involvement with the stage as stage was made persuasively emphatic, and the performances locked into its little paean of praise tightly, warmly.

Certain phenomena of 1927 had vanished and made us yearn a bit: managers who saw to it that their talented charges had fresh vehicles every season, two if need be; an available "road" that an elderly star could take to, for split weeks, whenever she chose to trundle old favorites out to a loyal citizenry. But "theater" itself seemed freshly in the air; *The Royal Family* reminded you that it had been here before and would be again.

2

Playing Fair with *Nanette*

The 1971 reconstruction of the 1925 musical *No, No, Nanette* had a secret. It lay in Ruby Keeler's sobriety. Actually, she wasn't the only one who possessed it, it had spread to infect the earnest, wide-eyed girls who danced on the tops of beach balls and the straight-faced, strait-laced boys in plus fours who lingered about the grand piano fingering their well-tempered ukuleles. And Miss Keeler, of course, wasn't onstage *all* of the time. She did only two numbers. (*Only* two, did I say? They could have donated one to practically any show in town and they'd still have had a smash.)

But the essence of the entertainment, its elegant giddiness and its glory, was contained in Miss Keeler's first entrance, which happened to be, as it ought to have been, down a staircase. There'd been a slight pause in the music. Someone else had finished a fine, forgotten Vincent Youmans song (perhaps "I've Confessed to the Breeze," with its curiously long, lovely, overlapping line). The stage held its breath, making a little pocket in time, as though listening for a clock-stroke or a doorbell or a love letter.

And, up on the balcony close to the foolish dewdrop chandeliers, a door opened. Miss Keeler entered, closed the door properly, immediately began to descend the staircase, on business. She didn't precisely seem to hear the applause. Her footsteps were even, her face was composed, and then, exactly halfway down, she stopped. She had to stop somewhere to acknowledge the thunder of welcome, both sentimental and sincere, that had gone up, and the exact center of the staircase was the logical place to stop in a setting that was everywhere symmetrical.

But she seemed to have *studied* where to stop, to have thought things through; she was serious about this entertainment and would move on again, good soldier that she was, in exactly one more moment, on cue. The voice of Warner Baxter still drove her, as in fact the voice of Busby Berkeley could be heard in the land, supervising the comings and goings of flappers and sheiks in the recaptured dawn of our lives. Miss Keeler, waiting for the beat that would bring her down to where Patsy Kelly and Jack Gilford and Helen Gallagher were waiting, smiled, and the smile was warm; behind it the eyes were grave and listening.

That was the first time she came down, to shake hands with the plot, a thing of nonchalant and perhaps unparalleled idiocy in which Mr. Gilford, who was Miss Keeler's husband, attempted to conceal the fact that he'd been supporting—though in entire innocence and out of the goodness of his haphazard heart—three different women in three different cities. The second time she came down, not too long after, was immediately after Mr. Gilford had joined his pretty niece, Susan Watson, in a deft, quiet chorus of "I Want to Be Happy" (had you known that "I Want to Be Happy" was sung to Nanette by her *uncle?*).

As Miss Watson and Mr. Gilford vanished like mice into the wings—and the wings were used much more often than doors in Burt Shevelove's admirably remembered staging—five young men strolled in from nowhere, unbidden but dressed to stun. They were wearing sweaters, designed by Raoul Pène du Bois, that resembled a trainload of tigers recently struck by lightning, and when they were joined by a chorus of perhaps a dozen more the stage seemed an explosion of Halloween colors, whorls and zigzags forever, putting psychedelic to shame. The boys' shoes were cleated beneath those diamond-patterned knee-socks, and as the fast tap began the stage floor flinched. It was jackhammer time. But it was also Ruby Keeler time, which meant something else.

Down the staircase once more, her beaverlike mind on her work, came the dancer, ready to lift, Swanee River style, her featherweight but fiercely concentrated person from right to left, left to right, across stage in front of the madness. There was no madness in *her*. She drifted from portal to portal like a paper doll that'd been blown from a desk because someone had opened a window, easy as eiderdown, attentive as a tot in first grade. Miss Keeler *minded* what she was doing, her eyes had a faraway look in them that saw some reward in the distance (a merit badge? a pat on the back? a minor place in heaven?) and because she was so dutiful while the men behind her were so demented the effect was just as hilarious as it ought to have been, and honorable besides.

This sense of playing fair with the "new musical of 1925" is what made it the enchanting thing it was. We'd become used to parodies, and pastiches that inevitably became parodies, of the period. We'd heard of high camp and learned how to kid. But *No, No, Nanette* wanted none of that, or a sly very little of it. Though the book had been tinkered with, it didn't try to outwit its original material. It accepted it, laughing of course but not snickering up its sleeve. Everything was out in the open, fair was fair, if Patsy Kelly had to answer the telephone every two minutes then *let* her answer the telephone every two minutes, if Miss Keeler asked for a phone number and got it immediately, let her do that too, gravely. Gravity is e'er the soul of wit in such cases.

And so Helen Gallagher came on stage from a shopping spree, purple packages from Bergdorf's piled high before her face, to permit a few chorus boys to snatch the packages away, one by one, thereby disclosing her startling, satiny, sunburst countenance. Picked up by the boys, she trilled instantly—and straight, which was the fun of it—into a song you might not have remembered but would not now forget. "Too Many Rings Around Rosie" was the name of it ("Too many rings around Rosie/Never got Rosie a ring" was how it went), it swiftly reminded you that Vincent Youmans had been a composer rather than a tunesmith (with that odd note on "*Rosie*" to dispel all doubts), it was performed on round pieces of furniture which eventually turned round by themselves, and it ended in a double group blossoming outward like morning petals that you might last have seen in *Whoopee* but instantly wished to see again tomorrow night.

Nor was Miss Gallagher through. Joining hands, or canes, with Bobby Van for a trim little exercise called "You Can Dance with Any Girl," she and her partner slipped imperceptibly from maxixe to hinted waltz to close-to-cakewalk to nervous breakdown in a spectacular experiment in footwork that may well have been the evening's most triumphant moment. A bit later I began to worry for the electrifying Miss Gallagher. As she began a traditional blues, I thought she couldn't possibly top—or even come near—what she'd been doing up to now, only to be surprised by Mr. Shevelove and choreographer Donald Saddler, who had really done all the dances, once more. Without warning, she was flanked by the boys in tuxedos in the moonlight, urged by a thrum of voices to suggest—in her sorrow—that broken-backed camel's walk that bespoke breeding in the twenties, brought at last to a weeping-willow finish, shoulder-length bob draped triangularly across her face, chiffon scarf dripping from bent wrist to the floor. Superb, this Miss Gallagher.

Tenderness and taste took care of the evening. Susan Watson glided through the softer-than-soft-shoe gauzerie of "Tea for Two," one gloved hand elegantly suspended behind her back. In fact, you heard "Tea for Two" as a ballad before you felt it as a fox trot. Jack Gilford, worrying about all those women and his nice wife besides, munched on his troubles like a squirrel preoccupied with a nut he distrusted. Didn't Patsy Kelly mug? Uh-huh. That's what stage maids used to do in 1925. And it had been arranged for her to do it all at once, in a sequence in which she could slap everything within reach, her own face, the nearest balustrade, a couple of suitcases that had to be hustled upstairs. Given the opportunity, she gave it the works; the result was a graduate course, short but exhaustive, in all the slow-burn, flat-palm possibilities developed in two-reel comedies by the masters and mistresses, herself included, of the form.

In front of it all Raoul Pène du Bois had hung an act curtain, properly chintzy, that seemed to have been composed of red peppers and snails; behind it all he had hung rafters and a starlit sky made of freshly poured fudge. Nell Brinkley would have approved. (And Mr. Pène du Bois could obviously market those sweaters, enriching himself enormously, any time he cared to.)

The roars that went up during the opening-night curtain calls—themselves most discreetly managed—were part nostalgia, part astonishment, part pain, part delight. Pain? Yes, a kind of mourning, not for our lost innocence but for our lost pleasure. By insisting on the innocence, and not taking too superior an attitude toward it, *No, No, Nanette* had momentarily restored the pleasure. We need to examine that achievement.

3

The Musicals That
Merely Made You Happy

I think somebody asked me the question. I was busy lighting Ruby Keeler's thirty-seventh cigarette (Miss Keeler smokes too much, winding herself not at all) and trying to hear, through the cross-clatter of voices, Helen Gallagher's impassioned defense of everything from old-fashioned melody to the social principles of her mother, and I couldn't be sure. But since I was the only reviewer present, and in theory the theorist, the question was probably mine to answer. Leo Lerman, the grand panjandrum of *Playbill*, had gathered together a tableful of New York business executives to cross compliments and challenges with some of those responsible for *No, No, Nanette*, and one executive wanted to know if the astonishing success of that 1925 musical wasn't *merely* a matter of nostalgia.

I muttered something about no, I thought the nostalgia came second, the fact that the *show* was good came first, that if the *show* hadn't been good mere nostalgia would have got it nowhere (remember a revival of *On Your Toes* a few years earlier, with the same Bobby Van who was so seraphically animated in *No, No, Nanette*, and how swiftly it failed?), and then started looking for more matches. (I smoke cigars now, and you don't have to carry as many matches for cigars as you do for Miss Keeler and those obviously undangerous cigarettes.)

But the question keeps bugging me. We could argue about the *mere* in "mere nostalgia." Why *mere*? Isn't nostalgia important? Isn't nostalgia respectable? Isn't it in the nature of the beast, the unhappy and forever unfulfilled human creature, to yearn a little after something, 'way back, that seemed like fulfillment, or an hour or two of happiness, at the time? If we couldn't remember the things that used to please us, would we continue to believe in a possible pleasure tomorrow? We know we haven't quite got hold of it today.

But never mind that. As the warm sigh of thanks began to go up nightly at the Forty-sixth Street Theater, where Miss Gallagher was finishing trim little dance numbers with the barest flick of her finger against the brim of her jaunty fedora and where Miss Keeler was rippling like a skipped pebble across the sea of chorus boys behind her, what, in heaven's name, were audiences being so nostalgic about? They were nostalgic, that's for sure. When Patsy Kelly, daring the entire company to do a fast clog she'd just slaughtered, let loose the triumphant cry, "Eat your heart out!" the audience knew that that was just what it was doing, eating its heart out. It was jealous of somebody over something that'd gone. Some people cried. What for?

The quick and easy assumption was that everyone was being nostalgic about the musical comedies of the 1920s. But who, out of all the people pouring into the Forty-sixth Street and out of it happier, had ever really and truly seen a 1920s musical? Max Gordon had, of course, because he was around at the time, though he hadn't produced his own chef d'oeuvre in the vein, *The Bandwagon*, until 1931. Brooks Atkinson had, because he'd discovered the Marx Brothers in *I'll Say She Is*, but he was retired and very busy in 1971. Richard Rodgers had, because he'd written more than his share of the shows of that decade, but he was now much more closely identified with the form that *replaced* the musicals of the twenties, the *Oklahoma!* boom that turned the *No, No, Nanette* school to dust.

All right, I'll admit it. *I* saw some of the musicals of the twenties. I saw the curtain go up on a living room with a great curved and cushioned divan smack in the middle of it and heard a comic maid start to grumble as she headed for the door or the telephone. That was *No, No, Nanette*, and I was a ripe ten at the time, being taken to the theater to see my very first show by two kindly maiden aunts. (I saw it in Chicago before they dared to bring it into New York.)

I saw an adorable clown in black face take her solo bow at matinee's end and grab at the house curtain as it started up for still another round of applause. Up she went with the curtain, heels kicking like crazy. That was *Topsy and Eva*, with Rosetta Duncan taking the ride.

I saw Harpo Marx come onto an otherwise unpopulated stage, lean against the proscenium in an enormous sombrero, and just laze there, leering at us, while he blew little puffs of cigarette smoke that looked like the anti-aircraft fire of World War I. He did it for a long time, alone, and, in some crazy conspiratorial way, we loved him for it. That was *Animal Crackers*, and you won't find the moment in the later film version no matter how hard you look. It was a stage moment, reserved for the aficionado; private theatrical property.

What *else* do I remember? Very, very little, alas. How much can you expect a man of ten, or twelve, or even thirteen to store in his head for future—let alone sentimental—reference? My point here is that even those of us who are old enough to root fragments of ancient happinesses out of our heads weren't old enough at the time to grasp the form whole or to conceive undying attachments to it. You can't be nostalgic about a way of walking (Helen Gallagher's John Held, Jr., slouch) or a way of getting the male chorus onstage (let them slip, all at once, from behind pillars that have been hiding them) that you honestly don't recall. Maybe you've heard about these things, maybe you've looked at old programs, maybe you've seen pastiches. But they don't add up to the first girl you loved, because you weren't loving girls yet, you were still messing around with the Boy Scouts. Of all the people who were washing love over *No, No, Nanette,* not more than ten percent could truly have been saluting a familiar, if long absent, face. In fact, people still don't remember one of the most important things about the musicals of the 1920s, but I'll get to that in a moment.

First we must make an allowance, rather a large one. There was no such thing, in any exclusive sense, as a musical comedy of the twenties. Do you know when the celebrated Princess musicals were done, with Jerome Kern supplying the tunes and P. G. Wodehouse and Guy Bolton the books and lyrics? They're certainly part of the tradition, what with Vivienne Segal and Oscar Shaw and Ernest Truex and all those people popping in and out of them, but they were over with by 1918. Yet *Smiles,* of 1930, in which Fred Astaire first danced in top hat and tails around the chorus boys while shooting them down with his cane, and *The Gay Divorce,* of 1932, in which Mr. Astaire passed himself off as the fellow who was supposed to compromise Claire Luce at a seaside resort, can't have been radically different from the Princess' *Oh, Lady, Lady!* Look at Victor Moore in 1926. *He* was passing himself off as a butler in order to conceal his bootlegging activities: *Oh, Kay!* Look at him again in 1934, passing himself off as a clergyman in order to gun down a rival gangster. Mr. Moore, and his new show, surely looked much like the old one.

The so-called musical comedy of the twenties really stretches all the way from 1915 to the arrival of *Oklahoma!* in 1943. Little changes along the way, oh, yes. Richard Rodgers was already *trying* to integrate the songs and dances, so that the score would be all of a piece, as early as *Chee-Chee* (1928). "The songs are going to be a definite part of the progress of the piece," Mr. Rodgers promised before that show arrived, "not extraneous interludes without rhyme or reason." In fact, the songs were so integrated that they couldn't be separated from one another, and so weren't listed on the program. Though *Chee-Chee* happened to prove a failure, Mr. Rodgers had kept his promise about integrating the *score*. But would you like to know what the plot of *Chee-Chee* had to do with? It had to do with the son of the Grand Eunuch of Old China. It seems that the son of the Grand Eunuch was taking all measures possible to avoid inheriting his father's job. Rhyme and reason, indeed!

Some musicals, like the Princess series, were called "intimate" and didn't have Roxy-sized chorus lines (though *Meet My Sister* in the thirties could scarcely have been less intimate than *Leave It To Jane* in 1917), some were multiple-star, Ziegfeld-scale extravaganzas (Ziegfeld originally intended to do three separate musicals for Marilyn Miller, Leon Errol, and Walter Catlett, then decided to whomp them all together in one supersmash called *Sally*). But big or small, pretend-integrated or "without rhyme or reason," they were fundamentally the same over a better than twenty-five-year span.

The songs weren't busy pushing a more or less sobersided plot, they were *songs*, independent, idiosyncratic, arrogant, detachable; a little ballad announcing that "He's just my Bill" could be dropped from *Oh, Lady, Lady!* in 1918 and be slipped with ease into even the relatively integrated *Show Boat* of 1927. People came into the theater to hear the latest melodies that Gershwin and Porter and Rodgers and Berlin and Kern and DeSylva, Brown, and Henderson had come up with, and two hours later they couldn't—not if their lives depended upon it—have told you how any one of their favorite numbers had been cued into the story going forward. ("I can write a song cue for *anything*," said the George Abbott of *Too Many Girls* and *Best Foot Forward* and *Where's Charley?*, and sure enough, he could.) It is just barely possible that the only celebrated song of the entire period that logically belonged to one show and not to another was "Alice Blue Gown." That was sung in *Irene* by a young fashion salon model who had surreptitiously sneaked out a gown (Alice blue) to wear to a dance. She was caught red handed, you'll be sorry to hear. It worked out all right, though. The rich hero loved her anyway, poor purloiner that she was.

Ditto the dances. The dances weren't connected to the narrative but to the latest notions sweeping the nation's dance floors, and so, in their clockwork routining, if they changed at all they changed ever so slightly to accommodate the shift from ragtime to jazz, Charleston to Black Bottom, occasionally venturing to originate a "Varsity Drag" on their own. (The "Varsity Drag" popped up in *Good News*, where the best things in life were free and what did *that* have to do with the fact that a campus football hero couldn't pass his exam in astronomy or whatever?) The dances were extensions of the music, not of the story line, and the music was a law unto itself. If you could hear "Swanee" or

"Sunny" or "Thou Swell" of an evening, did you really care what show it was in? ("Thou Swell" didn't *have* to take its "thou" from the King Arthur's court of *A Connecticut Yankee*. You could put it into *Good News* with no trouble at all. Just suppose that fellow was failing Chaucer.)

As I say, there are no vital distinctions to be made between the musicals of three decades, and the people who had put *No, No, Nanette* together knew that. As Mr. Saddler and Mr. Shevelove have freely admitted, the sleepy soft shoes and the piston taps and the sunburst endings of the numbers weren't derived directly from the twenties. Instead, they constituted a survey of everything from the youth of Irene Castle (there was a flash of the Castle walk in the show-stopper Miss Gallagher and Mr. Van did together) to the middle-age of Busby Berkeley (though there was rather less of Berkeley in it than you might have expected; the show eschewed his opulence and concentrated on friskiness). If *No, No, Nanette* was a period entertainment, it would be hard to put a period to the period it was playing with. Its reach really did stretch its memory span and ours; there was more than a single decade to be nostalgic about.

Even so. The sentiment that welled up seemed to me to have less to do with any one memory than it did with a general sense of loss. What we loved about the show, and what we had been missing for so long, was its *playfulness*. It was like a puppy without a purpose: free, and off and skipping. That seemed strange to us, and strangely appealing. Today we're accustomed to accepting responsibility, even when we go to musical comedies. (Responsibility for people who have been taught to hate and fear, for the end of Anatevka, for the idealism of that man of La Mancha, for the hostility of Jets and Sharks, for some sort of social or literary *sense*.) *No, No, Nanette* was irresponsible. Like all the musicals it grew up with, it just wanted to be happy and to make you happy, too, and it didn't give a hang how it swung it. Rule: *anything* goes, as a certain Cole Porter lyric once aptly insisted, so long as the evening takes off.

That brings me to the subject of earlier musical comedy books, those pre-*Oklahoma!* confections that liked rhyme well enough but defied reason, and to the one thing that everyone seems to have forgotten about them. We know that they weren't distinguished; sometimes they weren't even coherent. But they weren't *meant* to be. That's what's been forgotten. They were meant to be capers, improvisations, free-form doodles, handy pegs to hang better things on; they weren't to claim anything for themselves. And everyone understood that.

Oh, they were criticized occasionally at the time. Some doodles are better-looking than other doodles. But Robert Benchley grew impatient with people who were impatient about musical-comedy books. "If you're going in for books," he wrote, "you might as well stay home and tell stories every evening." What he knew, and what all the rest of us knew, was that the essential purpose of a musical comedy book was to be interrupted. Its very quality lay in its interruptibility. It wasn't supposed to *do* things; it was supposed to get out of the way of other things, as often and as nimbly as possible.

It was an endless series of open doors, an airy and unimportant artifice, an invitation to *freedom*. The question was not whether you had a "strong" book but whether you had a flexible book, one that could readily accommodate itself to all the treasures a composer and a choreographer and a clown could cook up, beforehand, in rehearsal, on the road, anytime. (The original *No, No, Nanette* had been on the road for forty-nine weeks before it came into New York, during which time Vincent Youmans managed to incorporate "Tea for Two" and "I Want To Be Happy." It would be difficult to do that with *West Side Story*.) Ideally, the form was as loose as a dashiki, not as tight as a Regency vest.

How loose? Noël Coward: "In most of these entertainments there was nearly always a bitter misunderstanding between the hero and the heroine at the end of the first act (if it was in two acts) or the second act (if it was in three acts). Either he would insult her publicly on discovering that she was a princess in her own right rather than the simple commoner he had imagined her to be, or she would wrench his engagement ring from her finger, fling it at his feet and faint dead away on hearing that he was not the humble tutor she had loved for himself alone, but a multimillionaire. The ultimate reconciliation was usually achieved a few seconds before the final curtain, after the leading comedian had sung a topical song and there was nothing left to do but forgive and forget."

Now you don't suppose that anyone, even in 1925, took that sort of thing to heart? They took it to humor, took it for fun, connived with its idiocy gleefully, made a happy deal with it. It could be as silly as it liked provided the songs and the jokes it so offhandedly made way for were good. What is particularly revealing in Mr. Coward's little resumé is not the princess-millionaire outline but the fact that the most important number just before these two were reconciled had absolutely nothing to do with them but was reserved for the principal comedian. The comic and his show-stopper got what was generally known in those days as the eleven o'clock spot, a tradition which absolutely demanded that before the nearly nonexistent story line of *Du Barry Was a Lady* could be wrapped up, Bert Lahr and Ethel Merman would have to come front and do "Friendship." The problem after that was to get the audience to stop applauding so that the story line *could* be wrapped up.

The blissfully irrelevant number, whether it belonged to the clowns or the lovers, could of course come anywhere, the plot being so open-ended. In *Oh, Lady, Lady!* P. G. Wodehouse and Guy Bolton had no difficulty at all in settling down to a duet between a loving ex-burglar named Spike Hudgins and his shoplifter fiancée, Fainting Fanny, part of which ran like this:

> *Since first I was a burglar, I have saved in every way*
> *Against the time when some nice girl should name the happy day.*
> *When I retired from active work and ceased at nights to roam*
> *I meant to have enough nice things to furnish up the home.*
>   *And I achieved, as you will find,*
>   *The object that I had in mind.*
>
> *Our home will be so bright and cheery*
> *That you will bless your burglar boy:*
> *I got some nifty silver, dearie,*
> *When I cracked that crib in Troy:*
> *And I got stuff enough in Yonkers*
> *To fill a fairly good-sized chest,*
> *And at a house in Mineola*
> *I got away with their victrola,*
> *So we'll have music in the evenings*
> *When we are in our little nest.*

Fanny, of course, responds in kind, having, in her various professional visits to stores, often said to herself, "There's something for the home." The number was not only one of the most popular in *Oh, Lady, Lady!*, it was a wow at Sing Sing when the inmates did it there.

To be able to use the songs and dances and gags you want to use (and that any audience in its right mind and out for an evening's pleasure will want you to use), you need a plot with removable pieces. That, probably, is why at least every *other* musical over a thirty-year span involved disguises. If one disguise didn't happen to provoke a particularly funny scene, you could always switch to another, or another three. William Gaxton, for instance, was almost never himself. In *Fifty Million Frenchmen* he pursued the girl he loved by pretending, successively, to be a Parisian guide, an Arabian magician, and a gigolo. In *Anything Goes*—in which Victor Moore was *already* disguised as a clergyman—Mr. Gaxton pretended to be a Chinaman, a sailor, American Public Enemy No. 1, and Nicholas Murray Butler. Female stars didn't work as hard, but they qualified. Marilyn Miller, a poor waitress, might easily be passed off as a Russian ballerina, rising to fame and fortune by the ruse. (I am indebted to Stanley Green's *The World of Musical Comedy* and to David Ewen's *Complete Book of the American Musical Theater* for many of these plot synopses; I couldn't see *everything*, not and pass eighth grade.)

What was needed, you see, was a minimal contrivance that didn't pretend to be anything but a contrivance and that could, with our genial approval, be used to start things off, wherever they might be going (to Paris, to college, to the court of Louis XIV, to jail). If the conceit was a joke in itself, so much the better. Victor Moore's side of *Anything Goes* works like this. Though he is disguised as a clergyman, he is actually Public Enemy No. 13. But he is superstitious. It is therefore necessary for him to try to eliminate one other public enemy so that he can become No. 12 and stop fretting. That's all it takes to take off, and fun from the start. *Something for the Boys*, if I remember correctly, was based on an actual incident: a woman who was having some dental work done began receiving shortwave broadcasts on her fillings; in no time at all it was Ethel Merman who was intercepting spy rings with her teeth.

The simplest way to tee off such a show was with a wager. The hero, probably a millionaire to begin with, would win a bet of $25,000 if he could live on absolutely nothing, in Paris, for one month. Or a girl would inherit millions if she could just keep her temper for half a year. If not a wager, then a slight displacement. A football player might inherit a dressmaking salon. A radio cowboy could be lured from his utterly safe microphone and forced by happenstance or by guile to trap an actual Mexican bandit. Premises like these lead to no logical second steps, except trouble, naturally. But the trouble can be of any sort, and if you're going to Mexico you can do Mexican dances. When I saw Al Jolson do *Hold Onto Your Hats*, which was the one about the radio cowboy, Jolson was feeling rather poorly. So he simply opened the second act by strolling onstage with a folding chair tucked under his arm, sat on the chair to rest his obviously weary bones, forgot about the bandit he was chasing and proceeded to sing all the songs he could think of, right there. Nobody minded. (Maybe the authors did. I never heard. But I surely don't have to repeat for you George S. Kaufman's stunned remark as he watched *The Cocoanuts* one night: "My God! I think I just heard one of the original lines!")

If the form didn't have to be quite that loose, it did have to be loose enough to accommodate the truly sainted among the musical-comedy greats, the star clowns. Even Ed Wynn and Bobby Clark and Joe Cook and Eddie Cantor usually moved in and out of hastily brushed-off plot lines involving a boy and a girl. They had to have a love story to help along, or inadvertently foul up, didn't they? But they also had to have room for whatever it was the audience demanded *they* do. They might have to turn up in blackface at least once, with any preposterous excuse, or the evening would be spoiled. They might have to occupy the entire stage for a while, as Joe Cook did, with a vast Rube Goldberg mechanism geared to hitting stooge Dave Chasen on the head at the precise moment he was to strike a single note, on a triangle, to complete "Three O'Clock in the Morning." They might have to appear as washerwomen, throwing clothes over their shoulders nonchalantly but so expertly that everything landed in place on a line strung up behind. Bobby Clark could do that.

"Isn't it rather a ghastly thing writing a show for a couple of comedians like Clark and McCullough?" someone once asked Guy Bolton, as reported in P. G. Wodehouse's cheerful salute to the time, *Bring On the Girls*. Wodehouse continues: "Guy said no. It could better be described as a series of block comedy scenes tied together by a plot. A 'block comedy scene' means one written like a revue sketch with a concentration on laughs and a final twist of 'blackout' value at the end. He enumerated some of the scenes, among them one in a sinister Mexican bedroom where Bobby Clark is stayed in the act of running away by the discovery of a diaphanous nightdress under his pillow, with which he runs about hopefully caroling, 'Marquita, Marquita.'" You don't derive the scenes from the plot. You see what good scenes you've got and use the plot as a bright red ribbon to wrap them together with, for delivery by Christmas.

What were the virtues of this kind of grab-baggery? Well, the virtues weren't *in* the librettos, they leaped out of them. (Let's face it. Musical-comedy librettos are never going to be all that good if only because first-rate playwrights generally won't write them, not wishing to play no-fiddle to the music; even *Oklahoma!*, with its glorious songs and dances intact, was beginning to sound lame in the libretto last time around at the New York State.) The old-style fantastifications didn't so much have virtues as spawn them. What, once more, were they? Music. Lyrics. Comedy. Clowns.

The fact that our own musical theater is simply not as richly endowed melodically as the theater that spawned Kern and Gershwin and Porter and Berlin and Schwartz and so many others may be the result of social change that can't be helped, may be just a freak of history. But the composer explosion of the earlier period may also have been due, in part at least, to the fact that its musical-comedy form offered so generous an invitation. It didn't require a composer to subject himself to a plot need. It invited him to compose what he wanted to compose, what was bubbling up inside him fastest, after which the plot could be fixed to suit. The lid was off. You could hear the corks popping.

Lyrics could be playful, having little else to do. (If, in one of our own musicals, you have a song about how the hero is going to have to change jobs, you can always change the song if it isn't good enough; but you can't change what the song *says*.) Larry Hart was perfectly free to write

> *You sew your trousseau,*
> *And Robinson Crusoe*
> *Is not so far from worldly cares*
> *As our blue room far away upstairs.*

But you couldn't square away that "Crusoe" rhyme in one of our responsible extravaganzas today. It's too impudent. It's poking fun at the fun it's having. You don't believe in love songs that behave like that, you just relish the trickery and accept it as mockery and hum it forever in your head. No one's going to rhyme "Mott Street" with "what street" in *Raisin* or *The Rothschilds*; there isn't even anything quite so nosethumbing as that in *Hello, Dolly!* You might, you just *might*, find something like it, or near it, in *Cabaret* or *Company* because producer Hal Prince and his colleagues have been making a new effort to stretch musical-comedy seams. But in the main we're still walking that narrow line that says we're not drunk.

Obviously our musicals aren't as funny as the musicals that could afford to stop while Bobby Clark caroled "Marquita" or Joe Cook, a man with sleepy eyes and a mouth like a cupcake, explained how he had become such a fine dancer:

"You may remember as far back as 300 years ago when the island of Manhattan spread out in the country among the tall trees and the high grass. At that time New York was ruled by the Indians, one of whom was Mikook, who had a pair of moccasins in which he used to dance and if I am not mistaken—I probably am mistaken—he tried to sell them for $24 so that the Mikook family could buy Manhattan, which was for sale at a reduced rate. You see, the owner was a brave named Wurzburger, who wanted to go South for his liver during the winter, it being impossible for him to wait any longer for it in the dining room of the Biltmore. But Mikook was unable to dispose of his famous moccasins so they were handed down in the Cook family from generation to generation until finally they fell into the hands of my father. He wore them for mittens the first three winters of his married life with my mother. I was born—of course, that's only hearsay—and my family was too poor to buy shoes for me, so when I was six years old my mother put the old Indian moccasins on my feet. From that time on I became the greatest dancer in the world, which seems an exaggeration, but of which I can assure you. At the age of seven I was better than Pat Rooney or George M. Cohan or any of the other boys who were then knocking them dead. At the age of ten I proposed to Irene Castle and became engaged to marry her, which is not generally known. I wrote her a letter telling her what a great dancer I was, and I said that unless I heard from her as of the 19th inst., I would consider myself engaged to her. No answer to mine of the 3rd inst. being received, I became engaged to Irene Castle and I remain engaged to this day. And so the years passed. . . ."

I won't go on. The clowns, the clowns, the clowns are gone. But we needn't play that record again. The once open door was simply shut in their faces.

No need to dismiss or diminish, to challenge or lament, the shows that came after. *Carousel* and *South Pacific* and *My Fair Lady* were— still are—wonderful musicals. But need we have insisted *only* on the one style, obviously bordering on operetta, during the years of our much advertised maturity? Must all librettos be sane, and all their songs sworn to allegiance?

Just as there are wise and foolish virgins—that is the rumor, anyway—can't there be wise and foolish musicals? I think it was the foolishness of *No, No, Nanette* that we loved, and that our love, long misplaced, was legitimate. Teilhard de Chardin pointed out that certain forms of nature, let's say the wasp or the dragonfly, achieve an absolute efficiency; everything in them is integrated, channeled to a specific end. When this is accomplished, growth stops; the form, with nothing loose left to rattle about in it, drops out of the evolutionary progression. The puppy, on the other hand, loves to play aimlessly, without practical purpose. He's the one that moves on; his responses aren't nailed down.

Here, Spot, here, Youmans, here, Harpo, here, boy.

4

Sherlock Holmes Foiled

Sherlock Holmes was so obviously intended for our pleasure, and for our pleasure alone, that it was a pity the show didn't provide more of it. This was heresy to say, I know. The Royal Shakespeare production of William Gillette's 1899 tampering with the Conan Doyle canon, subjected to a bit more tampering by director Frank Dunlop, had been vastly admired—on two continents—by the time I saw it in 1974. And, given the talent with which it fairly bulged, it did indeed provide us with lovely things to look at, a few turns of phrase calculated to make even the disappointed snort with glee.

There were Carl Toms's scenery and costumes to keep a ravished eye busy, paneled living rooms with stone turrets that shot straight up through them, bricked-in gas chambers so grimy you knew that any finger put to the walls would come away caked in two inches of dust, foggy London streets that dissolved into firelit studies eminently suitable for violin playing in solitude, a blond heroine whose blondness was most sweetly set off by a suit of demurest gray.

There were John Wood and Philip Locke, as Holmes and Moriarty respectively, to be listened to as carefully as if one were chasing, furtively and fruitlessly, a single elusive note dancing restlessly through all of Bach. These men made cadenzas of their haughty displays of intellect, Holmes racing through his celebrated deductions in an effort to outpace his infinite boredom, Moriarty separating his syllables as though each were too juicy to part with. I confess that I did snort aloud at the latter's "Touché! Auf wiedersehen!" it was so gloriously musical a concession to Holmes's genius, so sublimely ostentatious a muddle of tongues.

Yes, we had the stately Holmes of England, intact. Mr. Wood, his tight triangle of a mouth drawn in patient disdain, his oversize leprechaun's ears alert to faulty Chopin and little white lies, his curled hands drooping low at his sides as though he had at one time been hanged, was soulsickness itself in repose, the soulsickness of having found life, crime, love, and cocaine all so commonplace. In profile, shafts of stage light cut his face in two; he could have been pasted, cameolike, on *A Study in Scarlet*'s cover. When he spoke in profile, it was as though a tree trunk had acquired lips, and a snappish tree trunk at that. Listening to him say "el-e-*men*-ta-ry," with the last two sounds dying slowly of the wounds inflicted by the central emphasis, you understood the contempt he felt for a universe that kept asking for explanations. Impeccable.

Mr. Locke's arch-villain came from a gamier mold. Countenance drained of blood beneath twin tufts of white hair, he rather resembled an ostrich being born upside down. Or perhaps the Phantom of the Opera with a face-lift. I am certain he had no eyelashes, possibly no eyelids. There was a baleful glare at the center of a void, and it was approximately as alarming as a pair of headlights coming directly at you on a one-way street. It wasn't surprising to see him rising in solemnity on an iron elevator to his heavenly perch on a balcony; once he had finally been handcuffed, there was something of the martyred saint about him. He had been a spiritual fellow all along, just misguided in his profession.

With so much to admire, however dispassionately, why was I so dispassionate about the evening, so dry of tongue when I wanted to laugh, so unsubmerged in the potentially charming artifices of another and dottier time? I think that Gillette, and the particular theatrical period in which he worked, had a great deal to do with the stubborn matter.

There is a legend about actor-playwright Gillette, and there was a time of day about him. Legend has it that he invariably instructed his fellow actors to pull out all the stops, to "do it up brown," whereupon he strolled into their midst and underplayed them, seeming the sanest, the most controlled, the most "natural" of the group. The ploy would obviously have worked marvelously when he was doing Holmes, making a coil of quietness in the melodramatic maelstrom.

And there was a reason why some such tactic might have been perfectly feasible in 1899 and for a fairish time thereafter. Gillette wrote just as the theater was turning over, gradually surrendering its taste for opulent melodrama in favor of a more plausible restraint. But both options still existed, could stand side by side on stage—in the slightly earlier *Secret Service* as well as in *Holmes*. Plays were "realistic" and they weren't, for a while. Yet, no matter what delicate balances a given actor might strike in performance, this meant that the playwriting proper was trapped in a kind of limbo. It still had the external shape of melodrama—stolen letters, midnight confrontations, miraculous escapes—while trying on a voice of more reasonable inflections. A temporary crossbreed, half malarkey, half common sense.

But exactly how do you revive what was a bastard form to begin with? You can't do it as out-and-out pastiche, it's not quite florid enough, overripe enough, outlandish enough for that. You want *The Ticket-of-Leave Man* or *Nellie, the Beautiful Cloak Model* if you're going to be so openly playful. And you can't do it straight: even when the form is being laboriously rational about its exposition, it's still inherently foolish. Going back to *Sherlock Holmes* is going back to a bind. If the importation at the Broadhurst seemed to me caught in that bind—not funny enough as echo, not credible enough for tension—it was probably because its good people were caught in the halfway house Gillette built for them, *without being able to believe in it.* You see, Gillette, in a way, had believed. We couldn't. And so we insisted on something closer to sustained mirth.

That wasn't forthcoming as we attended to overdetailed plot turns, extended recapitulations, elaborate preparations for crises we couldn't care about because we knew they were going to be so effortlessly, even capriciously, resolved. A mechanical-doll effect, aimed at partial pastiche, cropped up now and again: butler and villainess each backing two steps away in opposite directions as Holmes made a shattering pronouncement. Outsize effects were occasionally indulged: signal rappings on the wall boomed loudly enough for the Castle of Otranto; the celebrated foiling of Moriarty by means of a cigar glowing in the dark was turned into something like a fireworks display, quite robbing the scene of its "naturalistic" surprise.

But this was no man's land, this brief patch of ground on which two understandings of theater once met, and it was not surprising that even so skilled a director as Mr. Dunlop should have whipped this way and that in search of a prevailing wind. I can't tell you he ever found one. *Holmes* was handsome as could be, and it left me half-hearted.

5

What James M. Barrie Knew

"Perhaps you need a sense of humor to be fond of me," says the mousey Maggie Wylie, bun piled severely on top of her primly carved face, in Sir James M. Barrie's *What Every Woman Knows*. And all you need to be fond of *What Every Woman Knows*, I think, is a shred of common decency.

Common decency for three reasons. One, the play works. Quaint as it may seem to be, sentimental as it may be accused of being, it works—and candor demands that one admit the fact. When the Roundabout Theater revived the piece in 1975, an audience was quickly lured into its narrative, made to laugh unexpectedly, hooked by the emotion the play so steadfastly refused to wear on its leg-of-mutton sleeve.

A second reason. How lovely it is to come across, in this day of playwriting arrogance, a dramatist who remembers he is in the theater and that something theatrical ought to be happening between the points the play is to make. I mean *fun* before the fustian, if fustian there is to be. Example. *What Every Woman Knows* has its points to score, of course—pretty plain ones about the vain and obtuse male and the woman who does his work for him without destroying his illusions. But first you've got to get such a man and such a woman together.

Set up a household in which the sole daughter, "getting on" at twenty-six, is a worry to her father and brothers: nobody's ever shown the least romantic interest in her. Give them a second worry: apparently someone's been breaking into the house nights, a burglar who must be caught red-handed. Arm the clan with clubs, turn out the lights, play for a little suspense in the moonlight, wait while the window rattles and a burly figure slips in between the lace curtains. Add a puzzlement, quickly. The intruder makes no move to ransack the neat North Scotland parlor, he filches a book from the shelf, lights a candle, and sits to read—which is what he is doing as the armed family posse surrounds him. Lights up, consternation. No burglar at all, but a poor young chap with political ambitions whose own family has long been at odds with the Wylies. The lad is brainy but has no books, no means of getting an education; he *should* be in university because he'll never amount to beans unless he gets there, but how?

The question, unthinkably but quite naturally, answers itself. There are two in the room—a boy and a girl—with needs. No one has ever supposed that the Scots aren't quick thinkers. Before any more wax has melted down, a proposition has been made. The family will provide university funds for five years, at the end of which period the promising boy will marry Maggie. Done and done.

Now Barrie *knows* he is playing with the theater in all of this midnight pussyfooting and cool plain dealing, but play, after all, is one of the things the theater is for. Is there a law against being amusing, and even a mite suspenseful, while getting around to the marriage-of-convenience plot? (And has anyone ever noticed that the marriage-of-convenience plot, which is so very stock, *never* fails?) Keep the touch light. Asked why he's come sneaking in windows, the boy stoutly replies that, given the feeling between families, he'd "never put foot in the Wylies' door." And don't let the line become coy. Make the boy just obtuse enough, rigid enough, defiant enough, to mean it. We're being offered a nice little layer cake of wry melodrama, the humor of the singleminded, and the art of nudging a narrative into being—sliced with a knife sharp enough to leave the icing intact. The machinations are all jolly before we've got to the crunch.

And the third reason you've got to respect Barrie's so "whimsical" work is that he's entirely aware of the tricks he's playing, is aware that *you're* aware of how the tricks work, and is prepared to undercut the artifice—shoring it up at the same time—by making the figures in his beguiling foolishness as level-headed as can be. Is there absurdity in the cake's tasty filling? Maggie, undisturbed over her knitting as the bargain is struck, sees both the absurdity and the sense in it, *makes* sense of it step by step. When there is some little discussion of whether a formal contract is needed—the boy is honorable and, after all, the family professes certainty that Maggie will surely be snatched up by some other suitor long before five years are done—Maggie is placid, submissive, and realistic. She wants a contract.

Throughout the engaging evening—I've been charting Barrie's deliberate sleight of hand for no more than the first of five scenes—whatever is sneaky or foreseeable or, shall we say, rigged is forced into the open, given a quick dose of daylight, justified by someone's instant sanity, usually Maggie's. If this was an acceptable kind of play for a man to write in 1908, it's still quick-witted enough in puncturing its improbabilities to keep it one wee step ahead in the 1970s. Call Barrie anything you like: old-fashioned, obvious, suspiciously childlike. You'll find him smiling at you.

III

LOOKING
FOR TOMORROW

1

The Legacy
of the Avant-Garde

A correspondent has sent me a clipping and I am fascinated by it for a very special reason. It is a *Variety* review of Thornton Wilder's *Our Town* written immediately after its out-of-town opening forty years ago, and it is highly unfavorable. Do you know why it is unfavorable? *Variety*'s man found the play far too avant-garde for his taste.

Our Town avant-garde? No one thinks of it that way anymore, not that homespun, endearing, down-to-earth account of everyday life and death in Grovers Corners, simple as bread being baked in a sunlit kitchen. As for those who hold it sentimental and self-consciously folksy, the notion of putting the adjective *experimental* to it must seem unreason itself. Yet it was avant-garde and it was experimental. It was so regarded and so damned. A few excerpts from the review:

"It will probably go down as the season's most extravagant waste of fine talent. . . . It probably represents an all-time high in experimental theater for Broadway. By comparison the modern-dress, sceneryless *Julius Caesar* [Orson Welles's] emerges as orthodox and conventional. It's the type of stuff put on here every now and then by the Princeton Theatre Intime, university experimental group, and other serious collegiate organizations. *Our Town* should have been left on the campus. . . ."

The piece goes on to specify just what was so novel about the venture (though the novelty is described as "thin"). "First tipoff on the experimental biz," it reports, "comes upon entering the theater. . . . There is no curtain and the full stage is bare, with only a few stray props resting against the back wall. At what corresponds to curtain time, out walks the stage manager . . . and leisurely sets down a few chairs and two small tables. These, together with two ladders used later for imaginary stairways, represent the only props or scenery used throughout the play." In point of fact, these usages *were* adventurous in an American play intended for Broadway. The use of ladders as acting areas seemed to echo the innovative techniques of Meyerhold in Russia; the narrator-cum-stagehand sounded a little bit Chinese and a little bit Brecht. After the triumphant Broadway success of *Our Town*, however, we never questioned the use of these particular devices again; they became tools casually available to any dramatist wishing to borrow them.

But what fascinates me so is not the ironies that grew out of the situation: the fact that an apparent failure in Princeton could become so solidly embedded in American drama and the American psyche that its fortieth anniversary would be celebrated on Memorial Day by its *fifth* separate production for television; or the fact that what was once rejected as far too far out could come to seem second nature. I'm interested, rather, in another irony, one that sheds some light on our own avant-garde, developed during the past fifteen to twenty years and just now making its way out of theaters *intime* and into the uptown Establishment.

You will notice that most of the techniques thought too daring in *Our Town* were visual techniques: open spaces, limited and arbitrary props, love scenes on ladders, and graveyards composed of nothing but folding chairs and umbrellas. Yet none of these things was considered an end in itself. The evening was not primarily, or even remotely, an improvisation arrived at by actors and director, working independently of a writer. The innovations of *Our Town* were meant to be functional, supportive: they were used to facilitate—indeed, to make possible—the movement of an all-important text. *Our Town* was the work of a literary man. The play was *written*.

Not so with our avant-garde, currently beginning to display its wares to mass rather than elite audiences. The man who has most recently cracked the Establishment is Andrei Serban, whose mountings of *The Cherry Orchard* and *Agamemnon* at the Vivian Beaumont in 1977 quickly became the talk, sometimes the quarrel, of the town. No gainsaying the impact Mr. Serban has had, however "controversial" that impact may be. By continuing and consolidating the inspirations born in lofts, garages, and church basements over the two decades past, and by adding an expansive vision of his own, he has Moved In. But attend: he has Moved In without bringing along a writer of his own. Yes, he does use texts, though not avant-garde texts: Chekhov and Aeschylus scarcely qualified as 1977 groundbreakers. Sometimes Mr. Serban respects the text at hand, as he did with *The Cherry Orchard*, magically amplifying but not erasing it. Sometimes he does not: what Aeschylus had written in the *Agamemnon* was deliberately, resolutely buried beneath dumb-show, processional, torchlight spectacle throughout.

For his thrust, like the central thrust of almost all of the experimentation directly preceding him, is primarily visual, profoundly *theatrical* rather than literary, derived not so much from the word as from the circus, from pantomime and the commedia dell'arte, from gymnastics and religious ritual, from painting and revue and Grand Guignol, from dance. In the sense that these things are almost always given precedence, our avant-garde is antitext, antiliterary. In the sense that dramatic logic and dramatic psychology have been superseded by theatrical spectacle, it is also anti-intellectual. Those who wish to put a pejorative term to it are free to do so: the avant-garde normally rejects conventional theater because it is too tainted with show biz, but our avant-garde has become show biz incarnate.

Think back a bit. What were we looking at ten or so years ago? The Living Theater, spelling out the title *Frankenstein* with the double-jointed bodies of the performers, for all the world like the corps de ballet at Radio City Music Hall. Andre Gregory rolling up his actors into spinning hoops for *Alice in Wonderland*, creating a caterpillar smoking a hookah while reclining on a toadstool composed of four actors bent double. Peter Brook slapping the text of *A Midsummer Night's Dream* about freely while he riveted our eyes upon the main business of the evening: aerialists in silver capes slithering down ropes from a balcony, trapeze artists spinning saucers as they swung high over the stage, Puck getting about on stilts, a hurricane of confetti and Frisbees bringing a scene to its close. Tom O'Horgan exhibiting, side-show style, nude bodies in glass cases, as Richard Foreman continues to do at his Ontological Hysteric Theater. Richard Schechner playing hob with the implications of Euripides' *The Bacchae* while audience attention was diverted by invitations to dance with the company, engage in group gropes. Charles Ludlum staging dances with thalidomide victims, dunking into toilet bowls the heads of actors in clown make-up.

Of them all—and there were more—only Joseph Chaikin of The Open Theater made a serious attempt to keep a writer at his side, seeking an ultimate fusion. It was the talented Jean-Claude van Itallie who provided him with the right chanted words to pave way for *The Serpent*'s remarkable passages of mime: Eve tempted in Eden, Cain killing Abel. But what Mr. van Itallie wrote played second fiddle—it was really a sort of accompaniment—to what was seen; the fusion didn't really take place, certainly the word did not win.

With Jerzy Grotowski it was told it could not win. For Grotowski, prepared words were the enemy of the actor, fetters falsely imposed upon him. An actor's gut impulse—a preverbal groan, a piggyback ride, a tongue lapping the lacquered floor—was the true stuff of theater and drama both, and no playwright was to be permitted to usurp his original, sacred right to create for himself. If texts were used, they were shredded, performed out of sequence or at rates of speed that made them incomprehensible to the most attentive of ears. Better no text at all. Let the magic of the body and the primal cry straining at the human vocal cords make direct, intuitive contact with those of us assembled above the pit, staring down. Were there strange moments in which such contact was made? Yes.

Values *were* discovered during these years of seething, sometimes foolish, sometimes startlingly provocative, activity. There was one value, however, that was not, could not, be developed in the circumstances: language, and all of the structures of thought and melody that arise from it.

Why *was* that? Usually avant-garde movements begin as literary revolutions and go on that way until their own *Finnegans Wake* exhausts them. Why was ours so determined to turn its back on the writer, dispense with him if possible? Were the directors of the period pigs, the performers narcissists, greedily bent on gratifying themselves alone? Not at all. The bias was built in. Ours may have been the first extended avant-garde period to have arranged, at the outset, its own lapse into silence, the first to use the word in order to get rid of the word.

Go back another ten years, roughly to the coming of Samuel Beckett and the noncoming of Godot. Beckett was of course a literary man, producing literary work; thus far our avant-garde began much as any earlier avant-garde had begun. Beckett had a message. The message was that there was no message. And right there were the seeds of an ultimate silence. Didi and Gogo waited through an eternity, as cheerfully as their respective pains permitted, for a promised word. They waited in vain. If existence had any meaning at all, it was not going to be conveyed to us in language.

Ionesco thumped the point home. In his *The Chairs* the expectant gathered in a circular room, awaiting the speaker who would tell them what they needed to hear. This speaker arrived. He spoke gibberish.

Beckett's Winnie, in *Happy Days*, did use words, hundreds and hundreds of them, as she sat chattering and primping, primping and chattering, while the sand rose about her, immobilizing her utterly. But these were pass-the-time words, pretty flights into futility. They accomplished nothing on the arid desert she inhabited; the sand would soon reach her mouth, it was silence that was coming. Beckett wrote some silent plays, as well as the silent *Film*.

Ionesco again hit harder, and less poetically. In *Rhinoceros* he parodied logic baldly, scoffing at the possibility that a syllogism could conceivably have meaning for us. Not content with dismantling verbal structures, he attacked not only the word in the gibberish of *The Chairs* but even the individual letter that went to make up the word: in *The Lesson* he questioned the sanity of anyone who thought that "f " was pronounced "f." Some of this was mild fun, to be sure, but one conclusion was inescapable: human beings were incapable of communicating with each other through language. An old couple sit together. The woman mourns the fact that their only son has left them. The man, agreeing, mourns the fact that they never had a son. Word cancels word, line cancels line, meaning cancels meaning.

The rash of "no communication" plays that followed, inspired by existentialist philosophy and generally offered under the heading of Theater of the Absurd, will be readily recalled; the plays *were* written. That is to say, the language was put down and swiftly shown to be profitless. For the most part, it was indeed profitless, both for the characters onstage and the audiences out front. I suppose I must have seen at least two hundred uncommunicative variants on, or imitations of, the genre in a three- to four-year period, virtually all of them by young would-be writers who were never heard of again. I can think of just three Absurdist or Absurdist-influenced American plays sturdy enough to survive the death of the vogue: Edward Albee's *The American Dream*, Arnold Weinstein's *The Red Eye of Love*, and, quite a bit later, John Guare's *House of Blue Leaves*. Otherwise, the form was simply too easy to fake; it didn't require talent to put random non-sense on paper and call it Absurdism; the fallout was inevitable.

So was the next step. If communication through words had been proved impossible—and a great many laborers in the theatrical vineyard, influenced not only by Beckett but by philosophers from Kierkegaard to Sartre, had now accepted the premise as so—then other means of communication would have to be found. Out went the text, no longer valid as a tool, and a movement that had begun as a literary one became subliterary or extraliterary at the behest of the literary men themselves. The writers had made writing suspect; it was time to send in the clowns.

Hence the explosion of mountebankery, of "plays" that were really painting or music or dance, of solemn investigations of time, space, and silence, of genuine mimetic inspiration and occasional successful gut contact. Sometimes something beautiful to look at, at least. And sometimes entertaining mockery of the theater that had been abandoned, the literary theater that had self-destructed in the manner of Jean Tingueley's machine. Quite a bonfire for a while, and though its blaze faded rather rapidly, it still casts shadows on a few out-of-the-way walls: in Robert Wilson's alternately funny, stunning, and unendurably tedious finger-painting to the sound of a clavichord; in Richard Foreman's Cabinet-of-Dr.-Caligari false perspectives; in the still-lifes and the disembodied dancing glass slippers (heels electrically lighted from within) of the Mabou Mines.

Most of the major companies that flourished while the flames leaped highest have vanished, and we're clearly now in a period of assimilation, a time when the Establishment reaches out and seizes whatever it can usefully incorporate into its own more traditional wares. In the assimilation the theater as a whole gains something: a livelier use of the eye, an increased awareness of the body, a heightened sense of the interrelationship between drama and all of the other arts.

It's also lost something. Writers. If Mr. Serban must use texts from Chekhov and Aeschylus, as Mr. Foreman has used Brecht and Peter Brook used Shakespeare and Richard Schechner used Euripides, it's because new playwrights, new texts, were of little or no concern to them during their years of adventure. We may very well have lost an entire generation of potential dramatists in the process, leaving us to stare in bewilderment and some distress at a void that may house performers readily enough but contains no one to provide them with fresh words to speak.

Less than a handful of playwrights who worked with, or were influenced by, the avant-garde at its peak continue to work, and they remain in outer orbit. Sam Shepard, Jean-Claude van Itallie, Israel Horovitz, John Guare are all there and all talented; but they're still on the theatrical periphery, not quite full-bodied enough to assert themselves as literary forces capable of commanding a large audience, of sustaining an entire evening with language and narrative of their own devising. Some will still make it; but it's a struggle, given the half-hearted value that was assigned them during their years of apprenticeship. Those who are now prying open the doors of the theatrical center—Albert Innaurato, David Mamet, David Rabe among them—are men who came along a bit late in the avant-garde's day, late enough to avail themselves of certain of its residual pleasures and/or treasures without feeling committed to its antiliterary drift. They were, and are, primarily word men.

We'll continue to take profit from all that has gone on. But all that has gone on has left many a potential dramatist crippled.

2

Improvisation for the Actor

At the Brooklyn Academy of Music, where in 1973 director Peter Brook permitted us daylong visits to observe the improvisational exercises of his International Center for Theater Research, I had to choose between believing my eyes and my ears. Ears it was.

The sessions began at ten-thirty in the morning, with a devoted, most often sobersided group of young performers slapping bare feet against the floor in increasingly agitated rhythms, unlimbering their bodies by slipping into gyrations that resembled everything from hornpipes to burlesque bumps, plunging into undulating mazes of bamboo rods to see whether they could gauge progress with sufficient accuracy to avoid being splintered to death.

The warming-up process was interesting enough; I noticed that among the several hundred observers on bleachers around me there were a fairish number surrendering to the occasional accompanying drumbeat, letting their heads and shoulders rock in response to the throbbing activity, not bothering to still their feet. The gyrations continued for an hour and twenty minutes before Mr. Brook, who had been studying his charges from the sidelines with the unwavering focus of a seer, strolled forward to speak.

What he had to say—and although we had heard sounds during the preparatory ritual, we had heard no intelligible words until now—made sense of several kinds. He spoke of the need to rediscover theater, in ourselves, for ourselves, without hand-me-down associations or assumptions that would turn the art stale before we could touch it. At a time when theater had virtually lost its power to command an audience, one was bound to listen to that with hope.

He dismissed the use of spontaneous improvisation as a form of personal therapy; yes, it could be employed in that way, used to disgorge pent-up emotions of a private sort, but his purpose in working with this company for three years (he had given it most of his time since his clown-white production of *A Midsummer Night's Dream* and his film version of *King Lear*) had not been to serve individual psyches, it had been to serve a common reality, a touchable truth, beyond those psyches.

Later, after a lunch break and a long afternoon experiment in which members of the company put their fingers tentatively to a large square made of wooden laths to discover—freshly—what wood was and what could be done with it, Mr. Brook spoke again, generously taking on any and all questions from the audience.

Mr. Brook is an exceedingly mild-mannered man, as pink as an Easter-morning rabbit and as soft-spoken as a vicar giving gentle benediction in a chapel. His composure on this occasion was so total and his blue eyes were so pale that when he *was* asked a question, he seemed to have been shot through the heart in one of those movies where people shot through the heart don't fall down right away. There was a long silence, stunned on both sides: Should I have asked? the questioner wondered. And then something unlocked: the answer, as well phrased as it would have been if he'd been writing a book, flowed like honey. Invariably it was sweet reason itself.

"Freedom and spontaneity don't necessarily bring quality," the master cautioned, warning enthusiasts that self-satisfaction was not the goal, something measurable had to be. Should one be thinking of the audience at all during improvisation, or simply forget that it is there? "Keep the audience in mind at all times; you are making it happen for *them*." Does it matter whether one gesture or another is used, so long as it is internally prompted? "There is no such thing as a meaningless gesture," came the quiet reply, with its obvious implication that meaning has as much to do with theater as uncontrolled urges do, that discipline and choice play a role in art.

Listening, one agreed all along—or almost all along. In insisting that nothing ever be wholly prepared in the theater—including the quasi-dramatic *The Convention of the Birds*, which served after dinner as a summary of work done by the group thus far—Mr. Brook did permit himself what seemed to me a seriously false equation. He spoke of the absurdity of preparing in advance all of the small talk one might wish to use at a dinner party, as though, while dressing to go out, one could rehearse one's responsive chatter to the lady on the right. "Anti-life," Mr. Brook called that, and of course it would be. He then compared such nonsense to rehearsing what one would do on a stage, calling it similar nonsense. But if there was to be no rehearsal for the stage, only freedom and spontaneity, how were we to arrive at "quali-

ty," or even know it when we found it? You can't weed something out
after you've *done* it. No matter. Fielding questions, the man was fascinating.

What I saw on the performing floor was something else again.
Midway through the afternoon I began to feel panic, panic for the
performers. There had been at least one mildly amusing improvisation
with that nailed-together square of wood: a Japanese lifted the skirt of
his kimono and almost dared step into the square, the square seemed to
turn into a well, echoes reverberated from it (including that bad old
vaudeville joke in which a wrong echo is returned), a man lowered
himself through the aperture to find a lonely seated figure at the base
of it, almost as though he'd found the shaman at the well-bottom of
Lascaux. Evocative, though cheapened every now and then in the
execution ("I'm lonely," the seated figure cried, only to cry again, when
kissed, "I'm not *that* lonely!").

But was this all, after three years of preparation? As others took
up the square, seeming to use it as mirror or cage, repetitive patterns
developed, patterns quickly as stale as anything conventional theater
might offer. The square was almost always used defensively, it seemed
to unleash no new imaginative impulses, it became an obstructive
fetish rather than a freeing force. Gradually one saw a real poverty of
inspiration at work: bamboo poles were rushed to the rescue again and
again, strewn on the floor, almost always to be treated as boundaries
not to be transgressed.

The physical vocabulary of these trainees was extraordinarily limited, and when Mr. Brook suggested that the company might try dividing the performing area into Broadway and Hollywood ("A wood
and a way—each has something the other hasn't got, let them make a
relationship with each other") the company sat immobile for a very
long time trying to think its way through *that* one. It never did.
Eventually a few performers rose and made use of the same leaps and
hop steps they'd been employing all day, "finding" nothing new, nothing distinctive, nothing illuminating. Matters weren't helped a bit by
inviting volunteers from the audience to see what they could make of
the suggested contrast and interplay. Spontaneously, the happening
didn't happen.

In the evening, with *The Convention of the Birds*, we were offered
less of the same. By this time certain things had become clear: though
the performers were constantly flirting with mime, they weren't skilled
mimes; though they had taken pains to release their bodies, they
weren't dancers, or anything like; and, when it was time to enunciate
simple enough sentences, they proved not to be trained actors, either.

Mr. Brook probably wanted no part of these three disciplines and was looking for a fourth. It wasn't there, not yet at any rate. I left exhausted and more concerned for the theater than ever. If we are to abandon playwrights and let the performer's creativity do all, where are we to find the creative performers? We may simply have compounded our problem.

3

Improvisation
for the Audience

I think the audience for experimental theater has simply got to have more rehearsal time. It is being asked to do so many things these days, and under such breathtaking circumstances, that in all fairness it must be given some opportunity to limber up, memorize its moves, get in fighting trim. It may also have a little money coming, if it can only unionize.

Take the case of the careworn customers of *Blood*, a very restless rock musical that opened at the Public Theater in 1971. To begin with, the Public Theater complex by then had, in addition to several handsome actual playhouses, three or four additional spaces which looked like empty ballrooms available for production, and the empty ballroom in which *Blood* was being shed just happened to be three flights up. Inasmuch as each of these flights involved *two* steep stairwells, for "three flights up" you could read "six." You could climb six, too.

The Public does have an elevator. In the case of *Blood*, however, that was out. Neither luck nor bribery would send you zooming directly to Flight Three. First you had to go to the second floor to pick up your seats. I don't mean your tickets. I mean your *seats*.

In the center of the second-floor lobby, where normally only espresso is served, representatives of the management were busy uncrating camp chairs and handing them out to patrons who prefer to sit on things during performance. (The seats hadn't come late or anything, it wasn't an accident; bear with me, and you'll see that it was the very principle of the enterprise.) Patrons were then asked to huddle together near a doorway, prior to the last ascent, seats in hand. Before the last ascent could begin, however, an announcement boomed through the lobby's amplifiers to the effect that reviewers didn't have to carry any seats at all, they could simply come forward ahead of the others and be escorted to prearranged comforts. The reviewers were, I think responsibly, hissed. I felt a cad, I can tell you, scaling those last two flights unburdened.

Above, reviewers were seated on narrow raised platforms, and on seats. Backs to the wall and looking down over the arena, they were in a fine position for a second St. Valentine's Day massacre, ducks in a shooting gallery if ever I saw ducks; they also and all too obviously resembled Nero, brooding over the amphitheater, thumbs-down at the ready. Then, into the extremely dark auditorium, guided only by pale blue flashlights in the hands of pale blue usherettes, the audience, equipped with furniture, made its way. I should perhaps stress that this furniture was not really heavy. Unfolded, the seats had no backs. This, whatever its disadvantages as the evening wore on, made them relatively easy to tote about.

And a wise thing, too. For the labor had barely begun. Once the members of the audience had staked out their respective squatter's rights, depositing themselves on either side of what seemed a vast permanent ramp, a kind of schoolmarm marched up the ramp, stomping heavily on its mottled red groundcloth to assign parts to the actors (not a word of what the audience was all too soon to do). One bearded chap in dungarees was to play Agamemnon; a bland youngster with a guitar who claimed he'd never been in a show before (at a rough guess, I'd say he was telling the truth) was assigned the role of Orestes; a girl in black was told she could be Clytemnestra and dream about snakes. All three then picked up the groundcloth and put it over their heads. A girl on a high balcony sang that we weren't to worry about logic tonight, we were simply to pray for the cause of mankind.

Then the ramp split. Again, no accident. Apart it came, swiftly maneuvered by the actors, who *had* rehearsed, dividing into fragments that turned outward and into the audience. Anyone who had seen, or been submerged by, an importation from Italy called *Orlando Furioso* under that bubble in Bryant Park now knew what to expect. In *Orlando Furioso* naked platforms on wheels, bearing actors but no helmsmen, raced down upon a standing audience at trolley-car clip, scattering people hither and yon and wherever else they could get to. The whole thing rather resembled Eisenstein's celebrated massacre on the Odessa steps.

The effect here was milder, say something like the opening of the Cherokee Strip. Up came the audience, up came the camp chairs, on came the actors ordering spectators to clear the way, out fanned the shreds of ramp until it had formed itself into a new, rather Busby

Berkeleyish, star-pattern. Once this was more or less settled—you could tell because the actors had begun to act on it again—the spectators, deciding that repose was now possibly safe, organized themselves afresh, conforming to the rearranged pattern and making new friends.

The play went on, with the actors temporarily doing the work. The spinsterish type had now become the grandmother of a boy (Orestes, watch for parallels now) who had just come home from Vietnam, where he'd had the unpleasant experience of having his senior officers order him to run so that they could shoot his ass off. His grandmother was waving a small flag while a plump girl in an apron waved coffee pots at him. For reasons I am unable to explain, the grandmother was soon lulled into a hot tub, where I believe she was drowned. At least she was pushed down a large hole at the point where the ramps met. Agamemnon, I think, went down the same hole later, though when other members of the company began fishing around in it all they seemed able to dredge from it was a large gray mop. (This may not have been a large gray mop; it may have been Agamemnon's military standard or something like that; the lights were kept terribly low except when it was time to chase the audience with the scenery again.) There continued to be songs, though I caught few lyrics after the opening statement.

And up again! I'm not going to wear you down with an exact accounting of the number of designs, floral or S-shaped or just plain ragged, the fractured ramp was thrust into, or the number of stampedes—less and less panic all the time, just increasing resignation—the customers were jostled into. Let's merely mention that at one point the customers were entirely inside the locked ramps, in diamond formation now, and at another they were bustled up *onto* the slopes so that the company could play on the floor. They were also getting quicker on their feet. They soon caught on—remember what little preparation they'd had—to the fact that whenever it got bright enough to see anything, chances were it was getting brighter for the benefit of those actors who had been trained under the Seven Santini Brothers and were about to shove the carpentry to new floor markings once more. Let the amber spots inch up a notch or two and these customers were on their toes. Until close to the very end.

Odd things had been happening along the way. For one, Grandma had turned up again, offering no explanation for her recent bath and rebirth, and she was now sitting in a rocking chair placed on the upward slant of a ramp. I don't know whether any of you have ever tried rocking a rocking chair on a ramp, but you can probably figure its hazards right off. Even the company could. Therefore they placed an actress directly alongside Granny's chair, one hand firmly gripping it to keep the old girl from flipping head over heels backward into the nearest pocket of patrons. I think this is what gave some members of the audience a clue to their next move.

When it came time for *them* to hoist their chairs onto the ramp—and theirs weren't even rocking chairs, mind—some of them plainly decided that they just didn't want to play anymore or that their insurance was inadequate. In any case, those of us on the reviewers' perch soon noticed that we were beginning to have company. Refugees were reaching us. They didn't say much as they slipped into place alongside us, nestling where they could. They didn't even ask if there were any reviewers' jobs open. They just sighed, sort of. I think they were resting up for the six flights down. They simply hadn't *known* what it took to be an audience these days—no one had told them, I'm writing this to remedy the oversight—and, being inexperienced, they needed time to regroup, consolidate, think over their sheltered lives. I thought of whispering something to them about The Performing Garage, where on a clear night you could swing from the rafters, but I decided against rushing them. We must walk before we can fly. And I'm sure they're home now, rehearsing, rehearsing, never to be caught napping again.

If Aeschylus was being rather oddly treated in *Blood*, old Henrik Ibsen took *his* lumps in a 1975 revival of *Ghosts*. The production was the work of a group known as the Shaliko Company, which seemed to have had its origins at New York University; Joseph Papp was simply "giving it shelter" in one of the tiniest playhouses in the Public. This *Ghosts* was, I would say, the closest we are ever likely to come to a Kung Fu version of Ibsen's play. Anyone really alert might have felt himself duly warned on entering the lobby of the first-floor auditorium: audiences were politely requested to hang up their coats before searching out their seats on carpeted stairwells. No room for excess baggage when actors and/or props were going to be directly over your head, beneath your feet, and crawling over narrow railings that straddled your knees. My own first brush with the "environment" came when I found Ibsen's housemaid, Regina, watering a plant that tended to lap over my toes; being quick of mind and body, I deftly avoided pneumonia.

Some things were difficult to avoid, some difficult to attend at all. I was very happy when Mrs. Alving, that free soul who had wrecked her life by submitting to the mores of the sternly respectable, tossed an exceedingly heavy book—a tome, let it be said—randomly over her shoulder and Pastor Manders actually caught it. If he hadn't, the spectator directly beside him might still be in bandages today. But the actor playing Pastor Manders had an exceptional eye for pop flies—he later snatched a wineglass similarly on the wing—and seemed to have a real future in the outfield.

He had no future at all on the wrestling mat. In this innovative production, Mrs. Alving was a highly sensual wench, a condition partly brought about by her long sexual deprivation and partly by the fact that she was to be seen sashaying around the premises with a wine bottle in her hand—rather as though *Ghosts* and *Ten Nights in a Barroom* were playing back to back in repertory and she'd got the performance dates confused. In any event, she made a headlong dive at poor Manders, pastor though he was, and kissed him with such cobra-like passion, slithering the while, that he felt himself compelled to hurl her to the floor.

This was a serious mistake. For he was, after all, a gentleman, with a gentleman's obligation to extend a hand to help her up again. Seizing his hand, she employed the karate that was the key to director Leonardo Shapiro's interpretation of the play, and promptly flopped him on his back, quite knocking the wind out of him though without dislodging his clerical collar. (Getting out my notepad after the first intermission, I found myself automatically writing "Round Two" as a prelude to what was to come.) While Mrs. Alving was doing all of this, she was speaking—there was a text, remember—of her late husband's depravity.

And there were other subjects to be discussed, other falls to be taken. At one point Pastor Manders found himself with carpenter Engstrand on his lap, both sobbing loudly as the minister offered solace: it sounded rather like a bad night in a barnyard, an impression reinforced shortly thereafter by the sight of the two men on their knees, butting heads together like tick-maddened sheep. But I don't really mean to dwell on the evening's eccentricities of performance, except to say that the actors seemed to imagine themselves housed in a heliport, convinced that if they made enough noise and waved their hands wildly enough one or another of them would soon take off. I had always supposed that it was Mrs. Alving's son, Osvald, who was on the verge of going mad; I seem to have been misinformed.

On to the "environmental" aspects. Scenes were played in small, raised pockets of space at the far corners of the miniature auditorium or on a balcony so narrow that spectators sitting on the edge of it—feet dangling into space—had to duck or take the damage whenever the performers waxed fierce. In the latter instance, spectators sitting *under* the balcony could, of course, see nothing at all. I noticed two of them rising from their padded benches and striding into what was otherwise an acting area in order to catch a glimpse of the contestants, apparently interested in what they were up to; five others simply remained congealed where they were, perhaps counting themselves lucky to be spared a moment or two of the performance. As for myself, I was having shoe trouble again. Carelessly permitting myself to be distracted by making a hasty note in the dark, I hadn't noticed that Pastor Manders had so maneuvered himself as to somehow or other get my foot embedded in his mane of white marcelled hair. I was able to remove my foot without at the same time removing shreds of his crowning glory, and all was well. As well as it was going to be that night.

Having spoken of two evenings at the Public, I must mention a third.

Not a man jack of us will ever get it through his head just how unpredictable stage life can be. The real thing can appear in the meanness of an eye, no more than that, in the sudden uncoiling of a body hitherto immobile against a pillar. It says, "Here I am, and you *listen*," and drama's with us without warning.

In *For Colored Girls Who Have Considered Suicide When the Rainbow Is Enuf,* the small miracle happened, and happened a number of times. There was a need for it to happen repeatedly because *For Colored Girls* wasn't a play that, once it had got its audience in its tigerish grip, could sustain its power, its presence, through narrative. It was a loosely linked collection of prose poems written by a stunning black woman named Ntozake Shange (who also appeared in the company) and simultaneously spoken and danced on an almost undecorated stage by six young accomplices who knew which veins Miss Shange had sliced open and how to convey to an audience the fact that the wounds hurt.

The evening was short (not more than ninety minutes, without intermission) and some passages were conventional ("I used to live in the world/Then I moved to Harlem and now my universe extends six blocks"). But spare as it was, it had drama hidden and boiling just beyond an apparently controlled surface, ready to be unleashed somewhere between the arrogant turn of a head and the infuriated stomp of a bare foot. Miss Shange herself, who seemed to seal her lips in wisdom with the completion of each thought, kept to a conversational tone, anger reined, as she formally rejected sorrow on the grounds that no girl could be sorry and colored at the same time.

But Trazana Beverley, in a blazing red variant of the chitons adopted by the players to free knees, arms, claws, and sinuous shoulders for a visual spelling-out of the seductions and rejections that had constituted their lives, was another, more explosive matter. You were apt to notice her midway through the evening as she snatched an orange butterfly from the sky to decorate her hair, created a rose "to dart from behind her ears," saw to it that her lips and elbows smelt of honey and Jack Daniel's. Making herself alluring for a night on the street that would end abruptly at 4:30 a.m., she was already self-mocking, secretly malicious in her masquerade. And when, her necessary night's work done, she furiously washed away everything calculated to disguise the fact that she was "an ordinary brown woman," her fury and her pride were spat out with equal, brusque and biting, venom.

More remarkable still, though, was the instant drama she created as a climax for the event. We didn't know what remembered story she was going to tell us as she seethed, through clenched teeth, that "there was no air," but a tension had been spun out of sound and taut stance that was going to grow and grow until its effect was nearly unbearable. This particular woman was going to lose her two children; the husband she had tried to rid herself of (he'd "caught her on the stairwell" when she was thirteen) would, in his own intense hatred born of frustration, drop them from a fifth-story window. It seemed to take place as we listened, made graphic step by step, inch by inch, pain by pain, through the actress' feverishly wrung hands, interlocked fingers, frozen silences, deep reluctant assents to a demand for love, impulsive tugs at children drawn to their "daddy." This was brilliant theatrical work, though we saw no one on stage but the woman remembering. A complete, chilling image had been born of a little language and a performer's secret wisdom; she spoke, and we walked into her words.

4

A Kiss in the Dark

The James Joyce Memorial Liquid Theater, visiting the Guggenheim Museum in 1971, was the only participatory theatrical event I had ever attended at which I got an elbow smack in the eye and a kiss to make up for it. The kiss was the difference.

Almost all of the groups that have for so long been inviting us to share the performance—to dance, to join the mystic circle on stage, to abandon our inhibitions along with our shoes—have done so on most peculiar terms. They have normally *ordered* us to get with it. They have come to where we were—on platforms or in cushioned seats—and jostled us, tugged at us, scolded us for a reluctance that was taken for granted. We were, in effect, accused of refusing an invitation before we had been extended one. We were embarrassed into saying no.

Inside the injunction there has sometimes been hostility. The performers have come to us as superior beings certain that we were among the unenlightened and wished to remain so. Sometimes they have screamed at us, damaging their voices—to say nothing of our ears—in the process. I was once screamed at (for what seemed a year or so and must have been a full ten minutes by the clock) by a member of The Living Theater who seemed more devoted to his rage than to my reluctance. I think if I'd given in he'd have been crushed. There'd have been nothing to spend his venom on. Love was always the message, but it was often delivered in tones of fury.

The Liquid Theater never raised its voice—or at least it did not until the entire audience was ready to join it, on impulse and impromptu, in a sound that suggested a thousand owls had taken up residence in the Guggenheim; but that came later. At the door you were greeted warmly but most politely, handed a bag in which to deposit your shoes and small change, told that you would be called to the next event by the color of the bag. (I was pale blue.)

While waiting for the reds and the navys around you to be summoned to the gauze-draped maze, you were allowed to lounge where you wished in the great rotunda—inflated zebra-striped cushions were provided for reasonable comfort—and listen to a guitarist make late-summer cricket sounds beneath the huge cement coil that seemed like the inside of a cool sauna.

Summoned, you might be asked to join in a game or two before closing your eyes. The games were very simple and you were allowed to choose partners, into whose eyes you were permitted to stare silently and whose shoulders you were invited to shake. I got a most attractive girl with green eyes and enjoyed shaking her; sorry to lose her a few moments later.

Entering the maze, you were asked—not ordered—to close your eyes, and closing your eyes—it turned out—was quite a simple thing to do. Nearly everyone I talked to about The Liquid Theater expressed apprehension about going. "Should I take a stick?" one normally courageous friend asked me. (An experience of earlier hostilities lingered, you see, and was hard to erase.) No sticks. The request was decently, gently made, it was instantly persuasive, you had no fear that you were going to be manhandled or mocked.

You were touched, it is true. (I find at this point that there is a long gap in my notes, and not only because my eyes were closed. My hands were occupied.) Hands were occupied by other hands, some male, some female, leading you through a passage of brushed cheeks, faintly felt feathers (while bells tinkled close to your ears), an opportunity to taste a grape without at first knowing what it was, easy embraces. I came away, and awake again, surprisingly soothed.

So, most apparently, did virtually all of the other guests present at the "performance" I attended. (It was the group's special genius to make you feel guests, even, I suspect, if you had paid your way in.) Many extended the experience by leading one another, eyes closed in turn, past and through the textures that were available to the finger-tips. Others engaged in shadow play against projections, some joined in encounter-group techniques and yoga variations with which you might or might not have been familiar. (I wasn't, much.)

Those who preferred group activity could once again play games. These games, as it happened, were the weakest, least imaginative aspect of the evening's assorted therapies (I agreed to adopt a turtle posture beneath an enveloping sheet and discovered, in my confinement, that I was merely tempted to smoke). They also went on too long.

In time, however, the gauzes that constituted the maze were flung away (it was during the flinging that I made that inadvertent contact with that nice girl's elbow) and the games melted into a show of sorts. On an improvised stage that looked rather like the underside of a flying saucer the boys and girls who had until now been agreeable escorts very gradually began to raise the temperature.

Hitherto the music, like the welcome, had been modest, on the soft side. Now at last great chords cleaved the suddenly spacious room; for the first time in my life I found the initial thrust of hard rock welcome, perhaps because I had been made to wait for it, tuned up to it.

There was, in the playing area, a bit of mime, a boy and a girl discovering sexual differences. The mime itself was familiar, naïve, nothing we hadn't seen before. But we were able to accept the loosely danced celebration of the body that erupted from it as genuine and exhilarating because some kind of trust had been established between the performers and ourselves. A simple liking had relaxed us.

Had, in fact, relaxed the entire group present so that, once the dancing had imperceptibly flowed from "stage" to audience, every last man and woman present rose, voluntarily and with pleasure, to join the chanting column snaking endlessly through the open space. I am told that, some evenings, the problem was not to get people into the theater, but to get them out of it. They wanted to stay on dancing.

To the last, by the way, you were free to behave as *you* wished. There were comfortable chairs along the curved walls. If you retired to one of them, as I eventually did because my knees were reminding me that I had never learned to sit cross-legged for long, no one would try to shame you into returning. You were still on hospitable ground.

Theater? No, not by any definition I would care to defend. But as communal therapy, participatory exercise, whatever you want to call it, it worked. The people in charge knew what they were about. And so I do report.

IV

THE PROBLEMS
OF NOW

1

The Grinling Gibbons Room

As the theater plunges on into heaven knows what, there is one thing I devoutly wish for each and every playwright: that he will be able to finish his Grinling Gibbons room.

Chances are that, unless you are a student of architecture or wood carving, you won't have the foggiest notion of what a Grinling Gibbons room is. I hadn't myself, being unversed in those particular arts, and it wasn't until I came face to face awhile back with a specter that's haunted me ever since that I began to ask questions.

A few are simply enough answered. Grinling Gibbons, principally a carver of ornamental woodwork for the stately homes of England, was born in 1648 and became so skilled and so fashionable while plying his trade, alone and in collaboration with the likes of Sir Christopher Wren, that late in life he was appointed "master carver in wood" to King George I. That was in 1714; he died seven years later, leaving many a ceiling, chapel, choir, statue, lintel, and decorated dado line behind him.

And what, you ask in your continuing confusion, has any of this to do with playwriting, or with my hopes for the theater's future? Two things, one of them frightening, one of them necessary. The fright came almost the moment I entered the odd forty-by-twenty-foot enclosed space that had been built onto dramatist Sidney Kingsley's guest cottage in New Jersey. The provisional space had been constructed as a blank; four bare walls and no more. But here and there about the four walls had risen the beginnings of what seemed a vast architectural jigsaw puzzle, doorways half formed, moldings running along the ceiling boldly for a time and then halting uncertainly, patches of paneling creeping jaggedly upward like the New York skyline.

Mr. Kingsley had bought himself, quite a long time before, a room that had once been designed, executed, and lived in, in London or mayhap in the Cotswolds—a Grinling Gibbons room. But he'd bought it in a crate, disassembled, a forest of matchsticks running to more than five thousand separate pieces. And he had no real clue as to what the completed room was supposed to look like. Or how he was to make it look like anything, anything at all. His actress wife, Madge Evans, was precisely as helpful as wives tend to be in such situations. "We have just acquired the world's greatest collection of seventeenth-century firewood," she announced.

To be sure, the individual pieces were marked. But they were sort of Buster Keaton–marked, identified by combinations of numerals and letters that could be read seven ways from Sunday and that would probably lead the innocent into erecting a structure that looked like a kaleidoscope gone mad. An intelligent man—Mr. Kingsley, let's say— could look at a painted labeling that ran something like S3B12R and deduce—or guess—that the initial S meant "South wall." But even supposing that he'd guessed right and that the S didn't stand for Southampton or Sandhurst or the name of the family that had commissioned the work, where did he go from there?

Where would you go? How do you decide which piece you dare affix to the naked wall first? Would your hand tremble as you chose, would your heart palpitate or your head swim, knowing that any false first move would compound itself until thirty or eighty or two hundred successfully fitted pieces had all accumulated about the wrong spot? Oh, yes, you could somehow assemble a most decorative doorway. You might even decide to place it on the S wall. Where? How far from which corner? And where were the corners anyway? Are you dead certain that all of the fragments of that handsome door belong to that handsome door and not to another? Neither chart nor ground plan, blueprint nor key, had been provided. A game of pin the tail on the donkey, with the donkey most likely being you.

But I said that tantalizing portions of the room had already climbed upward from the bases and surbases on which they rested: one beautiful door did display some confidence, though of course it might have belonged six inches, or six feet, to the right or to the left. Mr. Kingsley had been brave, and, being a man of the theater, had tackled the matter as a designer might. He'd first made miniature cardboard copies of all the pieces and then toyed with them, this way and that, just as Boris Aronson or Oliver Smith would probably do. When portions of the model had a sensible look to them, he'd tackled the real wood, fingers crossed and a prayer on his lips. The project struck me at the time as a magnificent form of therapy, something for a man to run to after a befogging day at the typewriter in order to soothe his fevered brow. Or overheat it further.

The image of that room has not only never left me, it has intensi
fied steadily as our theater has struggled on, producing newer, stranger
forms year after year, producing fewer new mature playwrights as
those same years have worn on. For the Kafkaesque truth is that all
our playwrights today stand in the dead centers of their Grinling
Gibbons rooms, utterly uncertain of what move to make next.

To a degree, this dilemma has always existed. Moss Hart, whose
work as a writer for the stage ranged from the early 1930s into the
1950s, used to point out that the fact that a man has managed to
produce one thoroughly workable play doesn't tell him a single thing
about how he is going to do the next one.

Whatever made the first jell is utterly irrelevant to the second, the
second to the third, and so on till career's end. *Every* new play is
unmapped territory, with a topography of its own and no street signs.
The writer enters it blindfolded, abandoning whatever rules he may
have picked up in another country, and gropes his way through thick-
ets and around boulders until he stumbles onto what he *thinks* is a
possible path. Whether or not the path is leading him anywhere will
remain a mystery until he gets there, at which point it may all be too
late.

Individual plays succeed because their individual secrets have been
deciphered, and every dramatist, no matter how experienced, feels
himself a trembling novice as he advances on new material. But if the
problem has always been there, it has become enormously intensified
during the past fifteen to twenty years. Earlier, if Mr. Hart *knew* that
he didn't know how to write his next play and that he'd have to go to
the mat with it to learn its private tricks through contact, he at least
knew what a comedy, or a farce, was supposed to look like, generically.
A comedy, then, looked like something Philip Barry or S. N. Behrman
might have written, a farce like something George S. Kaufman or
George Abbott might have done. The same thing held true for melodrama (*The Desperate Hours* or *Dial "M" for Murder*), for social drama (*All
My Sons*, *Dead End*), for genre pieces (*Awake and Sing*, *Morning's at
Seven*) and so on. Everyone had a rough idea of the *formal* universe in
which he meant to place his play, knew something of its overall look—
before he tackled the vital and unique details. He may have had
problems, but he wasn't going to fall off the edge of the world.

And then we all fell off the edge of the world. The rough-and-ready
conventions—call them blueprints of a kind—that had once guided our
writers, conventions that had dictated at least the outer shape of
comedy or melodrama, farce or "serious" drama, suddenly vanished or
were discredited as outmoded. Playwrights were no longer free to write
an Abbott farce or a tightly knit, melodrama-based *The Little Foxes*.

Neither were they given any new charts to go by. Instead they were hurled into the chartless worlds of Beckett, of Ionesco, of Pinter, of that Tom Stoppard who first attracted attention by shutting Rosencrantz and Guildenstern out of the rooms where everything was going on, worlds without boundaries, worlds whose pieces didn't fit, worlds that couldn't be finished because their dimensions extended beyond any horizons that Eugene O'Neill could have imagined. Mr. Stoppard, in fact, simply "fessed up." In *Travesties* he gamely, cavalierly, rather exuberantly tossed all the loose pieces of the jigsaw onto the table and let the audience make what it would, or could, of the scramble itself.

These men might be imitated—perhaps. The catch was that the moment a playwright imitated them, he was caught out. He didn't sound like himself and he didn't quite sound like them; they'd taken too great pains to establish themselves as unique, their work as *sui generis*. Certainly they offered no guidelines to entering a formal competition, a competition within rules that would help a struggling newcomer over the first obvious hurdles. If the new playwright was offered anything, it was an invitation to invent his own void. Or put it this way. The playwright now not only had to invent the particulars of a given play, he first had to invent the idea of what a play *was*. He had to create his materials and also a mold, an entirely new mold, to contain them. Small wonder, then, that new playwrights come to us so hesitatingly, so slowly, in such small numbers. They live, for the moment, in an unstructured universe. Build a play? How? On what authority?

And yet—I come to my second point now—it is absolutely essential that each playwright finish a room. The theater *is* a room, for a reason. Needless to say, I'm not thinking of a realistic box set with three walls and four floor lamps—a literalism I have never much liked or found necessary. I'm thinking of a room as an enclosure, not entirely airtight perhaps but effectively constricting. The ancient Greek theater was a room in this sense: the audience provided the enclosure, surrounding and corralling the play as it did, allowing only for an unimportant escape hatch at one side so that actors could change costumes occasionally. The Elizabethan theater was built to enclose everything but the sky, and who ever looked upward? *Equus* is supposed to take place in a room, a psychiatrist's office, but there is no shred of the office to be seen on the stage; the enclosure is once again supplied by those listening and crowding forward upon the play, members of the audience seated in a curve behind, as well as before, the actors. Neither do I say, out of some vague or academic architectural concern, that this enclosure is physically necessary—as though the actors might head for the hills if they weren't herded into a sheepfold. It is psychologically necessary.

Why? Because theater, if it is to be theater and not some limp makeshift substitute, is honor bound to create a most particular tension, to build up pressure as in a boiler, to close off safety valves and breathe in danger until palms moisten and scalps prickle. The pressure can't be primarily visual, as it is in films; there isn't enough space, and what space there is can only be prettied up here and there with pleasant clothes, arresting props. The essential pressure is intellectual, poetic, verbal; and this kind of intensity can be arrived at only where concentration, commitment, emotional and psychological attention are total, sealed off, in no danger of being dissipated. Even Sartre, who in his role as philosopher directed so many men toward the unchartable void, recognized the principle whenever he adopted the role of playwright. His best play confines three people to a room they can never leave. It is called, symbolically enough for our purposes, *No Exit*.

No exit. Today's playwright would do well to write the phrase on page one of every new play, at the beginning of each new scene. For he has fallen under an obligation to do more than imagine the minutes of the meeting to which he is inviting us. He must also imagine the chamber in which the meeting is to be held. Imagine it, get us inside it, and lock it.

Mr. Kingsley, by the way, has never completed his Grinling Gibbons room, just as many of our earnest young dramatists have never succeeded in conceiving the very special rooms they need to house the images haunting them in this new time of our lives. The discussions that immediately follow, however, mainly have to do with men who have managed—or nearly managed—to invent fresh structure and fresh substance simultaneously.

2

The Changing Room

Following David Storey's mysterious and ultimately mesmerizing *The Changing Room* was like watching the evolution of life on the planet. The evolution and then the disappearance. The play was about a room, a space, an initial void. Three moldering green walls—more fungus than paint—framed an emptiness, into which the first sluglike forms of life moved hesitantly. A feeble attendant, whose face had sourly congealed about the fear in his eyes, pushed a broom into the waiting world, brushing dust before him, pausing to put down towels for the more vigorous animals who would follow him.

Literally—let's speak of Mr. Storey's use of metaphor later—the scene was a cheap clubhouse locker room, somewhere in the north of England, used for the day by the overworked, underpaid members of a semipro Rugby League, men picking up forty dollars a day for bruising one another on a field nearly turned to ice. They appeared, out of the bitter cold, alone or in twos and threes, unlimber, swaddled in mufflers, at first uncommunicative, jaws working on chewing gum, dazed automatons heading for the coal stove and waiting for the flicker of blood or intelligence that would make them animate creatures.

Slowly, it came. There were clothes to be stripped away, hung like huddled bodies on a rack, bruised muscles to be strapped up against the violence of the play to come, stale and impolite jokes to be exchanged as signs of a beginning social intercourse, warm-ups to be got through on impulse and out of rhythm, fitful pauses of apprehension as though one and all were half wondering if the others were really there, footballs to be tossed more for the feel of the leather than for precision, maneuvers of play to be rehearsed in huddles still devoid of heart and of hurt, restlessness to be accommodated by shifting, shifting, shifting, from bench to wall to stove to toilet to bench.

Life expanded, like a flower caught in the act of opening by stop-motion photography, until it was game time. Now the room was a hive

of buzzing but still-leashed energy, now the bodies that had idly
brushed one another in passing began to differentiate themselves,
jogging, to faintly individualized interior beats as they danced into line-
up for the field, each man lowering his head and lifting his feet for the
run from the locker room in a tempo dictated by the private urge of his
flesh. They were a team, in their blue-and-white-striped jerseys and
socks, and they were persons, as strange to one another as they were—
seen so objectively, at such a cosmic distance—to us.

The violence of the field, the great central clash that both justified
and wasted life, followed, with a bloodied crew gasping for relief at the
half, a shattered nose to be put right while a heaving player was held to
the massage table, a dogged, drooping last return to quarters for mat-
ter-of-fact horseplay in the communal bath and a silent return to the
night, to the cold, to the job, to the moon. The place was being swept
again.

As staged by Michael Rudman—first at New Haven's Long Wharf
and then on Broadway in 1973—and as acted by twenty-two self-
effacing, physically and visually interlocked actors, the event was a
stunning piece of choreography. The play had to be taken, I think, as
choreography. It pretended to nothing else, or nothing other. There was
no narrative, no interest to be taken in who won, who lost, what. There
was no attempt at dimensional psychology, just enough identification to
let us see separate forms taking separate paths through the maze.
There was no theatrical heightening of language: the speech may have
been even *less* than naturalistic in that actual conversation in any
actual locker room would very probably have been both wittier and
coarser than this was (the level was established at "Some good qualities, that lad," "Don't know where he keeps them then"). There was, in
the end, *only* the design to attend to, and the design was no doubt what
the play had been written for.

Mr. Storey's plays can be taken as metaphorical puns. *Home*, which
John Gielgud and Ralph Richardson so brilliantly orchestrated in 1970,
does take place in a home, a mental institution. It is also home in the
sense that the people in it have returned to their origins: senility
returns us to infancy. *The Contractor*, produced here in 1973, devotes
itself to erecting, and then dismantling, the canopy for a wedding
reception. The contractor may of course be the man responsible for
getting the tent up. He may also, as literally as you like, be the party
contracting marriage. Marriages are put together, and come apart, like
awnings. *The Changing Room* is at once a space for dressing and
undressing and for being born, shaped, broken, and returned to dust.
No need to be strict about these puns. They simply hang in the air.

Suspended there, they are images to be looked at, inhaled whole, attended to without questions or demands for other satisfactions. Some audiences find the single satisfaction that is left minimal. I found myself, during *Changing Room*, increasingly engrossed in the sheer patterning, the incessant, varied, meshing animation of shoulders, knees, rumps, jaws. (The play, incidentally, was the first I had seen to wholly absorb the sometime nudity of its figures; any attempt to avoid it, given the circumstances and indeed the meaning of the piece, must have come out hopelessly coy.) *The Changing Room* is simply what it announces itself to be: the room in which men change, whether the change be meaningful or not. Holding change up to view is one of the primitive functions of the theater, here reduced to something like its first—and therefore vaguely magical—state. If the evening is to work for an audience at all, it must work something like magic: the invisible made visible, fluttering life plucked from empty air.

Whether the change that the occasion describes has meaning or not is left open. The trainer of the team would like to think that it has. Chatting wearily with his assistant once the game is done and the room all but cleared, he repeats to himself, "It counts, it counts." In production, his tone was dubious.

But that passage itself is not representative of the work at its best: in struggling toward symbolism, it hits too hard, tries to make literal and verbal what has come to us more kinetically, more intuitively, than that. There are other stresses, here and there, that ring false. "You'll wake up one day and find out that it's all too bloody late" seems, coming from the trainer, a bit of social moralizing, as though these men were careless fools who'd spent their Saturdays gaming when they ought to have been at the barricades.

And watching Mr. Rudman's production so intensely—because that is all there was to do—we became acutely aware of minor lapses. I couldn't imagine, for instance, why the obviously gifted director had permitted one of his actors, the chap who cleans up, to sweep his dust into a pile and then sweep the pile under a hamper: that is what conventional maids in the most conventional of domestic comedies do, and the laugh it stirred was an out-of-kilter laugh here. Similarly, having been given so much that was authentic, we became strict about authenticity ourselves. The play was to end with the stage being swept clean again. But the floor was still littered with the players' wet towels. Mr. Rudman, eager to get on with the business that would bring the evening full circle, set his attendant to sweeping up while the towels were still in his way. We at once disbelieved, became conscious of patterning divorced from probability. We had long since committed ourselves to the tempo and cadence of what we were seeing; we'd have waited, unprotesting, for the towels to be picked up.

Minor imperfections lodged like sand in the eye because so much else in the production had been perfect—and perfect *as* vibrating visual image. In going to *The Changing Room* a reviewer had to face up to what he *couldn't* have, this one evening. That done, the room swiftly filled with materialized substances—men, movement, a quivering shape in time and space—that suggested a rather remarkable medium at work.

3

The Meeting Room

Saint Joan heard voices, I hear voices, Harold Pinter hears voices. Joan tended to hear hers in the open fields, I hear mine mostly at intermission time on opening nights. During the single intermission for Harold Pinter's 1976 *No Man's Land*, I heard—clearly, out of the verbal crossfire—two distinct plaints from contrary directions, one on top of the other. The first voice, a woman's, was raised in arch inquiry to an escort: "You *are* going to explain this play to me tomorrow, aren't you?" The second, a man's, mused vaguely to a companion: "I seem to be spending an awful lot of time this evening saying hello to people I don't know."

It struck me on the spot that if I could just have reached out, one hand to the left and the other to the right, and pulled the two speakers together, we'd have had everybody's problems solved. For, you see, the second remark is, more or less precisely, the answer to the first. It does explain what Mr. Pinter's genially hypnotic play is all about: the fact that we must spend so much of our lives making animated conversation with other inhabitants of the planet whose faces we recognize but whose identities elude us. In fact, we may spend *all* of our lives doing just that.

Keep it simple. How many times, at parties, have you spent not just five or ten minutes but the entire evening sparring with obvious familiars you can't quite place, not daring to ask for names because introductions have been deemed unnecessary and the damage already done, trying subject after subject in hope of hitting on one that will offer a clue, desperately working to construct a tangible person out of the responses you get from an equally mystified companion who is laboring to label *you*?

Make it not so simple. What kind of conversations do you have with your own children? Fishing expeditions mainly, tentative and awkward, while you're trying to discover just who they've become while you weren't looking? How long can you talk with your husband or wife without being stunned by your mutual misconceptions of each other, misconceptions that call for revision all the way back to square one? And how much do you make up, how much of your own speech is trustworthy, while you're fencing?

Well, you've got the point, which is very much Pinter's—except that Pinter extends it toward infinity until it becomes a philosophical abstract, a threat, a majestic joke.

Pinter hears his voices in the dark. As the curtain rose on Ralph Richardson's circular, ceilingless though chandeliered study in *No Man's Land*, the green velvet drapes that followed the curve of the great windows were drawn and would remain drawn—if Mr. Richardson had anything to say about it—even when it was daytime. Mr. Richardson was fond of nightcaps and naps, feeling that he was stealing a march on the world by sleeping in the late afternoon while other folk were fussily preparing for the evening's meaningless rituals. He had, however, discovered himself lonely in his elegant, sealed-off chamber. Though he might have been a "man of letters" who had long since ceased to work, he still felt a need to *talk*.

"How nice to have company," he rumbled through his vodka or Scotch. "Can you imagine waking up, finding no one here, just furniture, staring at you? Most unpleasant. I've known that condition, I've been through that period. . . . I came round to human beings in the end . . . a wise move. I tried laughing alone. Pathetic." (To hear Mr. Richardson filling that "pathetic" with vigorous contempt was not to be chilled but thrilled by the arsenal of inflections a superb actor had at his almost military command.)

And the taste for human beings was, no doubt, what had caused him to bring John Gielgud home from a local, far from fashionable pub. Mr. Gielgud—whose character name was Spooner as Mr. Richardson's was Hirst, though character names were without meaning in this twilight wonderland of the unknowable—followed his host into the comfortable void most deferentially, shoulders at half mast, sandaled feet fearful of being trod on, an elongated pink mouse in trousers rumpled enough to have been filched from a charity bazaar. Mr. Gielgud was left standing, insecurely, during the amenities: drinks poured, conversational excavations begun. (To watch Mr. Gielgud deftly remove a topcoat from a chair and then stealthily seat himself without too much pretension was to watch genius, carefully nurtured, assert itself yet again.)

They did not know each other. Could they? With enormous affability and seedy charm, Mr. Gielgud offered dubious information, painting a portrait of himself as poet serving younger poets tea on his country

lawn, a wife rustling hospitably in the background. (A manservant and
a secretary who appeared now and again offered a conflicting report:
they had observed Mr. Gielgud as a menial, gathering up beer mugs at
the pub tables.) The exchanges were civilized, equivocal, abruptly intimate. Mr. Gielgud confessed that he derived his strength of mind from
never having been loved ("I looked up once into my mother's face. What
I saw there was nothing less than pure malevolence. I was fortunate to
escape with my life"). Asked whether *he* had ever been loved, Mr.
Richardson pondered, but not for long. "Oh, I don't suppose so," he
replied with a combination of candor, resignation, and rueful ferocity
that was, in the reading, sheer music.

The conversation was civilized until Mr. Richardson fell to the
floor, drunkenly crawling away on hands and knees. Returning after a
very brief, remarkably restorative nap, he asked his secretary, once he
had noticed Mr. Gielgud, "Who's that? A friend of yours? Won't someone introduce me?" Meetings, exploratory conversations, do not establish identity. Or perhaps they establish false ones. When Mr. Richardson reappeared in the second of the adventure's two acts, after Mr.
Gielgud had spent the night (locked in, in fact), he was instant bonhom-
ie, unhesitantly greeting his guest as "Charles" and inventing for good
old Charlie an entire history that might possibly have been someone
else's. He knew Charles's war record, Charles's old school. He had even
seduced, long ago, Charles's wife, though he was not apologetic about
the matter. To Charles's wife he had "admitted you were a damn fine
chap, but pointed out I would be taking nothing that belonged to you,
simply that portion of herself all women keep in reserve, for a rainy
day."

At this point in the confrontation, another Charles was likely to
pop into a listener's head, the Charles Chaplin of *City Lights*. For
Chaplin, in *City Lights*, was, after all, anticipating—in his own scam-
pering yet less elliptical way—Mr. Pinter's point: that no truly trustworthy identity can *ever* be established. Chaplin came to mind for a
second reason, once the first had occurred to us. *No Man's Land* was
comedy, comedy of a more direct and ample kind than Mr. Pinter had
ever offered us before.

There had always been a malicious wit to the more malicious plays.
Thugs waiting in basements to murder the next comer had often been
querulously funny while they waited. But *No Man's Land* was a departure for the playwright, on this and one other count. Here the menace,
the celebrated Pinter suspense, the violent happening that really happened though it did not resolve the mystery, were all muted or missing.
There were faint gestures in the direction of existential melodrama: the
secretary apparently carried a gun, Mr. Gielgud sensed "a touch of the

hostile" in the room. There was a beginning hint of the kind of power play, the struggle for possession of territory, that had marked such earlier work as *The Birthday Party* and *The Homecoming*: Mr. Gielgud, lingering a second day, was warned by the secretary, "Don't try to drive a wedge into a happy household."

But the so-called power play, when it came, was no earth-shaking struggle: it was pitiful, beautiful to listen to, and doomed to failure. Mr. Gielgud begged, with a passion that almost shattered his shabby dignity, to be taken on as secretary, cook, housekeeper, *anything* ("I am tender toward objects. I would take good care of your silver. I play chess, billiards, and the piano. I could play Chopin for you. I could read the Bible to you. I am a good companion"). But the plea was heartbreaking-amusing because the power wasn't there, only the feeble, yearning, indefinable humanity. And the hour that had preceded it, as two men fabricated backgrounds hilariously, had been comedy—parody of our habits, even self-parody on Pinter's part—through and through.

The other marked change was toward poetry. Mr. Pinter's texts had normally been spare, terse, very, very dry (though there had sometimes, as in *A Slight Ache,* been an ironic poetry of event). Here there was no holding back, almost a rush of rhythm, a reveling in metaphor. Sometimes it was pure T. S. Eliot: "I have known this before. The exit through the door, by way of belly and floor." More often it was doing Pinter's more idiosyncratic work. Mr. Richardson wished to show his guest his ancient photograph album; perhaps Mr. Gielgud would find his own face in it. Or, he continued:

"You might see the faces of others, in shadow, or cheeks of others, turning, or jaws, or backs of necks, or eyes, dark under hats, which might remind you of others, whom once you knew, whom you thought long dead, but from whom you will still receive a sidelong glance, if you can face the good ghost. Allow the love of the good ghost. They possess all that emotion, trapped. Bow to it. It will assuredly never release them, but who knows . . . what relief . . . it may give to them. . . . "

Thus the play, all sidelong glances, dark eyes beneath hats, the unidentified who will still be frozen in time and space when there are no more questions to be asked, no more subjects to be changed. Thus the two central performers, so brilliantly ambiguous, so filled with incandescent presence themselves that if darkness had been total they would have continued to gleam in it. And thus Mr. Pinter's subtly altered style, falling back at last on the one tool we have to work with: "All we have left is the English language."

If we cannot know the people we know, at least—in all good humor—there's that.

4

The Bear-Baiting Pit

I was about to say that if you'd been able to weld Simon Gray's *Otherwise Engaged* to his earlier play, *Butley*, you'd have had a double-edged razor blade in your hands. Except that you didn't really need *Butley* to do it. *Otherwise Engaged* was double-edged all on its own and when its witty, wounding words were whipped about in the air like a blade held between forefinger and thumb, it glittered, fascinated, and—in a mordantly comic way—frightened.

In one sense, it was *Butley* turned inside out. The chap named Butley, you'll recall, was a self-despising, job-despising schoolteacher with a fierce and necessary compulsion: he had to bait, bully, mock, betray, or in *some* way damage everyone within firing range. Only through his victims' howls of pain and rage could he feel himself alive.

The hero of *Otherwise Engaged* was another man, another matter, altogether. Called Simon and played by Tom Courtenay with the tough, resilient reserve of a boxer who has sworn never to fight again, his most intense desire was to offend no one, cause no scenes, stir no exacerbating emotions. He wasn't kindly, mind you. He was, rather, snugly if tensely wrapped in a self-protective web of his own spinning. All he wanted to do during the evening we met and came to know him was listen, quietly and with concentration, to a new recording of Wagner's *Parsifal*.

What happens to such a man? Victims come to him *begging* to be hurt. A brother desperately wants to be told that Simon despises him, despises the meanness of his ambition to become assistant headmaster of his school, despises the wife who has saddled him with five children. An old friend who is bored to death interviewing literary celebrities for the BBC (Australians are the worst, they write so much) is determined to be insulting, willing to concoct the most extravagant lies if only the lies will provoke Simon enough to hurl a glass of whiskey in his face.

An oily one-time schoolmate presses Simon into a corner from which there is no escape in order to make Simon say the one thing that will destroy him utterly; a sloppy young tenant who is being treated more than generously takes outrageous advantage of that generosity in an effort to touch Simon's breaking point; a casual visitor strips half her clothes off to force Simon's lust. Simon's wife, busy with an infidelity, is shocked that Simon should take her behavior so casually. "Ned's not going to leave his wife, you'll go on with it till he tires of you, why *have* this conversation?" is all that Simon says. Fury follows. It is the interlopers who feel they will never have identities until they succeed in making Simon boil over.

And Simon won't. He grimly, gamely, sardonically holds his peace, refuses the bait, rejects the invitation to wallow in all of those so human emotions by which people normally know themselves. The actor, mesmerizing throughout, didn't pretend that his task was easy. As he relaxed his head, it was clear that his hands were clawed until the knuckles showed white. His glazed eyes focused fiercely, with effort, on the irrationality around him until they gleamed brighter than the knuckles. Everlastingly at everyone's service, he mixed his unbidden guests' drinks, then stood poised and tentative as though if he ever sat down again a stranger or a friend or a wife might leave, or the world might end, or he might turn to stone. His mouth was granite, no doubt petrified from grinding his teeth; the lines beneath his eyes deepened and deepened with the strain of supporting his attentive forehead. The nerves were all there, screaming; but Mr. Courtenay wouldn't let you hear them.

He would, however, let you hear his incorruptible candor, which is why so much of the play was bitingly funny. "You think my wife is an imbecile, go on and say it!" his brother demanded. "I swear to you, Stephen, I've never told a soul!" came his lightning-quick reply, all earnestness. His own wife chose to announce that she and her lover wished "to be husband and wife to each other." He pondered her statement a moment, then repeated, with a faint question mark hovering over it, the phrase "husband *and* wife to each other?" It was clear that what worried him was not her conduct but her literacy. He was deliciously blunt where truth needed to be spoken; but it was spoken always as fact, not feeling.

And that is where the play as a whole acquires its double edge. Yes, many of the lines do it individually, slicing two ways at once, drawing blood from the speaker and the spoken-to. But the gradually displayed master design for the evening is challengingly ambiguous, open to two readings, both dangerous. Most of the time, nearly *all* of the time, you're on Simon's side: as successive leeches try to fatten themselves by embroiling him in their passions—they will become more intensely present, more important, if they can only make the dog bark—you admire the steel-trap mouth that keeps itself locked, the rigidly folded arms that seem pinned beneath a straitjacket, the intelligence that holds itself in check lest more idiocy be loosed upon the world. Most of the envy, greed, lust, and sheer opportunism that passes for feeling in the world *is* idiocy; Simon sees through all that and is well out of it.

Is he? If his patience is more than human, everything else about him is less than human, inevitably. Out of things, he is inaccessible, not entirely there; he might as well be a small relic of Easter Island propped up in a corner and flaking steadily, a male caryatid helping to hold up the Erechtheum. He speaks, wisely and often pungently; but there is something prerecorded about all that, set in a groove long ago and unalterable now. His wife, abusing him for refusing to entertain an emotion, has the poor taste to repeat her lover's assessment of him: "You only give permission for little bits of life to get through to you." And that is true. There is a most contrary sense—cunningly fostered by playwright Gray—in which the folk who badger Simon are not only working to define themselves by the fire they can draw from Simon, they are also working to define Simon, to kindle a blaze in him that will warm him and woo him back to what the rest of us call life.

The author takes no sides or both, call it as you wish. He simply sets up a subtle tension between two equally possible, mutually exclusive, attitudes, letting us hold them in balance as riskily as Simon does his own contraries. There's a moment when he almost breaks, and it's crucial in nearly every way. The brazenly cheerful young mess of a tenant, who has begun the evening by whistling a tune of his own against the opening strains of *Parsifal*, has gone on to borrow whatever he needs as he needs it. At last he is down from the upstairs flat again for some coffee. Simon sighs, but well and good. The coffee's not all, though. He'd like the coffeemaker, complete with special filter. With each pyramiding request, Simon's sealed valves seem to leak steam, threaten to burst. You know that the matter is trivial and not trivial. You know that Simon prizes the equipment, is fearful of having it mishandled. The young man knows there's an explosion coming, perhaps; and promptly multiplies his demands.

At the top of the crisis, there is an explosion. But it comes from the young lodger, who resents being resented and is willing to give his benefactor what for. This time, *this* time, we wish it had come from Simon. Having rooted for his funny but frigid rationality for most of the evening, we are suddenly healthy animals again, longing for him to do what we'd like to do: boot the young ingrate down the stairs and onto the street.

We're of two minds, then, and so is the play, successfully. Harold Pinter was undoubtedly the first best choice in all the world to direct it. Mr. Pinter is an old hand at keeping secrets while keeping the theatrical action blatantly moving along right under your nose, and he steadily tightened the noose around Simon without forcing us to swear allegiance either way. We felt the sting, coming and going, and liked it. Mr. Pinter, who learned gallows humor at the hangman's knee, never missed the treacherous comedy of a curved line. One chap had, on a certain occasion, insulted another. Simon explained that the offended party happened to be his brother. "I *am* sorry," smirked the offender, leaving it for us to decide whether he was sorry for the offense or even sorrier that Simon should be cursed with so revolting a sibling. A play, a blade, to be handled with care.

5

On the Moon

One of the most moving and one of the funniest plays of the decade, for me, is Michael Weller's 1972 *Moonchildren*, a deadpan nightmare about the day after the world died. Only the world died, you understand. The people didn't. They went right on living, on top of the craters, putting all of their wit and their energy and their love and their sublime playfulness into the task of inventing what no longer exists. If there isn't a life, why, you simply make one up—and you make it as bizarre and as natural, as intense and as preposterous, as you possibly can.

Five boys and two girls share an attic apartment near the university they attend, surrounded by 857 two-quart milk bottles, an assortment of recruiting posters, a box in which a mythical cat is about to give birth, and an icebox with Grant Wood's *American Gothic* plastered on its face. They share more than the apartment. They share hamburgers, though they shouldn't, because one of their number, Dick, has really bought the four dozen in the freezer for himself. Curiously, they do not share women. Kathy lives with Robert, shortly to become Jobert, until she stirs interest in Dick; but though no permanent claims are staked here, the shift never quite takes place. An awkward and stiff-necked decency keeps undercutting despair. The roommates *do* share one other thing. An inability to accept anything—hamburgers, cats, death, grades, the war, the future, even uncles—as real.

There is no bullion in the bank, anywhere, nothing to guarantee the value of a gesture or a commitment or a promise or a news bulletin. Neither are there maps of this terrain, discovered in 1965 or thereabouts, and so, in the absence of anything to put a foot or a finger to, they improvise, compulsively, frighteningly, hilariously, dancing with their tongues. They invent their own news bulletins: Norman is hostile (he isn't, he only wants to read his book), Cootie has been slaughtered by the pigs (Cootie returns hale and hearty in his ski cap and galoshes), Mike's father is a fur trapper (no comment). The world is ablaze with event that is all the better for being a known lie. A known lie, a put-on, is better than the one you can't track down.

Life is exhilarating at this level, no matter what subterranean pain lingers. Have the neighbors complained to the cops about the way these kids live? Mike explains that he was seen through the windows bare-assed because he so thoughtlessly came from the shower just to pick up an anchovy snack, with toast. Has an encyclopedia salesman foolishly stumbled into the apartment in the guise of a research worker, only gradually sneaking around to his true purpose? Never has a salesman had a more rapt, if secretly mocking, congregation. The children gather about him, mouths agape with awe and respect, listening as though he'd just come down from Mt. Sinai, creating for him the audience he has never, never had. There is no anger in them anymore, none that they will show, just a willingness to act out, and live up to, any role that isn't real. Ask them to perform, and they are on. There is only one rule: you must not ask them to believe in the performance.

"Do you think a guy could become a homosexual just by will power?" Cootie asks, stretched out blissfully on the mattress that interrupts the floor, making it clear that he has the will power but doesn't think it would take, anyhow. Robert is already dead. He has received his draft notice, it has been addressed to Jobert Rettie rather than Robert Rettie, and so he has become Jobert, burying Bob. He simply wants to see how it feels, being dead. It doesn't feel any different, he decides a bit later. That is because death exists for them all already, they fly above it, playing their pranks. Not simply death in a war, though there is that: one of the five boys, before the evening is out, sloshes the contents of a gasoline can over himself. Ordinary death, too. Bob's mother dies. Privately in anguish, he never reports the fact to his friends. Asked how he has been able to keep it to himself for so long, he replies that "a little cunning, a little fortitude, a little perseverance" will do the trick. He hasn't reported it because it *is* a fact in a universe that contains no facts; there is no way to deal with it. How can death have meaning if meaning is dead? The ache runs under the play like a frozen water pipe waiting to crack.

And the ache leads, after all the ebullient nonsense born of last-ditch desperation, to a final scene that is, in its indirection, unexpectedly touching. School is over, the place is being cleaned out. But it's not the *drama* of the group's dispersing that is now affecting. It is, rather, the muteness of the figures who have been so endlessly articulate; they refuse even the convention of saying good-bye. They have been togeth-

er. They will not be tomorrow. Out, without so much as a "See you."
Invented lives leave no grounding for emotion. And no one, by God, is
going to invent *that*. They simply part, brusquely, noncommittally,
heartbreakingly. Coming away from Alan Schneider's masterly Broadway production, I was halfway down the block before I found myself
choking back tears. I hadn't realized I'd taken these moonchildren so
seriously, or liked them so much.

Years from now, no one knows how many, we're going to want to
look back and define a time we lived through. *Moonchildren* is likely to
become one of the surveying instruments we use, an antic needle
pointing north to the chill.

6

Civilizing the Centaur

A true myth is a true bind. All the facts are in, and there is no way
out. Oedipus, an honorable man, can do whatever he likes to
avoid fulfilling the prophecy that he will kill his father and marry his
mother, but he will kill his father and marry his mother. We give
assent to the unresolvable, see that it is perfectly proportioned, perfectly just, perfectly terrifying.

If there is one thing more than another that a contemporary
playwright would like to do it is to make a myth. We feel a desperate
need these days for new icons, images, clothed symbols that will help us
come to terms with the "dark cave of the psyche," the cave that
thousands of years of reasoning haven't quite lighted after all. We want
a picture of ourselves that renders us whole, with all of the violent
contraries and inexplicable self-betrayals locked in. Not an explanation
but an intuition become flesh; not thinking, *seeing*. But, it turns out,
myths are extraordinarily hard to make just by the willing of it. We are
used to thinking now, used to explaining before we really see, and it's
not easy to wheel about and go back to magic.

The closest I have seen a contemporary play come to reanimating
the spirit of mystery that makes the stage a place of breathless discovery rather than a classroom for rational demonstration is Peter
Shaffer's *Equus*. Mr. Shaffer is the author of *The Royal Hunt of the
Sun,* and he may have been trying for just such iconography—a portrait of the drives that lead men to crucify themselves—there. Here, I
think, he has found it.

He's done it by using reason to despair of reason. We begin in what
looks like a lecture lab, a handy enough arena for dissecting the brain:
the center space is railed off, some members of the audience are seated
above it onstage as though they'd come for a scholarly demonstration.
It also looks, vaguely, like a horse ring in which winners might be put

through their paces. Then we notice that there are indeed horses about: from the rungs of steel ladders at both sides of the stage hang the silvered skeletons of horses' heads. They are handsome. They are already, in John Napier's exquisite design, oddly disturbing.

A doctor is waiting for a patient, one he doesn't want to take on. He is weary and wary of tampering with the psyches of children, though that is his job. The patient is seventeen, a part-time stable boy. He has rammed a metal spike through the eyes of six horses. It is the gratuitous, unfathomable horror of the act that leads the doctor to accept the charge.

At once we are lured, with infinite skill, into a psychiatric detective story, the tensions of which account for half the evening's force. Clues are grudgingly, suspensefully come by. The defiant boy, unkempt curls framing a face of stone, won't speak, he will only mockingly hum television commercials when prodded. At last tricked into speech by an adroit maneuver, he strikes a sly bargain he means to hold to. For every question of the doctor's that he answers, the doctor must answer one of his. Candor for candor, if we're going to get anywhere.

The process yields tantalizing bits of information. When he was a child his mother read to him: history, the New Testament, stories of horses in which horses spoke and felt. Under his mother's tutelage the boy has become religious enough to tack a cheap lithograph of the suffering Jesus, feet chained, back under the lash, to his bedroom wall. His atheist father, enraged, has torn it down and replaced it with the photograph of a horse, head-on, eyes staring.

A suspicion grows that horse and Christ have become one, the chains of the Savior the bit between the horse's teeth. The boy not only learns to love horses but to adore them: he is caught once by his father with wire forced into his own mouth, slashing at his body with a riding crop. On dark nights he slips into the stable, strips himself, and goes riding in the fields, sexually excited, joined to his god, self-made centaur.

But all the while that we are fitting bits and pieces together, still far from the sight of any answer, the questioning process has turned up something else: the hopelessly chained soul of the doctor himself. Tie loose, eyes tired, he is quickly vulnerable. One of the questions fired at him by the boy, which ought to be answered if the bargain is to be kept, is capable of infuriating him. Does he have any sex with his wife? In an unprofessional temper, he dismisses the boy for the day.

Yet the rage is other than it seems. In point of fact the doctor has no sex at all, having married an antiseptic Scotch dentist: the two "briskly wooed, briskly wed, were briskly disappointed, and turned briskly to their respective surgeries." It is the doctor's surgery—his genuine capacity for returning young minds to accepted norms—that frightens him. He dreams, on his unluckier nights, that he is Agamemnon applying the sacrificial scalpel to long lines of children, all waiting to have imagination, passion, individuality taken out of them. He is jealous of the boy he means to cure, jealous of his madness. While he, with his pallid fondness for all things Greek, has leafed through drawings of centaurs, the boy has become one. There is a bit between his own teeth that will never come out.

Civilization and its discontents again. Yes. And, as we move into the equally arresting second half of the play, on our way to the metal spike, we are not only aware that the theme is a common enough one in our time, we are also inclined—out of our restless logical impulses—to challenge, or at least think twice about, certain of the icon's ambiguities. Wishing for sex with a girl, the boy is temporarily impotent: "The Lord thy God is a jealous God." Only if the all-seeing god is blinded can the boy take a second step. Questions bother us here: is it wrong to cure impotence, wrong to dissolve a false and hurtful equation between one pair of eyes and another? And hasn't the decision to reject his god, to be no longer a centaur, been the boy's rather than the doctor's?

But that is logic at work again—really work for the next day, not while the second act is actually exerting its spell—and it is to be at least temporarily dismissed in view of the fact that the structure, the two terrible tensions pulling in contrary directions, the sense of myth slowly disclosing itself all do really function in the theater. They function in part because Mr. Shaffer has done his own work with the precision of Agamemnon's scalpel, in part because Alec McCowen, who created the role in London in 1973 with unparalleled brilliance, commanded us to believe without reserve in the agony and honesty of his man (Peter Firth, as the boy, kept pace perfectly with his mentor), and in part because director John Dexter had been able to make the psychological vise intensely visual.

There was, for instance, a superb effect at the first-act climax, the night ride of boy and horse unleashed. We might only have heard of this; it could have been narrated. A film would later do it literally and lose excitement in the doing. Here the boy simply mounted the shoulders of one of the five shadowy figures who had from time to time during the evening slipped beneath the brooding horses' masks. The hooves of the boy's alter ego began to paw the stage floor: they were spiky silver elevations that looked like inverted jeweled crowns. Then the stage floor itself began to move, turned on its axis by the nodding, neighing horse-men at hand so that the railings at first slipped by, then raced by. With the exultation of the boy's passion, the increasing speed of the spinning ground, the rush of air that both seemed to generate as track whirled away beneath the silver, we were left not only persuaded but spellbound by the clattering, crying, crop-whipping authenticity of the image.

Whenever I have seen the play produced—and I have seen four sets of performers by this time—it is the image that stands, and is complete. The boy, with his dangerous creativity, fills one half of it, forever driven, forever blocked. The doctor fills the other, feverishly unwilling to do what he must do, but doing it—only to block himself. The two fit together at unpredictable angles, like differently colored pieces in a stained-glass window, but they fit and use up all the space that there is. Any move either makes destroys the other. Locked horns, both right, no escape. The play is perfectly proportioned to its mutual pain.

7

Partygoing

Let's say you're at a party. The more talented raconteurs among the guests are apt to start things off with set pieces, long made-up jokes with calculated twists they have often used successfully before, artifices plain and complicated. You laugh, because the mechanics of the joke are tricky, because you're glad *someone* is doing the talking, because your first drink is watery and hasn't warmed you yet. Nothing wrong with your laughter: the contrivances you're listening to are often pleasantly ingenious.

Then, suddenly, someone pops in on the tag of a constructed joke with a spontaneous topper, possibly something he's thought of that happened to *him* along the very same lines, something all the funnier for the confessional air it has about it. And the flood is loosed, tongues tumble to get in, one impromptu sally becomes the fuse to explode another, hilarity mounts because some *truth* has crept into the open-hearted cackle. People are telling tales on themselves they may never have meant to shout into the night air, and someone is likely to spill a drink as the tears of hysteria take over, uncontrollably.

But there is an exhausted end to that. The laughter *has* been hysterical, and hysteria brings with it its own dampening effect: it has dared come too close to the dark side of the moon. The party doesn't fail, turn irredeemably sober. It simply subsides for a moment, riding out a thoughtful calm, while drinks are contemplatively revolved in their glasses and an occasional after-chuckle seeps through. In a moment, a raconteur will remember a story again, and an agreeable, if slightly subdued, babble will flutter about it. Home safe, and nothing too precious in the way of secrets—or stability—lost.

Alan Ayckbourn's *Absurd Person Singular*, brought here in 1974 after prolonged success in Britain and provided with an American company composed entirely of stars, was a virtual anatomy of social laughter, perhaps of the comic impulse itself, and not because it happened to take place at three successive Christmas parties. Instead of describing parties, it *functioned* as a party functions, complete with trigger, detonation, sighing but not dissatisfied aftermath.

Trigger: In the first of its three acts, hustler Larry Blyden kept making perspiring last-minute visits to his canary yellow kitchen—relieved by blue butterfly decals on every available partition—to make certain wife Carole Shelley was ready for the guests who might mean so much to his "dog-eat-dog" advancement in business. Miss Shelley was not exactly ready; there was still polishing to be done and she had not only forgotten to order the tonic water but was totally unaware that she was shod in fluffy mules as big as she while her evening shoes rested in the living room alongside a fireplace guests were already leaning on.

The act was perfect artifice, the skilled raconteur's bit. How were we to get the guests, one by one and then in mixed doubles, into the kitchen? And if there wasn't enough tonic water, how was Miss Shelley to slip down to the corner deli in a rainstorm that would have dismayed Noah? And if Mr. Blyden didn't want his upper-echelon guests to see Miss Shelley in a raincoat and slouch hat that made her look like a scruffy Cockney newsboy, how was he to conceal her except by locking her out? The chess moves were immaculate, the pair were superb farceurs capable of appearing and disappearing on metronome beat (Mr. Blyden managed to send a bag of potato chips skyward while precisely controlling the shape of its great flowering), and the spectacle of the sodden Miss Shelley tapping piteously against the glass-paneled back door like the Ghost of Christmas Drowned was just the lunatic, logically-arrived-at cap the whole canny contrivance wanted.

Detonation: We spent the second act, and the second Christmas, in the shapelier, if rather untended, kitchen of architect Tony Roberts and his stubbornly suicidal spouse, Sandy Dennis. (Miss Dennis, hallelujah, had shed her mannerisms along with her lust for life, and had never put her stricken-Madonna face to more endearingly convulsing use.) You see, we'd moved into truth-telling territory now, though it was truth-telling blown up to party-balloon proportions, embroidered with every shade of the self-denigrating absurd.

Miss Dennis, silently bent on her own spectacular destruction and still clad in a red bathrobe though guests had arrived, would have hurled herself from the kitchen window if only her entire body had been cooperative and if only Mr. Roberts hadn't stopped talking fatuously through his nasal passages long enough to notice what she was doing. When he did notice, and pried her loose from the sill, she came away with eyes blazing and fingers locked in leaping position. She would, while not even straying guests paid her mind, do her hara-kiri best to run headlong onto a carving knife, asphyxiate herself in a stove that looked as if a waterfall of burnt meringue had engulfed it, hang herself from a lighting fixture that nearly electrocuted a dear friend instead.

And she couldn't even get her damned suicide note written; others kept appropriating it to sketch necessary household repair work on its back. High madness had taken over, humor had risked its outer limits. Ferociously, Miss Dennis nailed her note to the kitchen table. Laughter had been nailed, too: a spike was driven right through its heart when its noise was heartiest. *Absurd Person Singular* had one of the funniest second acts I have ever seen; and death was the joke.

Aftermath: The pause in comedy's occupations that is known as the adult's hour came in banker Richard Kiley's kitchen, while wife Geraldine Page huddled drunkenly in bed (though not for long). The walls, the very lighting, were pea green on this Christmas; artifice was over, hysteria was over, the celebrants now needed to recoup from a joke grown near-dangerous. Mr. Kiley was a beached cod, distancing himself from his fellow clowns as though reading a newspaper at arm's length, flexing his mouth to change the taste, waiting patiently for the running paint of Miss Page's face to make a little farewell puddle on the floor.

The party wasn't over, though; Mr. Blyden, who had "made it" by this time, would come furtively out of the night in his clubman's fez to freshly roil the stilled waters, conduct a game that involved "forfeits." All would end dancing with apples chucked under their chins, oranges tucked between knees. Macabre, and yet mellow, too. Laughter renewed itself in desperation; after all, that's where it had come from, hadn't it?

Mr. Ayckbourn's touch was light, his sympathies warm, his vision the vision of a zoom lens: broad as a field when it was time for a field day, pinpointed precisely when a lip twisted in wry regret. The very structure of laughter was caught in his range finder.

I admired his comedy about comedy very much.

8

A Self-Conscious
Neil Simon

Whatever else Neil Simon may do, he must never begin apologizing for the fact that he is funny. I thought I detected traces of just this in his play *Chapter Two*, though none at all in his simultaneously released and wonderfully exuberant film, *The Goodbye Girl*, and I hoped at once he'd have done with it. The traces weren't much, but they offered small clues to the ultimate instability of *Chapter Two*. Once Judd Hirsch, as a novelist whose wife of twelve years had died and left him inconsolable, had entangled recent divorcee Anita Gillette in a series of four or five phone calls that were gracefully witty and increasingly warm, he skipped a beat as though listening to himself and then remarked to the girl he hadn't even seen yet, "I don't know if you know this, but we both talk in the same rhythm."

What, pray tell, was that line doing in the play? In the first place, it wasn't true. The two forlorn people who had been encouraged to date but had no intention of doing any such thing did *not* speak in the same cadence or indulge in the same kinds of verbal gamesmanship. They were adroitly individualized, they were attractive people rather than handy puppets, they semed perfectly well able to use their own tongues. Was Mr. Simon self-conscious, then, *afraid* he'd be accused for the six hundredth time of shuffling a fast deck of one-liners, each cut to the same shape of plastic, each stamped with his own compulsively gagging imprint? It sounded like a cover-up, and it was utterly unnecessary. Of *course* there were jokes in the play, gags in the play, even one-liners in the play. The play was a comedy, overall. But jokes, gags, even one-liners are entirely acceptable provided they come from the defined personalities, the urgent needs, the cockeyed perceptions of the contestants delivering them. (I swear to heaven that if I hear Mr. Simon put down one more time for his facility at coining swiftly relevant retorts, I am going to fill an entire page with one-liners every reader can recite along with me. They will all be by William Shakespeare.)

Later in the play, Miss Gillette inadvertently walked in on a floundering extramarital fling her unhappily married best friend was having with Mr. Hirsch's unhappily married brother. *In flagrante*, and all that. Miss Gillette's friend promptly announced,"This is one of those situations in life that a lot of people find humor in." You see what Mr. Simon was being half sheepish, half assertive about here. He knew exactly how stock the situation was. And he was papering over his mild embarrassment at using it by first pointing out that it *was* stock and then reminding us that life itself can be pretty stock, at times. I suppose that this cagily inserted bit of self-justification was more understandable than the one quoted earlier. Though he'd planted the situation carefully—Miss Gillette had given her friend the key to the apartment for just such hanky-panky, which meant that there was nothing illogical about her forgetful overlap—it was indeed old hat.

But just a minute. All comedy, including Mr. Simon's, makes use of artifice. Calculated, open, obvious artifice. (*The School for Scandal* has no copyright on the screen scene, and long-lost children run all the way from Plautus to *The Waltz of the Toreadors*.) The point in using a dash of the old ready-mix is that it's the quickest way to get you where you're going. If you're headed for nothing more than some caustically romantic, slaphappy high jinks among show folk, as *The Goodbye Girl* is, then a transparent contrivance will—quite literally—get the door open to let the fun in. Artifice: Unemployed dancer Marsha Mason has not only been ditched by her latest lover but has just discovered that the lout has sublet the apartment; new tenant Richard Dreyfuss, wet and tired, is even now howling in the hallway, demanding sanctuary. Inasmuch as neither of them has anywhere else to go this midnight, it makes sense for Miss Mason, with the highly skeptical approval of her ten-year-old daughter, to let him stay.

The device patent, but not patented—also makes way for instant merriment. The remarkable Mr. Dreyfuss, looking like a bearded and bespectacled Paul Newman and seeming constantly to work on a trapeze, strikes an immediate blow for men's lib, stipulating his right to go nude in his own cramped quarters, to meditate mornings (with incense and without interruption), to do the cooking. Miss Mason, creature of mishap, redecorates the tattered premises from a magazine illustration, getting everything just off-center and just off-tone. Daughter Quinn Cummings, movie buff and a sprig of deadly nightshade if ever there was one, gives interloper Dreyfuss due warning of her own powers ("Did you see *The Exorcist?*" she asks menacingly. "Then you'd better get out of the room").

The invention bubbles: As part of an off-Broadway improvisation, actor Dreyfuss has taken the names and addresses of everyone in the audience and thinks "we should have them all over to dinner real soon." The backstage shoptalk is dryly authentic, though Mr. Dreyfuss's lone, surprising failure is his inability to camp persuasively in a homosexually oriented production of *Richard III.* Even the domestic infighting becomes endearing ("Meet me downstairs." "Why?" "Because I'm the *mother*, that's why"). Upshot: though we've got ourselves entangled with this trio most arbitrarily, we're glad to be there.

But artifice can open the door to other things: to the melancholia of *Waltz of the Toreadors*, remember, *and* to the traumatic effects of having abruptly lost a wife in *Chapter Two.* The opening rounds of Mr. Simon's play expertly managed the infiltration of good gags by real grief. We knew that novelist Hirsch had just returned from a fruitless tour of the places he and his wife had once been happy in: he'd gone, as he told us, because he was sure "She's not dead, she's in London waiting for me." We knew that all he wanted to do now, while brother Cliff Gorman rattled off a bright line of patter meant to cheer him up, was to read, and reread, the letters of condolence he'd received. How, then, was he to be trapped into the first of those cumulatively hilarious phone calls, calls to a girl he didn't care to meet? Simple, and, if you wish, a stage trick. In the course of doing research on his new book he'd jotted down the phone number of a helpful, and elderly, librarian. On the back of the slip of paper brother Gorman had scribbled the number of the divorcee he was presently pushing. Mr. Hirsch got the wrong side of the memo, that's all—and we were off.

Off into intelligent, plausible, and explosively entertaining sparring between two wary people whose wits happened to fit. Off into a first tentative meeting (scheduled to last for exactly five minutes, or, if she should be interested, six), comedy growing steadily out of the caginess. Off all too quickly—by everyone else's lights—into marriage, after two weeks' acquaintance.

Yet the banter, delightful as it was, didn't destroy the undertone of mourning. In the middle of all that was so breezily engaging, and even as he contemplated the new marriage he now wanted, Mr. Hirsch was apprehensive, suddenly worried that the miracle wouldn't work. Why should he have been apprehensive? "Because it's not supposed to happen twice in your life," he said. The line functioned well, as seriousness. It also condensed the entire play, with all of its psychological givings and misgivings, into ten words. But there was no clash between the dominant sunniness and the sobriety threaded through it. The moods met and meshed easily, ready partners in a complex venture, and the evening's first half rolled along handily.

If something went awry in the second—and it did, with a wild wrench—it wasn't because of Mr. Simon's one-liners and it wasn't because he was willing to use a standard farce gimmick and it wasn't because these things couldn't pave the way to genuine feeling. It was for a surprisingly elementary reason. Mr. Simon had simply failed to dramatize the center, the heart and soul, of his play. The center was this: the honeymoon fell apart because Mr. Hirsch *would* not surrender his earlier sorrow or his self-pity; happiness, he felt, would be a betrayal of his first wife. And so he returned not as the engagingly reasonable fellow we'd watched pursue and carry off a prize but as a virtual latter-day Mr. Hyde, a dour and bitter malcontent. The man had been transformed into an ogre.

But *we* hadn't seen it happen. We hadn't been there. Not as the seed took root, not as it grew subtly from occasional warning to constant threat, not as it brought the house of cards tumbling down. The likelihood that all of this would happen had been laid out for us by Mr. Gorman in an impassioned warning beforehand; thus we knew what was *supposed* to have taken place. But it was over, past us now, and all we had left on our hands was an unfamiliar and unappeasable fellow we didn't like. The evening instantly degenerated into bouts of abrasive recrimination, with the stalemate finally being half resolved by a haymaker of a speech that the fed-up Miss Gillette let fly with. The speech was a good one; but it didn't make up for the intimacy, the dramatic progression, we'd been denied.

Mr. Simon himself had told us that the play was in part autobiographical—*no* play is entirely autobiographical—and it is conceivable that the trials he'd gone through had immersed him so totally, had been so truly traumatic, that he had forgotten the steps in the process; shock obliterates. Having been unable to analyze his own bewildered behavior at the time, he may still have lacked the detachment, the complete objectivity, that would have helped him lead a stage character through the maze. However that may be—and I don't like playing psychoanalyst—it was obvious that he'd sensed something missing and had attempted to plug the gap by giving us more, and then more, of the misguided affair his brother was having with Miss Gillette's friend. That affair was irrelevant, it didn't address itself to the actual difficulty, and much of it could and should have been trimmed away.

Laughter—and there remained a lot of honest laughter in *Chapter Two*—had never been the problem.

9

Stoppard, Non-Stop

The stage has ample room for caprice, but is cagy about incoherence. The difficulty, sometimes, is to tell the difference between them.

Lenin, James Joyce, and Tristan Tzara all appeared as characters in Tom Stoppard's 1975 *Travesties*. But the play, it would seem, was really about an actor named John Wood, who is surely the champion chatterbox of our already unruly time. As the author explained in interviews (to be believed at one's own risk), he'd been determined to write a play for Mr. Wood for some time when he happened to come across the odd, though not necessarily meaningful, fact that Lenin, Joyce, and Tzara all lived in Zurich at the same time during World War I.

Sensing an opportunity for his special brand of cerebral impertinence, and speculating on what it might or mightn't have been like if any two of the three had met, he'd first thought of turning Wood into Tzara, though he discarded that notion (he said) upon discovering that they didn't look alike.

Wood was next to be cast as Joyce, whose riverspill of language he'd have been so capable of managing; no dice there, either, possibly because Joyce just wasn't going to become all that important to the verbal pyrotechnics (for very good reasons, as we'll see in a moment).

Hence he had no part for him, which led to the one real inspiration that hit him. He'd give him *no* part, no part to play at all, make him a nobody at a time when the world was coming to nothing, and let him talk a blue streak—fantastifications, furies, lies—that would make the sudden emptiness of 1917, together with the disintegration of society and even of language that followed the war years, blitheringly, blatheringly transparent onstage.

What worked in *Travesties*—made it occasionally crackle and always insist that you listen to it—stemmed from this decision. Mr. Stoppard had got Mr. Wood up there, seedy and garrulous in a sloppily belted greatcoat, sucking at cigarettes between syllables though there was no room between syllables, banging away at an already ravished piano in a red spotlight for openers, going on to strip off his gray bundling (and his rattling senility with it) to disport himself in the lawn-party tans of the period with white socks beneath, arguing vehemently with Tzara over the merits of shellfire (was war fought for the freedom of poets or for capitalism with the Dardanelles thrown in?), crossing his grasshopper's legs and slipping without warning into scenes from an amateur production of *The Importance of Being Earnest* that Joyce had proposed. All of this in run-on overlap, motion-picture laboratory dissolves, café-floor maxixes, and music-hall turns (with "Louise," "My Blue Heaven," and "Mr. Gallagher and Mr. Shean" sharing a jangling soundtrack with an extremely noisy cuckoo-clock). Bravura was put to shame alongside Mr. Wood's fortissimo, pianissimo, and machine-gun spatters. He was even intelligible, no matter what he was not saying.

And the nobodiness of the man became the perfect central symbol of the occasion. In 1917 the modern world was dissolving as Mr. Wood was dissolving, as Russia was dissolving to make a loophole for Lenin, as logic, sequence, and the formal structures of art were dissolving under the impact of Dadaism and its iconoclastic fellows, as words were dissolving and rearranging themselves in Joyce's head, Joyce's hands. As dramatic shapes continued to dissolve in Mr. Stoppard's play.

We were never to forget the war that shattered sense in the body politic and consistency of style in the toys of art. The evening began in darkness dominated by a cannonade, significant noises saying farewell to a great many things—as a faintly trailing whistle of "Auld Lang Syne" reminded us. Every so often the kaleidoscopic whirl collapsed into a single shaft of light, pinpointing Mr. Wood so that he could go on, rabidly, about warfare. One of the occasion's most satisfying passages found nobody Wood and no-art Tzara raging at each other over the virtues and vices of ruin simply as ruin. Tzara was exalted by the ruin of academic form in art, which had amounted to nothing more than cleverness. What *he* produced, as he shredded a sonnet into strips of paper and poured its words at random from a hat, might be nonsense "but at least it's not clever nonsense." Mr. Wood, in hot retort, held that anyone indifferent to what was being lost must possess "a degree of self-absorption that would have glazed over the eyes of Narcissus." In the general dislocation, even Joyce's clothes had got out of sync. He'd once mismatched his jacket and trousers and they'd kept passing each other without meeting ever since. Nothing had held, and fury would not bring it back.

Having an argumentative nonentity on the premises also served to define, dizzily, the esthetic positions of the historic entities about him: the men who knew what they were after. Lenin wanted a politically useful art: "Literature must be partisan, and under party control." Tzara wanted to wipe away the illusion of usefulness, the pretense that the existence of art in any way changed man; art was whatever it said it was, a glory of irrelevance. Joyce, biding his time and keeping a bit mum about it all, was really after something else. Accepting the destruction of traditional forms, he was engaged in reconstruction—on his own terms. Because he was the quietly and immediately productive one—we saw him literally pull a rabbit out of a hat, and did not miss the implication—he wouldn't have been a good part for Mr. Wood. Aside from a jovial habit of speaking in limericks, he was too busy working to have much to say. Or even be around that often.

And Mr. Stoppard wanted the sputtering confusion, not achieved coherence. He got it—sleekly, brazenly, amusingly. We got it, too, as we were meant to do. We also, from time to time, got the bends. For every liberty costs something, and the liberties Mr. Stoppard had taken with language and shape did cost us certain of the pleasures we count on in the presence of drama. The fact that there was no real interaction between the urgent mouthpieces staking out positions, the fact that some of them never even met, diffused our attention dangerously. Lenin, played straight, functioned entirely alone, outside the prankish fevers in which most of the others were engaged. His material was, as a result, familiar and dull. Joyce was skimped in the writing, as we've said. When actor Wood wanted to get away from Dadaism for a bit, he had to seek out the ladies, either his sister in a sequined ball cape of kelly green or one Cecily Carruthers, who seemed to have escaped Oscar Wilde's play only to turn into a platitudinously rabid revolutionary.

One thing in particular needed watching if Mr. Stoppard was to continue to make us sit still with his wit, and that was the wit itself. *Travesties* struck me as being a bit lazier than the earlier *Rosencrantz and Guildenstern* and *Jumpers*, as though Mr. Stoppard were now too quick to give us what was on the very tip of his tongue. Aside from endless replays on the meaning and use of the syllables *Da-da* (Mr. Wood was to be heard wondering if someone had a stammer), there were too many soft semipuns, glib portmanteau words, simple inversions: "comraderaderie" in Red Square, "the entente cordiality" of war, "belles litter" applied to Tzara's hat-poetry, whole lines like "Oh, the yes-noes of yesteryear" and "It takes courage to sit down and be counted." These were parlor tricks, and cute enough for titters. But, excepting for the single battle royal between the nonentity and Tzara, there was nothing of the keen intellectual interest that attached to the out-of-kilter philosophizing of *Jumpers*, just as there were none of the underlying structural tensions that kept the badinage of *Rosencrantz and Guildenstern* alive and hurting. In the latter play—still the author's best play—Mr. Stoppard had been somewhat protected. Though poor Rosencrantz and Guildenstern were unable to understand what was going on at Elsinore, *we* knew; we had the familiar outline of *Hamlet* safely filed in our heads. We were thus provided with a structure inside which we could follow Rosencrantz and Guildenstern's vain groping for meaning in a universe turned meaningless. When Mr. Stoppard is entirely on his own, however, there is always the danger that his footing will become as insecure as ours is. He is an intellectual prankster, yes; and we can, much of the time, enjoy the gamesmanship. Much of the time, in *Travesties*, we still did. But how random, how carefree, how catch-as-catch-can dare a playwright be with the planking that must support even a comic passion? Is playwriting, in this time of perceived discontinuity, condemned, or confined, to unabashed doodling?

Stoppard's habit of thinking that three bad jokes will do as well as one good joke provided they follow one another rapidly enough finally proved fatal in the case of his 1977 *Dirty Linen*. The piece—it was really two short plays, one tucked with highhanded irrelevance inside the other—had been publicized before its arrival in New York as what the British call a "knickers farce," meaning that a girl's panties, slip, and dress were all apt to be snatched from her in a manner that obviously had not gone out with *Getting Gertie's Garter*. The snatching would take place during meetings of a House of Commons committee investigating sexual immorality in the government, a subject not entirely unfamiliar to our own body politic. Pastiche sex comedy and political satire joining hands? Possible.

But the gap in Mr. Stoppard's gift that had somewhat damaged his longer plays yawned wide enough this time to swallow us all. An audience prepared to enjoy either the parodistic plotting or the author's nimbleness of tongue, or both, found itself listening to a handful of M.P.s drifting into the conference room to exchange elaborately pronounced French and Latin phrases as coyly as possible. Two of them attempted to place their identical derbies on the same hook of the hatrack. Apologetically, one murmured, "Mea culpa," having already disposed of "toujours la politesse" and "noblesse oblige." The simple-minded game went on for three or four or five minutes. There was no real attitude behind it: the committee members weren't being idly impish or leadenly learned with one another. Nor was the author being satirical about *them*. He was simply being giddily offhand about what line he put down next, not caring in the least whether the presumed joke had a starting point or an angle of flight.

Tiring of this rather later than we did, he shifted to the beginning business at hand and to a joke that was meant to be a joke, all right, but that was what I think of as a "joke-joke," an obvious and easy piece of manufacture. A Titian-haired chick named Maddie Gotobed (no need to hold this against the author, stylized character names have an honorable enough history) was to serve as recording secretary during the session, always provided she could take shorthand. An M.P. asked her if she used the Gregg or Pitman method. She answered that she was on the pill.

Shortly even the joke-jokes disappeared, to be replaced by devices still more slapdash. With Miss Gotobed conspicuously present, Freudian word-substitutions of the most primitive sort began to pop up everywhere. A gentleman who wished to say "tut, tut" said "tit, tit." (Variations on this one soon became as common, and about as amusing, as cockroaches.) The government was concerned about "the unbuttoned behavior both in and out of the trousers of Parliament." (Surely I don't have to translate for you, but "houses" was intended.) A chap who wished to propose "having dinner in some out-of-the-way nook" proposed instead "having some out-of-the-way nookie" and then, inexplicably flustered considering what had been going on around him, pawed the air in embarrassment until he was red in the face. A reference to Pecksniff was objected to as a dirty word until it was explained to the offended party that Pecksniff was a character in *Dombey and Son*. Subsiding, the complainant agreed that of *course* he was in *Dumbo and Son*. (Note to readers, reaching for their pens: the title was corrected to *Martin Chuzzlewit* a moment or two later.) And words were played upon, pressed upon, simply for their sounds: "Volvo," for instance, was so lovingly italicized by the person enunciating it that we resented being thought stupid enough not to have picked up its associations without all of that effortful articulation. Most of the acting was imitation British, and everybody waited for the laughs that were meant to come.

The first sizable enough one actually to come on opening night arrived with a misspelling: a chairman ready to take "Aye" and "No" votes divided a blackboard in two and chalked in his columns, "Ayes/ Nose." The first genuinely good one came exceedingly late in the frameplay, *Dirty Linen*: an outraged M.P. turned on his fellow investigators, shook a mightily reproving finger at them, and let fly with the accusation "One of you is telling the truth!" The audience found that it could come up for air with that, and it did: for once, a hollow sound was replaced by a hearty one, and the house sighed with a quiet relief for a few minutes thereafter.

Exception had to be made for a single long speech in the evening's insert, *New-Found-Land*, which thrust itself into the tower chambers just under Big Ben while the Gotobed committee was taking a ten-minute recess. *New-Found-Land* had nothing at all to do with *Dirty Linen*, except that Mr. Stoppard's director had required something about America to complete his announced intentions for the original London program and Mr. Stoppard had readily obliged, possessing no structure to violate.

The small sketch was really a monologue delivered to a deaf and drowsing superior by a chap painting, with toothy enthusiasm and fire in his eyes, a portrait of America that sounded like Walt Whitman anticipating *The March of Time*, with piano accompaniment by Stephen Foster. The sheer tumble of travel-brochure phrases cribbed from Mark Twain and Tin Pan Alley in approximately equal portions struck the kind of sparks that Mr. Stoppard's teeming brain *can* give off, and all of us were pretty much bound to grow giddy as the *Twentieth Century Limited*, with "the wind slamming off the Great Lake as we pull into Chicago," turned mysteriously into the *Chattanooga* somewhere across Pennsylvania on its way to Kentucky, where, without pause, we were invited to "climb through mountain ash and hickory into the hills of Tennessee." From this vantage point we were able to see "the last of the riverboats working out of Natchez," "octoroon lovelies," and "far below, a boy on a raft." Actor Jacob Brooke was briefly transfixing as he caught clichés by the tail and tied them all together into a monstrously lyric bouquet.

Even here, though, there was an indifference in Stoppard that was disturbing: a refusal to be selective about his own effects, to distinguish between inspiration and childlike scribbling. For instance, it was of no help to the monologue to toss in hasty reference to America's idealistic determination "to put strychnine in every pot." This kind of clumsy satirical punning simply undercut the humor that was already being built into a series of folksy platitudes. Not all kinds of tomfoolery go together.

It is important that Mr. Stoppard take more care with the improvisations he chooses to let us see and hear. He has a reputation to sustain and to further, as he has an audience to honor. His audience, at this point, is somewhat limited. *Travesties*, in spite of mainly favorable reviews, could not get through a single New York season; I assume that what is called poor word of mouth, an audience dissatisfaction with the failure of the play's pleasantries to seek some sort of focus, did it in. A talented playwright cannot really wish to court disenchantment and narrow his base ever more dangerously by neglecting to exercise a reasonable critical control over the words from his own mouth.

10

A Memory of Champions

Jason Miller's *That Championship Season,* first produced at the Public Theater in 1972, proved a fine play so superbly detailed in the writing, staging, and performing that you missed a gesture or an inflection—any gesture or inflection—at your own peril.

The format of the evening was at first sight familiar. The limp lace curtains and the steeply ascending balustrade provided by designer Santo Loquasto at once suggested the conventional naturalism of *The Dark at the Top of the Stairs* (though the play made it clear that the dark, in all our lives, is at the bottom of the stairs now, even in broad daylight). The reunion of old buddies, in this case that of four basketball players with the coach who'd made them winners twenty years earlier, was already an archetypal stage gambit of our time. We like to assemble the disillusioned in order to let them discover that present failure is directly traceable to what were once thought virtues. All true enough.

But *That Championship Season*, under A. J. Antoon's sensitive direction, was a play that commanded, and seemed to possess, a second sight. Its people were not just stand-ins for the rest of us, handy pegs to make a pattern or point a moral. They were people who didn't want to get their shirts wet. I'd better explain that. A trivial, utterly unaccented bit of business riveted me so during the play's first, initially genial, act that I still find myself remembering it more emphatically than some of the open violence that followed.

Paul Sorvino, as the one member of the squad who had managed to make himself filthy rich, was breaking out a can of beer. The first greetings were over, backs had been thumped, Polish jokes had been swapped, festering minds were just beginning to turn inward. Mr. Sorvino, hoisting the can to his lips, carefully placed his free hand directly over his shirt front, to catch the drip. It was a reflex, scarcely more than that, the kind of thing some men do. What sort of men? No doubt all sorts. Yet in the single, simple, almost thoughtless move of his hand, the actor surreptitiously set off a warning bell. One member of the group wasn't thinking about the group, wasn't attending to the raffish reminiscences of the slippered coach, wasn't here for the fun of it. His concerns were elsewhere, they were alert and protective, they were going to come out—perhaps disturbingly—when the time was right. He was wearing a shield, and we noticed it.

Disturbance was not long coming. Another of the four was mayor of the town, up for reelection, likely to lose to a Jew who'd changed his name, sorely in need of money only Mr. Sorvino could provide. And Mr. Sorvino, who hadn't got rich backing losers, was ready to defect, team or no team. He had more than that to hide. He'd been having an affair with the mayor's wife and he knew that another of the firm friends, for practical reasons of his own, was on the verge of blurting out the truth. The coach, long ago, had taught all of his charges to be "lean and mean," and though they had by no means grown leaner, the meanness had stayed with them.

When the news *was* out, writer and director found odd, glancing, unexpected responses to the hurt, fresh theatrical images for a not uncommon theatrical situation. The mayor, played by Charles Durning with the face of a lost boy peeping out through his cradle of chins, was not a very bright fellow. He was known as Sabu around town because his only achievement during four years in office had been to provide the local zoo with an elephant—which quickly died. Relations with his wife had long been strained: a mongoloid child took care of that. But, curly hair turning wet with perspiration, he was brought close to breakdown by the new revelation. He had not expected betrayal, not this sort. Why not? "I'm the *mayor*, for Crissake!" he screamed, abandoning in his hysteria all other claims to being a man. The rage, like so much else in the play, was as quickly touching in its inappropriate phrasing as it was bitterly funny.

Now author and director took the shaken fellow out of doors, just beyond the half-open windows, where a friend might steady him by walking, cool him with reasonable advice. As the conniving continued in the living room, we did not lose the suffering, overweight, tantrum-prone victim. In spurts of childlike outrage, he was half in at the window, accusing and crying and being forcibly pulled away again, a broken life-rhythm reasserting itself no matter what might go forward. The effect was astonishingly right and original. Though we have had stage windows before, and by the thousands, I don't think I have ever seen this particular use made of them: the sense of air, of night-fright beyond the walls, of extended dimension was so palpable that you believed in the continuing world past the leaded-glass door, half imagined you could remember the street address tacked over it.

You almost knew the telephone number. At one point the affluent Mr. Sorvino made up his mind. He would back the Jew, make a comfortable deal with him. He went to the phone, called, offered his curt, we-all-understand-don't-we proposition. The few things we heard him say thereafter conveyed very little. But the actor's fingers, slowly extending themselves into space as though there were a fog coming on and a new path to be found through it, the weight of his body shifting from one leg to another in the rhythm of a boxer trying to steady himself from a blow, told us everything we needed to know about the conversation. He was being turned down, affably but bluntly, sent back to the sorry fellowship he'd nerved himself to ditch.

Everything that was openly physical, even melodramatic, in the play—a drunken tumble down that stairwell, a tussle with a rifle from the gun rack, a crack across the face that literally took a man's teeth out—was in effect certified as authentic by the nuance, the subliminally registered byplay, that had preceded it. Images lingered long after they had dissolved into fury, or into heartbreaking comedy: Michael McGuire as a junior-high-school principal drawing his tapering hands down his face to ease the pain in his eyes but ready, on the instant, to accept praise, most modestly, for a speech on democracy he'd once delivered in high school; Richard A. Dysart as the coach, towel still slung over his shoulder, lovingly and persuasively remembering the clear mountain pools of his youth, only to muddy them instantly with equally affectionate memories of Joe McCarthy and Father Coughlin; Mr. Sorvino again, musing aloud on the deep and grim satisfaction he derived from driving his Porsche, past midnight, at 140 miles an hour, married only to speed.

But perhaps no one represented the play, and the meticulously musical styling of its production, better than Walter McGinn, tossed into a corner like an old coat, peering at the group from behind a permanently moist nose, smiling and smiling and smiling. Mr. McGinn was the loner of the outfit, the one who'd substituted drink (he had no drinking problem, he explained, he could get booze anywhere) for the values drummed into his teammates. He listened to the coach renewing the peptalk that had done them all in ("Exploiting a man's weakness is the name of the game"), a peptalk that took anti-Semitism in stride, ate rumored Communists for dinner, roughed up "niggers" on the basketball floor. And, having no part in it, he saw the joke clearly, clearly enough to cruelly caution the mayor to conceal the fate of his child

("You'll lose the mongoloid vote right there"), clearly enough at the end to turn the creed that had killed them into a savage dance at stage center, the spastic tangle of his feet echoing everything that was at once ruthless and rubbery in their lives.

Strong work. The familiar surface of the play hadn't prevented a writer from finding valid new life, astonishing energy, at its core. Even old shapes are renewable if a man knows how to dig.

11

Dying Together

There's a curious locution used frequently toward the end of David Rabe's *Streamers,* together with one unexpected epithet that seems to have attracted very little notice. The locution and the epithet may both be important in trying to grasp the metaphor that Mr. Rabe has been struggling to capture in his fist during his constantly promising but thus far unsolidified young career.

The odd word is *house,* the unexpected one *nigger.* Three men share the cots and footlockers of a Virginia army barracks during the Vietnam war; they may be shipped out at any time. One, a dedicated if naïve white liberal, has managed to make a good friend of the easygoing black in the next bed ("You was just the first person to talk back friendly," the black tells him simply). The third, white, proclaims himself a homosexual and camps amusingly to prove it, though for a long time neither of his roommates wants to believe that he is speaking the plain truth. Into the barracks at odd hours, and once after lights-out—slithering drunkenly on his belly by the feeble glow filtered through a transom—comes an unstable black named Carlyle, sorry for himself in his loneliness ("You guys got it made and I got nothin'"), provocatively menacing with his instantly triggered temper, spastically clawed fingers, out-of-kilter lower lip. Carlyle hates the army, hates the war, hates KP—more or less equally. "The army ain't a house," he says, using the term first.

As the play narrows down to a significant homosexual incident, with the white "queer" taking on the black "beast" for want of a better companion to ease his frustrations, the odd word crops up again. The white liberal, who was once a Catholic and even thought of becoming a priest to "help" others where he could, discovers that there are limits to his liberalism. The homosexual has aroused himself by playing footsie with Carlyle and he asks the others to leave so that the two can have their "fun." The liberal is swiftly in a fury. Carlyle and friend can go outside into the bushes, if they wish to; that's their business, none of his. But what they plan to do, what they have already begun doing, is not to happen, the boy rages, "in my house!" The homosexual, unevasive throughout, snaps back, "This is my house, too!"

Now that's a peculiar word, really, to be describing a barren shed, mere planking thrown up in a prefab rush, with a couple of tin lamps overhead to make a naked glare of its white walls, unpainted rafters. What does Mr. Rabe mean by it? And what does he mean a few minutes later when the interfering liberal, having had the palm of his hand slashed and his gut pierced by Carlyle's knife, is writhing on the floor in his own blood, piteously pulling a blanket over himself as though humiliated? His black buddy, the one he once talked "friendly" to, makes a gesture of comfort, of assistance. He is screamed at, called a "nigger," for his pains. Has the liberal's liberalism been a posture, something a white boy has forcibly imposed on himself to cover over an actual felt bias?

As I listened to Mr. Rabe's play for a second time—it had been brought from New Haven's Long Wharf to New York's Lincoln Center in a tighter, emotionally clearer 1976 Mike Nichols production—I thought I began to see what the author has been brooding about in the trio that includes *The Basic Training of Pavlo Hummel, Sticks and Bones,* and now *Streamers.* I thought I also glimpsed what it was about his subtext that has so often given him audience trouble: *Sticks and Bones* suffered regular intermission walkouts and failed on Broadway when Joseph Papp transferred it there from his Public; a mass desertion startled me the night I saw *Streamers* in New Haven, and there were still solo escapes taking place at Lincoln Center (just one on opening night). Mr. Rabe has a consistent view of his otherwise varied universe, and, whether that view is right or wrong, there is something intuitively unpalatable to a good many spectators somewhere inside it.

Mr. Rabe's view has nothing to do, really, with the Vietnam war as such, often as the playwright has used that suicidal folly as background; Vietnam is, in fact, simply the most readily available background for his purpose. What I think he is saying is simple, simpler than the multiple symbols he keeps offering us to explain the bloody violence he invariably arrives at. (There are two repeated symbols in *Streamers.* One has to do with parachutes that fail to open, the "streamers" of the title, senselessly dropping men to quite pointless deaths. The other concerns a pit in which a sergeant, during his wartime duty, has trapped a Vietcong: he's thrown a grenade into the pit and sat himself heavily on its lid, listening to the victim's mad scramble to free himself of the certain death with which he shares quarters.)

The author's message, if I read it correctly, is this. We are all—

black, white, straight, queer, parents, children, friends, foes, stable, unstable—living together in the same "house." And we can't do it.

We aren't doing it, ever. In *Sticks and Bones* cartoon-strip parents try to make contact with a blinded son home from battle, as the son himself has tried to behave honorably toward a Eurasian mistress. Failure all round, with the son slitting his wrists and letting his blood drain into a basin before the unfeeling family's eyes. In *Streamers*, which is Mr. Rabe's most effective play to date—rich in character nuance, tense in its close-quarter hostilities—three buddies and one interloper reach out to one another in a variety of ways; but the variety is too unpredictable for safety and, in this smallest of small worlds where adaptation should be feasible, a knife is suddenly drawn to turn the "house" into a slaughterhouse.

While edginess is growing among un-alikes, among human beings thrown together as they *must* be thrown together if they are to survive a universal loneliness, *Streamers* is taut as a bowstring, provocative as the unfathomable mystery of personality is always provocative. Then, a little better than three-quarters through the play, the blood begins to spurt. We are neither surprised nor shocked that some sort of violence should erupt; we have felt the fuse lighted, the hand grenade tossed into the pit. We are unsettled by it nonetheless and for a reason: the explosion seems to exceed its own defined boundaries. It's not confined to the men quarreling over a homosexual act, it extends to at least one total innocent who has played no part in the abrasive contest; a helpless sergeant has his belly slit open simply for good, or bad, measure. The wantonness takes us aback, insults our sense of dramatic cohesiveness.

But that, in turn, forces us to face up to Mr. Rabe's sense of life, of our joint occupancy of the "house." Our attempts to live together in this universe with some chance of ultimate harmony are hopeless. For our flare-ups *are* irrational, in excess of any possible motive. We violate one another at random simply because we are here and because we are what we are. We *cannot* coexist. Or so the pits of our stomachs tell us as we sit in numb horror.

That we cannot coexist, that man cannot make a home of the universe, may be true. It is not a usual dramatic truth. Normally, no matter what ghastly things men and women may be seen doing to one another, we assume a possible rectitude, a natural inner harmony that has been temporarily and intelligibly shattered but can somehow be restored; we may not always see it restored in a play, but we are permitted to scent its return, accept its existence as a postulate.

Not here. And so, to the degree that we admire the play, to the degree that we believe in it, we despair. We may take a considerable admiration home from the theater with us, as I did. But how many of us are willing to take despair for a bedmate?

12

The Last Chance Saloon

For quite some time before I went to see Arthur Kopit's *Wings*, I'd been puzzling over the contemporary theater's increasing preoccupation with illness and age, with senility and death. Mr. Kopit's 1978 play took us, with graphic persuasiveness, inside the stroke-damaged brain of a silver-haired former aviatrix, charting each rugged, ragged step made by patient, doctors, and nurses toward regaining the woman's power of speech before death could impose a permanent silence.

Certainly we'd been in this hospital, this sanitarium, this nursing home before. In Peter Nichols's *The National Health* we'd shared quarters for the evening with a dozen such victims, some terminal, some salvageable, watching protective white screens glide into place about the cots of those who might not last out the long night. In Michael Cristopher's *The Shadow Box*, we'd been permitted access to the private quarters of the ill, scattered cozily here and there about the hospital grounds; all of the cases were terminal. In Ronald Ribman's *Cold Storage*, we'd been taken to the hospital roof, where a garrulous chap in a wheelchair who'd come to terms with the cancer eating away at him prodded a younger fellow-patient for secrets he wished to keep.

David Storey's *Home* had invited us to listen in on the affable non sequiturs of two elderly chaps cocooned in senility, while *The Gin Game* charted for us the quirks of a nursing-home couple whose congealed temperaments first drew them to one another and then wrenched them apart again. Bernard Slade's *Tribute* centered our attention on an incorrigible middle-aged fellow who'd played the clown all his life and was now face to face with certain death from leukemia. I could lengthen the list—the most moving moment in Hugh Leonard's *Da* was one in which a dying man momentarily lost himself in time and imagined himself begging for a bride again—but there's no need. There *is* a doctor in the house these nights, but he's onstage, or waiting in the wings.

The preoccupation, let it be said at once, is not morbid. These plays, virtually all of them, are laced through and through with humor: in the cocky, robust jocularity Martin Balsam displayed in *Cold Storage*, in the quick, flippant wit Laurence Luckinbill tossed at unwelcome visitors in *The Shadow Box*, in Ralph Richardson and John Gielgud's politely woolly exchanges in *Home*, in Jack Lemmon's compulsive vaudeville throughout *Tribute*. As for *The Gin Game*, Hume Cronyn and Jessica Tandy made the very angers that estranged them endearingly funny.

No surprise in this. Age and illness—in the theater, at least—belong rather more to comedy than to pathos. Comedy is made of man's unavoidable limitations, of everything that simply can't be helped: of hunger, thirst, nakedness (including Jack Lemmon's dropped trousers), sexual urgencies, failing powers. Many of Shakespeare's very best clowns are in their dotage, and if Mrs. Malaprop hasn't had a stroke she might as well have had one. When Molière was dying he made fun of himself and death both, writing and appearing in a play about a fool who merely *fancied* himself ill. You may say that he died in comedy's arms. Comedy doesn't mean to humiliate or to hurt its unfortunates; it simply means to say that the human condition is—in its ultimate impotence—preposterous; and at least half the time the observation *is* funny. Take away the laugh and what is left would be no more than bathetic.

But why the prolonged emphasis, just now, on mortality? Snap answers pop up. We've arrived at a society in which people live longer, which means that a great many more of them are going to die of wasting diseases; the subject is much on our minds. There are other sociological phenomena plaguing us at the moment, though, and we don't give them anywhere near the stage time we seem to be giving to geriatrics. Something subtler, perhaps? Living in a nuclear age and fearful of holocaust, are we shielding ourselves psychologically by reminding ourselves that our bodies, after all, are going to self-destruct anyway? Far-fetched.

I did think I came upon a possible clue, however, as I listened to Constance Cummings groping with her bafflement in the Yale Repertory Theater's production of *Wings*. Miss Cummings played the one-time aviatrix who had been reading alone in her room when, without warning, the lamp nearest her had gone out and come on again, the ticking clock beside her had halted, started, then been drowned out in an earthquake of mind-shattering sound. Recovering consciousness in a maze of transparent screens that were somehow her brain and somehow a hospital, she forced herself to still the cascade of disjointed syllables that rattled violently in her head and patiently, slowly extracted single concepts from the jammed circuitry. "What's my name?" she murmured softly to herself, inside herself. "Where is my arm? What's an arm?" But when she asked these and other questions of her doctors, or answered questions they ever so carefully put to her, she discovered something: the words she heard in her head and believed she was using were not the sounds her lips were producing; to all around her, she was unintelligible. Stalemate. Contact broken. Utter isolation.

Still, there was a shaft of steel inside the admirable Miss Cummings's tremors. Alone, she counseled herself firmly: "They will find me. I am still intact. In here."

You will notice she said nothing about death. In the entire play she never feared it, never even seemed to think of it. She spoke and thought of being found, of restoring contact, of achieving communication.

Wings wasn't a play about death. Neither, I think, were any of the other plays mentioned earlier. All of them were plays about communication, about getting in touch. But let's go back a bit.

If any other play leapt instantly to mind it was William Gibson's 1959 *The Miracle Worker*, in which the young Helen Keller, deaf and blind from infancy, was "found" after painstaking effort. A nurse, Annie Sullivan, penetrated the isolation and brought forth an intact person.

There is, however, an enormous difference between these two plays, as there is between 1959 and today. *The Miracle Worker* began with an assumption, the assumption that communication was possible. No matter how tough the shell that sealed one person away from another, the job could be done, the promise of open contact was real. The body of the play was devoted to making the promise come true. It did come true, triumphantly. In *Wings* Miss Cummings made progress, began to find limited conversation quite possible, then—again without warning—was clapped into final imprisonment by a second stroke. In 1978 the effort at communication was aborted.

You see, during the nineteen years between the two pieces we have been told and told and told—by philosophers and by dramatists—that genuine communication is *not* possible, not even to the youthful, the hale, the readily articulate. And we have come to believe it, or at least dramatists have written as though they believed it. Working from the existentialist premise that we lack adequate tools for making direct contact—words are deceptive, logic is fallacious, the notion that we can "know" someone is an illusion—the stage has offered us not only the directionless banter of Samuel Beckett's two principal clowns in *Waiting for Godot* but a strangled example of an otherwise silent slave's effort to make himself heard. The slave's nonstop tirade begins with

"Given the existence as uttered forth in the public works of Puncher and Wattmann of a personal God quaquaquaqua with white beard quaquaquaqua outside time without extension who from the heights of divine apathia divine athambia divine aphasia loves us dearly," and the passage does not sound unlike the terrible tumble of mismatched fragments Miss Cummings's aviatrix produced so helplessly, so unintentionally. Eugene Ionesco, ushering us into the heyday of the so-called Theater of the Absurd, took time to destroy the syllogism in one play, the value of individual letters that help form words in another, and, in yet another, delivered the only redemptive message we were ever likely to hear: "He, mme, mm, mm. Ju, gou, hou, hou. Heu, heu, gu gou, gueue."

Younger and younger writers picked up the thread—the threat, really, that all our efforts at finding one another were doomed to failure—though each made a stage picture of the premise in his own way. Harold Pinter's people, for instance, weren't idlers, they *did* things to other people; but they rarely understood precisely what it was they were doing, didn't really quite know to whom they were doing it.

Edward Albee more or less provided the American stage model for the message in *The Zoo Story*. Two strangers meet on a park bench. One is prim, private, and conservative, immersed in his newspaper; the other, risen up out of the "beat" generation, tries to reach him through words. The words are spent, but no meaningful contact is established. In the end, and in desperation, physical contact is made—with a switchblade. During the ten or twelve years after *The Zoo Story* the model it offered must have been imitated hundreds of times, giving rise to what I still think of as the Park Bench Play.

But two unreachables *could* stand erect and face front for their empty exchanges as well, as Richardson and Gielgud so often did in *Home*. Because both men were senile, their conversation was necessarily wayward; because they were senile, they could also affect to enjoy it. Playwright Storey rammed the irony home in this fragment:

"So rare, these days, to meet someone to whom one can actually talk."

"I know what you mean."

"One works. One looks around. One meets people. But very little communication actually takes place."

"Very."

"None at all in most cases!"

"Oh, absolutely."

"The agonies and frustrations. I can assure you. In the end one gives up in absolute despair."

Did a generation of attentive listeners give up in despair some-where along the line? Is it conceivable that the drug culture of the sixties sprang from the endlessly driven home insistence that the "other" was unreachable and only the self could be experienced? We won't press that.

But, over a span of nearly twenty years, all of us—of whatever age—could not help but be influenced by the omnipresent information that we were isolates, adopting "roles" that did not truly represent us, accepting others in *their* "roles" as masks to be nodded to, forever denied the possibility of a valid meeting of minds. Most of us, I suppose, accepted the news calmly and simply went on living with it, choosing *not* to bang our heads against walls that couldn't be breached.

The root question recurs. Why, in these past few years, should the renewed, determined effort to reach out, get in touch, *make* contact turn up almost exclusively in plays devoted to those whose brains and bodies are on the verge of flickering out? Why the intense focus on this single, very late moment in the time of our lives? The answer, no doubt, is simple enough. So long as we are in middle life, and busy about our chores, the need for absolute communion can rather readily be by-passed, waived. We can communicate just enough for present purposes, and present purposes fill our hearts and heads, hurry us on past felt personal failures, past vacancies we know are there. But as twilight descends, and purposes have been accomplished or forcibly discarded, we become aware of something missed, of something neglected, of an effort that ought to have been made. When we are finally alone, alone isn't good enough. *Was* union possible? Should we have tried harder to find out? Is there time enough left now to extend a hand, a thought, an offering of any sort that might be received and understood and re-turned? Now or never.

Look at what actually happens in the plays we've been talking about. Throughout *Tribute* Jack Lemmon devoted every ounce of his failing energies to one thing: reestablishing, before it was too late, an honest intimacy with his son. Author Bernard Slade had handled the final transformation hokily; but the dogged attempt succeeded, and father and son left the spotlight arm in arm. In *The Shadow Box* Laurence Luckinbill might have failed permanently to establish a relationship with his wife; but he had, with great determination, forged a new one with a homosexual companion, and that became a success of sorts. In *Cold Storage* Martin Balsam kept at it and at it until, through baiting and badgering and his own terrible candor, he forced from companion Len Cariou the naked truth about himself. Needless to say, not every stab at fusion has succeeded. In *The Gin Game* the querulous partners at the card table came within inches of rapport, then stumbled over crotchets too deeply embedded for erasure. In *Wings* Miss Cummings's courage carried her to the very threshold of contact, at which point the door was slammed mercilessly in her face. But the try had been made.

All these plays about the sere and yellow leaf? Plays of last-minute awakening, last-ditch drives for a breakthrough. It's when we find ourselves together in The Last Chance Saloon that we hoist glasses, clink them, and do our broken but earnest best to probe for the conversation we were told we couldn't have, the conversation we'd never had time for, the conversation we know we were born to.

V

OVERBOARD

1

The Uneasy Audience

The line between life and the theater is a notoriously narrow one; I don't think I have ever seen it crossed so subtly, so frequently, in some ways so frighteningly, as it was at the performance of *Short Eyes* I attended in 1974.

First a word about what *Short Eyes is*. Miguel Pinero's quasi-documentary play has its roots in a considerable experience of prisons. The author has served time at Sing Sing, many of his performers first came together as part of a workshop at the men's division of the Bedford Hills Correctional Facility in Westchester. Once freed, and finding theater exhilarating above and beyond mere therapy, the former convicts elected to stay together in an acting ensemble called The Family. Given a sympathetic director in Marvin Felix Camillo, and with some professional actors added, The Family's production of *Short Eyes* was finally offered house room at the Public.

The play is no simple slice of life but an ambitious construct centered about a single irony. The narrative introduces us, inside a tiled, double-tiered cellblock, to a half-dozen or so richly ribald inmates who are essentially tolerant of one another's aberrations. Homosexual rape is taken for granted, beatings are commonplace, murder is not necessarily out of bounds. But one thing *is* out of bounds. Let a man be booked—not convicted, just booked—for child molestation and all camaraderie vanishes. When a trembling, clean-cut, psychologically naked young man is led into the day room, introduced as a pervert who has compulsively pursued little girls, and has heard the barred doors slide shut behind him, he senses that he is irrevocably marked for death. First he will be spat upon, in time he will be hoisted high in the air and then lowered headfirst into a toilet bowl. But more is inevitably coming. Among outcasts, there is only one true outcast. The aversion is primal, unquestioned, absolute.

It was about halfway through the first act, which I was finding genuinely interesting, that I first became aware of the audience. I don't know precisely why I happened to glance about me at the faces on three sides of the Anspacher auditorium. Perhaps the young man's monologue—an edgy, run-on catalogue of the little girls he had pursued— had gone on just a shade too long. Perhaps it had become too plainly a monologue, schematically set off against the rambunctious choral outbursts of the clan, gratuitously delivered to a listener who would indeed ask "Why are you telling me all this?" before it was done. But I did happen to glance about, and what I saw startled me. Approximately half of the audience was deliberately Not Looking.

It was listening, I feel quite sure; I doubt that anyone missed much of the nervous confession. But here were people deep in study of their programs, for undue lengths of time—not bored, avoiding. And here were others perfectly erect in their seats but with eyes turned away from the disclosure on stage. I had the feeling that they would sooner or later turn back, but not until they had suppressed something, come to terms with something. And I suddenly realized that they were—instinctively, unconsciously, in silence—confirming the irony on stage. The convicts' aversion was their aversion, the convicts' exclusion their exclusion.

This sort of thing does not normally happen in the theater. Playgoers normally detach themselves to a considerable degree, formalize what they are looking at—with help from a playwright who is formalizing it for them. They are accustomed to every sort of violence, every sort of transgression of taboos, and in fact are—as a rule—scarcely able to take their eyes off vivid demonstrations of the unthinkable. I don't have to tell you that.

Something else was happening here. Instead of responding dramatically to the material set before them, they had been thrown back onto their life responses; instead of provisionally sharing an emotion onstage in the ordinary way, they were testing—maybe attempting to tame—an emotion they would actually have felt in their living rooms, or on the streets. The line had been crossed: imagination had surrendered to an actual, and disturbing, possibility.

The line was crossed in another way, not long after. As onstage brutality increased, yet another segment of the audience—perhaps a third of it—began literally to scream encouragement, encouragement *of* the man doing the brutalizing. If an inmate was attempting to rape a boyish newcomer, he was, in effect, cheered on. If a junkie reported that he was on drugs not because he was black or the victim of a "personality disorder" but simply because he liked the stuff enormously, he was applauded. I don't pretend to be able to identify the portion of the audience that was volubly reversing drama's traditional sympathy for the underdog, or for the innocent. So far as I could tell, it was composed of pretty much the same racial mix—black, white, Puerto Rican—that stirred restlessly about onstage. Conceivably these rooters were simply rooters for The Family, had followed its rough struggle upward; conceivably they were among the once dispossessed themselves, hardheaded survivors intimate with street law. Whatever may have prompted their responses, these were once again not dramatic responses as we have known them; they were more nearly acknowledgments that this is The Way It Is for the unlucky, and let every man guard his own groin. The arena was truly an arena, not a showcase.

Short Eyes, then, was a promising piece of work that had not yet freed itself of its initial debt to life, hadn't reshaped events in such a way as to invite objective judgment. The members of the audience sat through the experience without ever *becoming* an audience: reactions were private, singular, subjective, and unshared, dependent on individual lifestyles. Too great a reliance on fact as fact tends to fragment; only form can fuse.

The playwright-audience confrontation can end in other ways. For instance, the most interesting thing that happened the night I attended Edward Bond's *Lear* at the Yale Repertory Theater in 1973 took place in the auditorium, not onstage. Theoretically, interesting things were happening onstage. Workers who accidentally dropped tools while building a wall that looked like Agamemnon's at Mycenae were being shot down in cold blood. Tattered statesmen dripping gore were creeping about after a new sort of King Lear with daggers in their hands, only to be discovered drowned in wells discolored with what blood they had left. Pregnant women were being raped, Lear's daughters bayoneted and disemboweled—with Lear dipping his hands into the entrails of one to raise stained red fingers into view. Lear himself was being strapped to a chair and crowned with a newfangled electronic device designed to remove his eyes without damaging them for possible later use elsewhere.

It was at this last point that, first as a slight rustle, then as something closer to the sound of a landslide, the wooden chairs of the Yale Repertory auditorium could be heard scraping this way and that as members of the audience rose and raced for the exits. The departure was highly dramatic, and was no doubt meant to be. But it might have been easily misread.

The obvious explanation for the sizable exodus was that the evening's bloodbath had at last come within inches of drowning those watching it, that their stomachs had turned first, then their backs. Outrage? Disgust? A refusal, any longer, to look on the face of violence?

No such thing, I think. It wasn't a steadily mounting horror that was driving people away—weak people, unable to tolerate an author's insistent vision. Rather the contrary. No one had believed in a bit of the blood all evening long—the evening was now about two hours deep into its three hours' carnage—any more than they had been led to care a fig for the figures bathing in it. There had been no controlling principle to account for the deeds being done, nothing intimately human or narratively necessary to engage us. We were only being invited to watch violence as violence, to accept it as the occasion's *sole* activity, to endure without explanation Mr. Bond's image of life as a succession of random guttings.

But purely gratuitous bloodletting—as in Paris's old Grand Guignol—produces the most contrary effects. One of them is laughter, which didn't happen here; either the enterprise was too transparently earnest or the Yale audience too polite for that. The other is exasperation—exasperation with our failure to respond as we are being so ruthlessly ordered to respond. The audience was *supposed* to be harrowed by the horror of it all; but it wasn't being harrowed, it was being allowed to lapse into indifference, or perhaps into wishing it had a piece of the red-paint concession.

Unable to react appropriately, and finally arriving at an event so monstrous that *not* to react appropriately would brand it as unfeeling, the audience—or a goodly portion of it—simply rose and fled. An audience was being asked to react in a way the play could not persuade it to react, and to linger any longer would have been something like hypocrisy. We can pretend to an unbelieved belief for a certain length of time; after that the sense that we are lying to ourselves makes us impatient with ourselves and we cut bait.

I don't think that those who left were rudely expressing their displeasure with the play, certainly not with its deliberately savage excesses. I think they were trying to get straight with themselves again, trying to get real responses back in line with real stimuli, refusing to signal by their continued, submissive presence that the mayhem onstage was disturbing them. In what may seem a perverse way, they were striking a blow for honesty.

2

Prying

During the two or three days that passed after I'd sat on bleachers in Brooklyn listening to three white-gowned women, impersonal as sea gulls, chant fragments of the poetry of Sylvia Plath, and before I'd pushed myself to my desk to record my impressions of the event, I found myself dodging people. Dodging questions. How was it? Did you like it? What was it like? Picking up *Ariel* in the interim, and rereading Robert Lowell's introduction to the volume published after Sylvia Plath's suicide in 1963, I came upon this: "Probably many, after reading 'Ariel,' will recoil from their first overawed shock, and painfully wonder why so much of it leaves them feeling empty, evasive, and inarticulate." Yes, that's how I'd been feeling.

Not from shock, because the facts of Miss Plath's experience of "viciousness in the kitchen," her exacerbated sensitivity to tulips as much as to the dark, her proudly announced "talent" for death and the perhaps unintended death that came of it, were long since well known, absorbed to the degree that they could be. Not because I did not think the poetry poetry, or found it a burden I did not care to take on. One had only to hear the stark and shaking opening phrase, "The tulips are too excitable," to sit up sharply and await another line as abrasively satisfying.

No, I had been evasive, I think, because—modest and honorable as the performance was—I found something about the occasion itself in part gratuitous, in greater part morbid. Had we really come to hear fifteen lyrics read aloud, all but two of which we might have better grasped by sitting down with *Ariel* at home? Or had we come because we hoped to hear a celebrated illness diagnosed, its unthinkable termination explained—hopes that were certain to be defeated no matter how hard we might pry?

To its credit, the Royal Shakespeare Company's intimate evening at the Brooklyn Academy of Music did its best to dismiss a merely morbid, or foolishly romantic, or queasily sentimental interest in a young woman's putting her head into a gas oven. A. Alvarez's *The Savage God* was quoted early, deprecating the myth that had grown up imagining the poet as sacrificial victim of her work and urging us to listen to the work simply as work, something done for its own sake, breathing independent life.

We were not to suppose that the only way Miss Plath could possibly have "validated" what she'd written was by putting an end to dead fathers, baby brothers, hissing potatoes, herself. As Mr. Lowell said, "Sylvia Plath's poems are not the celebration of some savage and debauched existence, that of the 'damned' poet, glad to burn out his body for a few years of continuous intensity." We were to attend to the music rather than the madness, even when the music seemed half mad.

Right and proper. Yet as the three superbly trained performers glided barefoot about the stage to offer us snippets of biography, excerpts from Miss Plath's novel *The Bell Jar*, and the fifteen lyrics that were sandwiched between, we found ourselves reading the lot as possible preparations for a suicide note. What light was shed here, what there? The rhythm of the moment might be the bitter drumbeat, really coffin nails, of "Daddy," a superb requiem for a father who had died before the poet could kill him. "A cleft in your chin instead of your foot," the performer intoned, while another member of the trio prepared to jab pins into the black doll that represented the Polish-German "brute" who "bit my pretty red heart in two."

But what were we making of this as we leaned forward intently, chins on our hands, wanting to miss nothing? Were we afraid of missing the design of the piece, a design admittedly charged with virulent emotion but, more than anything, a design? I think not.

We were working out our own amateur analysis, catching hints for a case history. We were asking if hatred for a dead father—or love-hatred for a dead father—explained what had happened to a woman in 1963. Our behavior was too simplistic for words, certainly for this woman's words, which were written to shape an emotion when she was in full possession of her powers of feeling and shaping. But it was, I think, the way we behaved.

So with her resentment of her baby brother, her resentment of her mother's being three weeks away in hospital, her resentment of "fluorescent light wincing on and off like a terrible migraine," her ravaged conviction that "the tulips should be behind bars like dangerous animals." Indeed we were so intent on trying to put together a woman that we came very close to forgetting that what she wanted to do was put together verses. We got in her way, as resolutely as death itself.

At the same time neither we nor the Royal Shakespeare Company were entirely guilty of voyeurism. For even if we could have pulled away from our preoccupations, the poems would often enough have brought us back to them. "These poems," Mr. Lowell had said, "are playing Russian roulette with six cartridges in the cylinder" and "they tell that life, even when disciplined, is simply not worth it."

We heard what they told. We might have tried to distract ourselves, and succeeded temporarily in distracting ourselves, with a mother's confidence to a baby: "You are the solid the spaces lean on." We could feel the irony of "My boy, it's your last resort/Will you marry it, marry it, marry it?" We could be caught up in the arrow-flight of a girl's fusion with her horse, laugh aloud at a description of the Roman-mob noise that caged bees make. But always, always, we were hearing that the poet had a "call" for death and thought herself very good at it, hearing the blunt, bleak tag, "Somebody's done for."

What were we to do, then, except surrender—sympathetic ghouls that we were and are—to the sickness in all of us that seeks sickness in others? I doubt that anyone was bored by the production of *Sylvia Plath* in 1974. But I did question the profit to any of us of mounting in dramatic format what was not essentially dramatic and then allowing our inquisitiveness to take up the slack. The poems—and more of them—were at hand, at home.

3

The Death of Comedy

I once spent an evening with a celebrated comedian who was in what is called a state of high dudgeon. Seriously. Something had happened to him that had offended him—more than that, humiliated him—deeply, and his sense of injury filled the air for a good forty minutes. The next night I saw him doing a guest spot on television. He was saying all of the things he'd said the night before, nearly word for word. The routine was hilarious. In a brief twenty-four hours he'd stepped back from himself, measured his anger, discovered its disproportions, and acknowledged its absurdity. Now he was acting his outrage, mocking the fool he'd made of himself in caring about the silly business at all. He had, in record-breaking time, created comedy out of his hurt.

Well, we all know that, don't we? That comedy begins in pain and deprivation and magically transmutes itself into laughter by a slight overemphasis here and there? It's all a matter of taking another look, of altering the perspective. And that, for a time, is what teacher Milo O'Shea seemed to be trying to drum into his night-class students, aspiring comics all, in Trevor Griffiths's *Comedians*. The play, brought from England in 1976 but largely recast and restaged here by Mike Nichols, spent its first hour in a Manchester classroom setting up a reasonably clear, even too familiar, opposition between two kinds of comedy.

The kind Mr. O'Shea espoused was the kind I've been talking about. Begin with the truth. Indeed, Mr. O'Shea drilled his would-be funnymen endlessly in a litany chanted by the group: "The traitor distrusts the truth." Yes, "speed and detail" are valuable, but, as he told his charges, "you'd better be good before you're rich and famous, because you'll never be good later." And being good now meant digging into perfectly real terrors and perfectly real resentments as roots for the humor to come, not merely manufacturing slick *shtik*.

He had one caution, sternly insisted on. No hate. A gaunt, fidgety, balding student who had just composed an obscene limerick was roundly dressed down not because the limerick was obscene but because "it's a joke that hates women and sex." It was perfectly all right—good, even—for the student to recognize the hatred and fear that clung to him. But they still dominated the joke, the joke hadn't wriggled free of its malice and taken that one leap into merriment. "You haven't done anything to change it" was the message. Mr. O'Shea carried his injunctions beyond the gags themselves: "Hate your audience and you'll wind up hating yourselves." The truth, by all means; but freed of spite.

The play's other prescription for comedy was that promoted by a theatrical agent who'd come down to audition these tyros. It was simple: constructed setups leading to kickers, ethnic jokes but not too many, sex but not too much, the standard grab bag. "Perhaps we can't all be Bob Hopes but at least we can try," he said with a conspiratorial, lantern-jawed grin and a cheery wave of his umbrella as he headed for the tryout hall. The amateurs, doing menial work by day, all wanted jobs. Once onstage and auditioning, were they to stand by Mr. O'Shea or give a prospective employer what he'd asked for?

In the seedy cabaret monitored by a grim M.C., most opted for the latter—and it was here that whatever intellectual interest the first act might have generated gasped and died. The stock routines the six aspirants adopted at the microphone were meant to be either bad or very tired. But it was surely the author's task to invent his own awfulness, to approximate staleness by creating new bad jokes that might afford us the kind of pleasure we get from parody. Neil Simon had managed the trick beautifully in *The Sunshine Boys*, devising a Smith and Dale "Dr. Kronkite" routine that delectably resurrected an outdated style without borrowing a word. Mr. Griffiths had instead settled for everybody's chestnuts and our groans. (Quick, now; what fabricated constructions lead up to the tag lines "I'll take ten," "I'm talking as quietly as I can," "But he couldn't get his mouth around the funnel"?) Literal datedness could only make us feel older and older as the second act played itself out.

There was one real exception, and it blew what was left of the meticulously staged, well-acted evening. The chap who had earlier been rebuked for his limerick began his turn on the platform doing tricks with a tiny, intractable violin. Not for long, however. Two life-size dummies—in tuxedo and tiara—were wheeled on, and the "comic" began to bait them, familiarly and viciously, spitting out his lower-class venom on their stuffed, silent forms ("Who needs them?"), pinning a flower to the female's cleavage with such seething violence that the gown was soon dripping blood. He concluded with a song: "The people's flag is deepest red."

There was a classroom post mortem later. The agent offered application forms to two of the drearier contenders, was merely embarrassed at having to face the stubborn rebel. When he was gone, instructor O'Shea was patient with his pupil. "You were brilliant," he acknowledged, "but it wasn't humor. Despise people and you're not telling the truth." But this bit of philosophy—call it moralizing, if you wish—was not permitted to stand. The offender erupted into a climactic attack on Mr. O'Shea ("So we've got to love the enemy, have we?"), suggesting that Mr. O'Shea had faltered in his own career as vaudevillian precisely because he'd lost his hate. The play's contest ended there, seeming to say that honest comedians must begin and remain where Lenny Bruce ended, with the rage on full display, untranslated.

The tragedy of Lenny Bruce, the subject and would-be hero of a 1971 floor-show spectacular called *Lenny* was that he became the very same obsessed creature he ought to have been satirizing. Comedy is indeed made of obsession, of compulsion. The great fools we laugh at— in literature or in vaudeville—are victims of urges they can do nothing to abate.

Harpagon is a compulsive miser. Goldoni's Lelio is a compulsive liar. Tartuffe and Horner are compulsive lechers, willing to go to any lengths to disguise their libidinous energies the better to give them a workout. These are all monomaniacal clowns. Their heads are programmed like one-way streets. They can think of only one thing at a time, all the time. One or another gross disproportion has galloped away with the lot of them.

But they are the *characters* of comedy, not the makers of it. The maker—whether he is a playwright or a saloon entertainer or a parlor raconteur—is another kind of fellow altogether. He is the sane man, the norm, the champion of common sense, the fellow who sees the clown's disproportion *as* a disproportion and puts it into a proper, and hence hilarious, perspective for us. Making his own sanity the measure of the insanity all about him, he serves as cool distancer, standing securely on the brink of the abyss and pointing his finger at the clown who teeters over, and finally into, it.

Lenny Bruce, somewhere along the way, lost his cool, lost his place on the brink, toppled right over into the quicksand in which the characters of comedy forever mire themselves. He became as compulsive, as single-minded, as insistent, finally as *boring* as a Tartuffe or a Horner would be if we had to cope with him in real life without an intermediary to make him funny for us.

I am prepared to believe that at one time Lenny Bruce was funny. I never heard him on a nightclub floor and so cannot offer any opinion out of early personal experience. When I did hear tapes and recordings of performances, and when I looked over transcripts of the appearances for which he was brought to trial in New York, I did not find the material or the manner genuinely amusing. (Neither did I think it obscene; it simply seemed to me out of control.) The man had already become the victim of passion rather than the parodist of passion.

In the long compilation of routines that Julian Barry had now put together and called a "play," there were fleeting indications of the quick-witted double vision that makes comedy possible (you see the absurdity and you put it in a commonplace light). There was a throw-away line that plainly had the makings. As Cliff Gorman, a fine actor doing his best to approximate a run-on saloon gabble, spoke idly and rapidly to his new bride of the exceedingly smart home they'd have together, he said, "I'll get a coffee table and make a door out of it."

That's funny. The man has impaled one decorative fetish of a pseudo-*chic* segment of society as surely as he has indicated that he himself is outside that society. It's a joke not only because he's turned the practice inside out, but because he *is* out of it. *They*—the fools—do this sort of thing. Lenny remains iconoclast.

There was another whiff, drifting off into agreeable fantasy now, as Lenny prattled on about telephone operators, particularly Tijuana telephone operators—who, it would seem, are the most helpful in the world. Just tell them you haven't the four bucks to make this particular long-distance call and they'll cheerfully settle for whatever you've got in your pockets. "They'll take anything—even Chiclets." This was easy exaggeration based on a small trait the comedian had observed. But he remained the observer, happily detailing an absurdity. He hadn't yet been trapped in other people's excesses.

Then the wind began to change. Why, he asked, do comics make so many fag jokes and none about dykes? Because dykes are liable to beat the shit out of you. "The only true anonymous giver is the guy that knocks up your daughter." At the nightclub tables around him were "two kikes, three niggers, one spick." The Leopold and Loeb case? "Bobby Frank was probably a snotty kid anyway." He'd rather have had his own kid see a stag movie than *King of Kings* because he didn't want him coming home to kill Christ, and that's what was in that movie.

From being the genially sane observer, Mr. Bruce was passing over into the insane, or at least rabid, partisan. He was becoming part of his material rather than its analyst. He was preoccupied now with a cause, immersed in his needs and determined that we should all serve them;

he was committed to an angry apostolate. His task: to say the unsayable. To say all the words we have normally suppressed and to say them and say them and say them. To say all the thoughts anyone may have had at any time, founded or unfounded, whatever they might be: to say that when Jackie Kennedy scrambled over the back of that car in Dallas she wasn't trying to summon help, she was trying to save her own skin. To say everything directly, uninverted, uncurved, uncovered.

When Dorothy Parker remarked that if all the girls at a college-prom weekend were laid end to end she wouldn't be surprised, she was doing two things: she was making a pun and she was making a show of making it politely. (The pun is a two-track device; it is the politeness that creates distance, establishes proportion, and these are the things that make the line funny.)

As we came to know him in *Lenny*, Mr. Bruce was no longer interested in giving such a thought form. He wanted to describe each copulation plainly, in graffiti garishness, one after the other, same terms each time. He wanted to rub our noses in the names for things—only certain names, only the ones he thought we would most resist hearing—because he had acquired the impulses of a prophet, a desperate need to hurl anathemas. ("All of my humor is based on destruction and despair," he'd been quoted as saying.)

Where the compulsion came from, and why it took over so totally, is impossible to say: he didn't seem, on the evidence offered during the evening, to have been sexually frustrated, though there may have been a hint of sexual disorientation in his background. He made almost-jokes about his mother and aunt constantly coming home, when he was a child, to report men rushing out from behind bushes to expose themselves; the reports had been too constant to be true. But he was already less than amused by the memory, less than amused by the sexual fantasies of elderly women. He could not put them by, or put them down, as a stock human foible. He was more nearly enraged by them, as he was enraged by our unwillingness to use the "right" word for fellatio. It was easy to see, though, what the compulsion did to his comedy: it killed it. Yet *Lenny* had not been made into a play about the disintegration and death of comedy, comedy done in by becoming as intolerant as the crazy creatures it first set out to lampoon. Instead, from beginning to bitter end, playwright Barry and director Tom O'Horgan had elected to celebrate Lenny Bruce, to offer him as culture hero, to deify him as a humorist wrecked by *other* people, by social pressures.

There was no acknowledgment along the way that humor itself had suffered. Bruce was compared to Aristophanes and Swift; his enemies were symbolized by a massively booted Hitler on stilts. Where laughs were probably not going to be forthcoming, dodges were used. A policeman, asked to read a transcript of a Lenny Bruce performance in court, began by saying "I'm not going to get any laughs with this, I know that," sheepishly acknowledging his incompetence as a performer; the implication was that Bruce *had* got laughs with it, though it was hard now to see where. The last line of the evening was spoken by the performer's long-abandoned wife: "He was a damned funny guy." But, at the last, that was the last thing he was.

The stance of comedy had long since vanished and only its content—obsessiveness—remained. The comedian had dissolved into his joke. To continue to justify him *as a comedian*, as the production unflaggingly did, was a great deal like trying to persuade us that Harpagon was really a very generous man, that Tartuffe was truly pious, that Lelio was telling the truth by his own lights.

Mr. Gorman, in the demanding and virtually exhausting title role, wasn't truly a *shtik* man; he was no master of swiftly slipped-in Yiddish or Irish. But he was surely an actor of range and intelligence; he was himself likable; and, in one of the rare moments when we were able to see Bruce at a loss, he was moving. Fumbling with his prepared defense brief, then losing himself in a terrible tangle of recording tape as he knelt in bewilderment on the floor, he suggested the play that might have been.

Mr. O'Horgan's work was visually more disciplined than usual: stage compositions were sharp, movement was generally well focused. But intellectually the director was bent on pandering, pouring gratuitous and question-begging devices over the stage with a lavish, leering hand. Ceiling-high puppets of Orphan Annie, the Lone Ranger, Dracula, and Jacqueline Kennedy dangled in space to no great purpose; the granite heads of four recent presidents loomed in Mt. Rushmore solidity to less. When Lenny Bruce was discovered nude and dead in his bathroom, the bathroom moved forward out of Richard Nixon's mouth. The image traded on an actual disaffection, but it was quite irrelevant. When Mr. O'Horgan offered us a nude Jesus and a nude Moses at the end of Act One, as though the world hadn't moved an inch since *Hair* first proclaimed itself, the effect was merely naïve.

There was decoration everywhere, presumed explanation everywhere. But neither Hitler nor Nixon had destroyed this particular entertainer. His inability to hold himself at or near the common-sense center of things—the comedian's center—had destroyed him. He had forgotten, even when he was telling the truth, how to make us laugh at the wild things he was saying.

4

Surrender?

In a column written in 1971 I expressed some surprise that members of the younger generation should find themselves enjoying a Broadway comedy as conventional as Leonard Gershe's *Butterflies Are Free.* Shortly thereafter a press agent called me to suggest that conventional comedy was by no means the only thing the younger generation was ready to enjoy. If I wanted to find out for myself how else the land might lie I could drop down to East 3rd Street and see *One Flew Over the Cuckoo's Nest.*

I'd missed this off-Broadway revival when it opened, and, having disliked the earlier production uptown, was obviously dragging my feet. But this new mounting had caught on enough to have run for more than six months, it was obviously appealing to *some* audience in substantial numbers, and it was plainly my business to go. I went. The press agent, so far from simply trying to engineer a plug for his show, was quite right. The audience for *One Flew Over the Cuckoo's Nest* was almost entirely composed of the very young, teeners, early twenties at most—not of people the age of Ken Kesey, who wrote the novel, or of Dale Wasserman, who had made a play of it.

They were all about me—seas of golden hair, wave crests of sunny laughter, buckets of applause. They weren't far-out kids, particularly; no ostentatious sloppiness. They were the young as the young have always been. But with a difference. The difference was in the play, and in the meanings they took from it.

You may remember—perhaps from the still later film version— that *One Flew Over the Cuckoo's Nest* takes place in a ward in a state mental hospital, presided over by a rabbity doctor and a much stronger, at first sweetly solicitous nurse. One of the patients is apparently catatonic, the son of an Indian chief whose manhood had been destroyed; another fastens himself to the blank white walls in crucifixion postures; most are as near-normal as the prim and bespectacled chap in a bathrobe who cheerfully divides his companions into "the curables, the chronics, and the vegetables."

There are group-therapy sessions. It soon becomes apparent—too soon for my dramatic taste, but let that wait—that Nurse Ratched is not so much engaged in the process of relieving the guilt feelings her crippled patients may have as she is determined to fix her charges forever in doubly guilt-ridden states. A boy who probably loves his mother and is hounded by fear of failing her is persuaded that he really loathes her and has become ill as a means of punishing her. Our prim friend, patently as sound of mind and spirit as anyone walking the streets of today's cities, is persuaded that he is effeminate or has been emasculated by his wife. The therapy is geared to make the psychosis permanent. One and all are being conditioned to regard themselves as helpless.

A swaggering fellow named Randle Patrick McMurphy arrives, simian grin at the ready when he isn't solemnly chewing gum. He has escaped the drudgery of a prison sentence at a work farm by shamming mental illness, and though he isn't very bright—he hasn't realized, for instance, that in having himself committed to an institution he has extended his term of confinement indefinitely, become a prisoner until medical rather than legal authorities decide to let him out—he is quite bright enough to see through the whole sorry operation. He immediately decides to lead a revolt against it.

His revolt takes various forms: he runs a kind of gambling syndicate despite regulations against gambling, he conducts a campaign for longer television hours, he secretly helps the Indian to overcome his therapy-induced muteness and deafness, he takes bets that he can best Nurse Ratched in open conflict.

With each bravura challenge to the "system," with each bracing thrust of a man's shoulders as he threw off his "conditioning," the audience broke into delighted cheers and applause. I don't think the rather awkward dramaturgy of the play bothered them in the least. Mr. Wasserman's adaptation still seemed to me jaggedly put together; episodes didn't build upon one another but jerked back and forth, with trivial developments following larger ones as puzzling anticlimaxes; everything was arranged for the author's convenience, including McMurphy's capacity for quickly detecting the truth. Nor did it help to tell me, in a program note, that the play was in some sense a cartoon; it was not consistently a cartoon. No matter. Dramaturgy, I think, was the last thing these young men and women had come for.

They had come to attend to an image of what they most fear in their own lives, perhaps with some hope of exorcising it by the energy of their applause. What they most fear is just that "conditioning" that is the central action of the play. They are afraid that they are conditioned, will be conditioned, have been conditioned. They have been taught to make responses that are not their own, and have so been robbed of individuality.

The fear is not entirely new, of course. In the introduction to his fascinating study of recent American fiction, *City of Words*, Tony Tanner has pointed out that a tension has always existed in American life between the concept of freedom and the concept of social form, of shape or contour. Unlimited freedom has been sought as a good; to find it, the shackles of social shape must be thrown off; but once they are all thrown off man may have no shape at all, may end as a jellyfish, without identity. Conversely, if he accepts existing social contours in order to give himself an identity through shape, the imposed contours may make him rigid and false to himself, destroying identity again. A constantly recurring problem for the prototypical American hero has been, in Mr. Tanner's question: "Can he find a freedom which is not a jelly, and can he establish an identity which is not a prison?" The setting here is a prison, and we see how it functions.

But there is something more here, something closer to the once extravagant science-fiction speculations of Kurt Vonnegut, Jr.'s *Sirens of Titan* and to the soberly proposed recommendations of scientist B. F. Skinner. We are already beyond choice, beyond the tension of options. Somebody has got hold of the machinery and no matter how much we rebel or struggle or defy or cry out we can always be conditioned a little further.

Nurse Ratched is the key to the piece, its prime force and ultimate symbol. I do not like her as a character in a play because I grew up in a humanistic tradition, was trained in a humanistic theater, and therefore like my characters to be recognizably human. Nurse Ratched isn't human. She is entirely malevolent, without any saving softnesses or familiar margins for error. She is herself a computer. And she is all-powerful.

When McMurphy gets a bit out of hand, and is having rather too much success in restoring identities to his companions, he is whisked to the laboratory and given shock treatments. When the shock treatments do not tranquilize him ("Sin while you may," the victim in the bathrobe cries, "for tomorrow we shall be tranquilized!"), he is subjected to a frontal lobotomy. Nurse Ratched, with the controls at her fingertips, has made him a vegetable.

But who is Nurse Ratched, and why should a young audience

believe in her (I assume that it did and does)? Why is she a woman? (There are other such women in the background of the play: the Indian's father has had his manhood destroyed by a white wife.) Where did she get her absolute power and what, in the end, is her motive? Why does she wish to condition all living things to her will?

Perhaps she is simply the mythical "they" who are always out to get us, in which case any audience's belief in her is apt to be a bit paranoid. But the boys and girls I sat with and watched certainly did not seem paranoid. They seemed amused and, after a certain point, resigned. I wanted answers to my questions. I don't think they asked any questions. Are they, then, persuaded that we are all already manipulated by some unidentifiable hostile force, without power to comprehend the "system," let alone do battle with it? Scary, if you think of it that way.

5

Deadly, Male or Female

At what point did the contemporary world, enlightened as it is, come to regard sex as poison, deadly no matter what the dosage? The question crossed my mind, fleetingly, as I came away from Albert Innaurato's short thoroughly unpleasant, undeniably powerful *The Transfiguration of Benno Blimpie,* offered as part of a double bill called *Monsters* at the Astor Place in 1977. If I didn't pursue it at the time, I suppose it was because it seemed so easy to answer: *Benno* is such a disturbing play—I felt as though I'd been mauled in the play-house, and by experts—because we have at last been willing to face up to the nature of the sensual beast inside us, to acknowledge candidly that beast's indiscriminate taste for sodomy, child molestation, homo-sexual attack, castration, fetishism in its fanciest forms, what have you. If our experiences when dealing with sex in the theater have grown more troubling (the audience with which I saw *Benno* did not relax its attention for a moment, but it attempted to relieve its unease by shifting about in its seats to a most remarkable degree), it is because the theater itself has grown more honest. It has, hasn't it?

Later the same week, and after I'd seen Mr. Innaurato's longer, gentler, but still sexually anguished *Gemini* at the Circle Repertory's home off Sheridan Square, I moved uptown for Theodore Mann's pro-duction of *Romeo and Juliet,* expecting simply to listen to *Romeo and Juliet* again and perhaps relish freshly that lovely lyricism we're al-ways going on about. I didn't waste much time on the lyricism. Instead, I found myself hearing an attitude toward sex—composed of two simul-taneous strands meshing without effort—that quite made hash of the "honesty" theory I'd been nursing.

We are neither more honest nor more knowing about sex than Shakespeare was. Of course I ought to have realized that, did realize it; schoolboys quickly catch on to the bawdry that so regularly and so easily salts and peppers the play, commonplace and matter-of-fact as the Monday wash. Our noses are not rubbed in its grubbier aspects, to be sure. But familiarity with what boys and girls, men and women, are apt to be up to, or at least fantasizing about, is well-nigh total and freely made light of.

Juliet's nurse is not unaware of, or the least bit embarrassed by, the fleshly stirrings that surely rise unbidden in her thirteen-year-old charge. She assumes them, could not possibly be shocked by them. "Now comes the wanton blood up in your cheeks," she tells the mere child, rather enjoying the spectacle. Homosexuality is touched on, turned into a joke. When a mooning Romeo is prodded by Benvolio to say what ails him, Romeo's confession, "I do love a woman," is instantly countered by a ribald sally from his friend: "I aimed so near when I supposed you loved." Mercutio and that street gang of his use five-letter words that continue to convey their messages in the twentieth century, and there's not a character in the play who doesn't take lust, natural or "unnatural," for granted. We can't really claim much that is new in the way of information for ourselves.

But mark two things. The candor is casual, its content laughed off as inevitable. Furtive urges of the flesh have nothing to do with the horrors that follow in the play: the poison that is responsible for so much fatal swordplay and so many threatened and actual suicides is a social poison, distilled from the senseless hatreds of feuding families. Sex as such is no villain; vengeance is. And sex, raw sex if you like, does not by its very existence rule out the possibility of genuine, selfless, idealized love. Most of the play *is* lyrical, rhapsodic even, undisturbed by the bawdry that is its natural companion. That is to say, Shakespeare permitted the two a reasonably peaceful coexistence, one extending the other a cheerfully helping hand. If romance had its underside, it was a rather jolly underside. Wantonness came with the package; if anything, Shakespeare *liked* it.

My question stands, then: why, in our presumed wisdom that is not really all that new, are we so determined to find sex repellent? Sex is the mortal enemy of love in *Benno Blimpie*; it is, in the end, the enemy Benno wishes to kill.

Benno is an enormously fat boy, sprawled like a giant jellyfish over the pyramid the play's scenes make, dribbling chocolate ice cream down his vast white shirt as he methodically, purposively eats himself to death. He has sought love, from his parents, from his grandfather, perhaps from schoolyard acquaintances. His mother shoos him from the table, from the house, as "fat and ugly"; she is preoccupied with the fact that his father is now impotent though his grandfather is not. The

psychologically castrated father is appalled that Benno is so sexually
passive, not at all the son he wanted. The grandfather will have Benno
nowhere near him; he is far too busy seducing, or being seduced by, a
nymphet bold and skilled enough to give Lolita cold chills; instead of
delivering the promised sex, however, the young slut puts a knife in the
old man before she has done with him. Three boys in the schoolyard
assault Benno homosexually. When we last see him, he is holding a
meat cleaver high above his head, ready to bring it down upon his
genitals.

I haven't used the notion of sex as a poison randomly. Halfway
through Mr. Innaurato's nightmare, Benno promises himself that he
will blind himself, lock himself in a room with the household rodents,
and eat rat poison. "I will be a sexual object to them," he says bitterly,
maliciously, knowing that as the rats indulge themselves they will also
be killing themselves. Sex as killer. We come upon the image more and
more often these days.

Its function is nowhere near so lethal in the full-length *Gemini*,
though once again we meet an unloved fat boy who, this time, does take
rat poison (unsuccessfully). The thread that comes close to holding
together the backyard celebrations and caterwaulings of an Italian
neighborhood is here homosexual. A twenty-one-year-old who has been
having an affair with a friend's sister fears that it is the friend he really
loves, and the subject must be aired, to the dismay of one and all. Sex as
anxiety, as a disruptive force viewed with uniform distaste.

Strictly speaking, *Gemini* makes no clear statements, morose or
otherwise; as the piece stands, a last-minute and insufficiently motivat-
ed change of heart leaves all members of the trio happy. The trio have
not, in any case, provided us with the real body of the play: that comes
from the sidelines, from the sometimes too extravagant but often very
amusing portraits of family and friends, of a monarch-mother who
rules the garden with a fly swatter until she climbs a telephone pole
bent on spectacular but rather inefficient suicide, of a father's woebegone mistress who isn't hungry enough to be served a helping of pasta
but who manages to make a holocaust of everyone else's plate. The
resolute single-mindedness of *Benno Blimpie* makes it unmistakably
the stronger play, abrasive as it means to be, abrasive as it is. Its
structure is rigidly economical (having just one thing to say), its language is atonally musical, taut and tough as piano wire. The author is
clearly someone to be reckoned with, even as we are attempting to cope
with the wrecked sexuality of his vision, a vision that increasingly
dominates twentieth-century literature and that Shakespeare, lucky
soul, would scarcely have recognized.

Romeo and Juliet was not otherwise very illuminating in its Circle in the Square mounting. During its first half, airy and rapidly spoken, Shakespeare's youngsters were eager to get on with things, rattling off their moonstruck metaphors for the charmingly giddy glories they are and blushing very little about their hurry—once properly blessed—to be abed. Unhappily, the very speed, the lightness of foot and line, that had made a pleasant enough breeze of the evening's beginnings put down no foundation for the emotional storms that followed, particularly since the Romeo of the occasion tended to adopt the postures of passion without ever seeming to feel very personally about what was happening to him. As the evening grew more serious, we didn't grow more serious along with it. I know I spent part of my time wondering why these two foolish children couldn't have devised some expedient means of getting themselves out of the whole mess (couldn't they *both* have slipped away to Mantua?). The rest of the time I spent admiring the late sixteenth century's easy embrace of sex in its totality, as a given.

But the sixteenth century is not ours and we now live with the revulsions of *Benno Blimpie*. Being of our time, *Benno Blimpie* speaks to our time, to that rift in the contemporary psyche that led Susan Sontag to speculate a little while back on whether there mightn't, after all, be something "wrong" with sex (functionally, not morally). Someone—I name no villain, because I am not at all prepared to isolate one—has taken a cleaver to our instincts, neatly and rather nastily severing sensuality from affection. The matter certainly wants looking into, even if the inquiry leaves us temporarily shaken.

VI

A SECOND LOOK

1

The Mystery
of George and Martha

I wish that Edward Albee hadn't directed the 1976 revival of his *Who's Afraid of Virginia Woolf?*, because then he'd have been able to see it. Seeing it with detachment, without having to worry personally about its specific stage effects, I think he'd have felt two things. Enormous pleasure, to begin with. For the excitement that the play had engendered when it first appeared in 1962 proved to have been not in the least dependent upon the shock value of the then forbidden words he'd used or even upon the outrage he'd stirred in many audiences by presenting the twenty-three-years-married George and Martha as vampires steadily at each other's throats.

The play had profited from its language, all right, but from language in which bile had become wit and the wit had become a knotted whip and the knotted whip hadn't merely been snapped in midair to show what a crackle it could give off but had been applied instead directly to the problem of exposing the raw life beneath torn flesh.

The words were weapons, the weapons were used in battle, and the battle was as gratifyingly malicious as it is mysteriously meaningful today. We have been through so much since it first appeared—dramatically and otherwise—that the play can have no taint of scandal about it now; the play stuns, and remains a stunning achievement, because its strength comes from actual pain, its demonic energy from real despair. Mr. Albee's intuition had played him fair and square.

The second thing he might have felt is that he could shut up about the play now, that he was under no further compulsion to explain it. It is understandable that he should have felt annoyed, and in some way demeaned, by a rumor that went the eternal rounds shortly after the piece became the talk of the town: a rumor that the caged and clawing principals were not really man and wife, or man and woman, but disguised homosexuals. It's also understandable that such a reading should have been offered. The most puzzling aspect of the gin-soaked nightmare, then as now, is the fantasy child that historian George and faculty-wife Martha once created for themselves and have kept, until this savagely loquacious moment, their secret.

For a heterosexual couple to invent a child they cannot physically create would be a sentimental gesture; and, as it happens, Martha does have one extended passage in which she permits herself sentimental reminiscence of the infant boy's delivery, his robust health, his black hair that turned blond as the sun, his teddy bear, his summertime tan. But at most other times the mythical child is used as a club: each accuses the other of molesting the boy sexually, with Martha breaking down bathroom doors to get at him nude in the tub. To heterosexual audiences, at least, this particular form of most unsentimental spite does smack of homosexuality rather than heterosexuality. And so an explanation for something that seemed to require explanation had been devised by gossips, surreptitiously imposed upon the play.

Mr. Albee has since been much concerned with killing off the superimposition, and quite rightly: the play's two women—here Colleen Dewhurst's blood-goddess taking on consorts for the pleasure of the kill and Maureen Anderman's soppy schoolgirl in an infantile jumper—are, on the evidence of our eyes and ears, incontestably women, women of a dark imagination perhaps but not of an inaccurate one. Feeling an obligation to offer an explanation of his own, Mr. Albee seized upon the often remarked circumstance that the principal contenders in the feverish bout were named George and Martha. He began intimating in interviews that yes, the illusory offspring was indeed the vaunted American dream, given spurious birth by the legend of the Washingtons, hotly debated thereafter, now dead (and Mr. Albee had earlier written a play about just such a nonexistent boy, called *The American Dream*, hadn't he?).

But, as we watched the sparks fly and felt the heat from the evening's anvil anew, we realized that this was so much nonsense. Symbolically, the exegesis doesn't work. It *never* occurs to us, as we take relish in the very personal infighting, that we are attending the creation and the demise of anything so abstract, so remote, so specifically political, so unfleshed. If it did occur to us, we shouldn't see the relevance: though George is a historian, this isn't a history lesson, it is an immediate human probing—a slashing and cutting—into live tissue, not sociological theory. There is no earthly reason why an "American" dream should go down to failure because of this George's, this

Martha's, attempts to flay each other as the only means of touching each other. *Their* savage story is both larger and deeper than facile, two-dimensional political cartooning. And if Mr. Albee had walked into the theater "cold," prepared—like the rest of us—to see only what was happening up there onstage, I think he'd have noticed something: that the most inexplicable thing about his play is the thing that needs least explaining.

In revival the puzzle resolved itself without effort. Most of the play's hypnotic quality, its outsize humor above all, depended on an eerie literalism. Ben Gazzara, brilliant as the apparently defeated but trigger-tongued George, was asked whether he minded getting a drink for a new colleague who'd dropped by—after midnight—with his baby-doll wife. Mr. Gazzara considered, soliloquized, made an intensely reflective, outrageously funny philosophical question out of whether or not he *minded*. He was going to get the drink, of course; he was already reaching for the makings. But a literal question had been put to him: did he *mind*? And that needed answering, exploring, if one were to take conversation at all seriously. Later, in a burst of anger at all the baiting he'd been subjected to, the colleague made a move to strike Mr. Gazzara, then desisted on the deliberately insulting premise that he would never hit an older man. Mr. Gazzara's programmed reflexes shot back: "Oh, you just hit younger men, and children, women, birds?" The headlong rush of the evening, much of its hilarity, came from an obsession with semantic precision, from the practice of offering instant retort to questions and statements that ought never to have been phrased. Make a fool of fools, as quickly as you can.

Underneath all of this, though, its opposite was slowly building up: the inexplicit, the ambiguous, the unreal. Speaking of the child before strangers was taboo: but speech slipped out, almost unbidden, and flashes of contention over why the child so often ran away from home, over whether the child was really George's, glittered like knife blades over so briefly during the nonstop, increasingly vicious, banter. Was this subtext functioning properly, in spite of its amorphous nature? We knew that it was, for certain, when Mr. Gazzara affected to have heard, near the end of the second act, the door chimes ringing (Miss Dewhurst had merely brushed against them a few seconds earlier).

When Mr. Gazzara went to the door, with his bewildered colleague looking on, to whip it open, welcome a messenger who wasn't there, and receive—in the void filled only with the night air—a message announcing the death of the imagined son, tension was absolute. In this moment of obvious emptiness, we believed—believed that what was not happening was in some sense happening; believed in an emptiness between George and Martha that required the invention of a son; believed in the necessity of the child's death if that terrifying emptiness, filled only with violently exact speech, were ever to be ended.

Sometimes it is best to let the mysterious *be* mysterious. What isn't defined can take on all the overtones there are, in actors' inflected voices, in our own receptive heads. Given the intensity of that vacuum described by the open door, we were ready for the extravagance of the third act's exorcism, ready to see what could be made of George and Martha once the fiction that had kept them apart had been interred. Now it was Miss Dewhurst's turn to be brilliant, rebelling against the requiem Mr. Gazzara was reading quietly from a missal, surrendering her child by speaking the last necessary words ("We couldn't have any"), resigning herself to a life lived openly with her husband (no illusion to separate them, "Just us").

The child had not been a bind but a deliberately built barrier. To keep from surrendering to each other, they had invented a third object on which both could focus, evasively so that their eyes would never meet, abrasively so that their mutual emptiness could be filled with *something* (the snarling filled them with energy, kept them alive). This entirely human story, for all its oddities, was quite enough; it played on the stage with force, with a subliminal credibility, with a more nearly universal thrust than its original audiences were inclined to credit. And so we could be grateful, and let be.

2

How Does Your Garden Grow?

Lillian Hellman's *The Autumn Garden* is an extraordinarily perceptive play—tart-tongued, too, and touching when it is being toughest—but what may be its most important insight is an odd one indeed. The play, given what must in honesty be called an exquisite revival by New Haven's Long Wharf Theater in 1976, is—as its title has always made plain enough—a glance at what is called middle life. And middle life, notoriously, is a time when people, relationships, come unstuck.

But *The Autumn Garden* will not have it that way. *Its* people, whether they are bound by marital or maternal or merely imagined ties of long standing, are—almost all of them—trying desperately to unglue themselves from one another, to face facts and break free. And they simply cannot do it. They are not held in place, kicking and screaming, by the strengths of those to whom they once committed themselves. That would be easily remediable: faced with strength, a man or a woman can always fight back and, with determination, win. They are held in place, altogether helplessly, by the weaknesses of their partners, impaled on the stake—the terrible stake—of compassion. Only the young can sever bonds easily; their inexperience has kept them ignorant of pity.

Of the nine or ten acquaintances who have gathered for a few weeks in a going-to-seed summer resort, a fiftyish but still strong-minded general is burdened with by far the most intolerable wife. His Rose is a faded buttercup, petals fluttering about giddily in the light September breeze, relentlessly wired for sound. Her incessant, still-girlish chatter—no sentence ever seems to have a subject, it simply leapfrogs to the next verb—can be deciphered only by an iconoclastic, clearheaded grandmother and she does it as she would a crossword puzzle, for pleasure—with a little malice thrown in. Rose does not resent being ridiculed; she is accustomed to ridicule and quietly absorbs it, pursing her mouth briefly as though to stifle the hurt and plunging on with the pluckiness of a one-time belle of the ball. As her husband says of her, "Every professional soldier marries Rose; it's in the army manual."

He *will* now, have a divorce; he is urgent and blunt about that. Offering her grounds for divorce by confessing to an earlier affair, he is countered by the eternal child in Rose. Wistfully half improvising (how much of what she says can anyone take for true?), she confesses to an indiscretion of her own. Even things out and there's no cause for parting, is there? The ploy is infantile, yearning, proud and prepared for defeat all at once.

In time, she submits; she will see her brother, a lawyer, to make arrangements. Returning, reassuring her husband that he will have his freedom, she is surprisingly, somewhat evasively, calm. No tears, a cold little laugh instead. The general instantly announces himself frightened by her manner; there's a trick in reserve, isn't there? No, no trick, she replies as she faces him, eyes wide, countenance candid, composed. She has also been to a doctor, to confirm what she has for some time suspected: she is seriously ill, has not long to live. Thrashing his way through doubt and dismay until he has exhausted his emotional alternatives, the victim finds himself embracing the inevitable victor. There is no triumph in Rose, though, only reflective gratitude. She did know he'd feel sorry for her, she tells him, adding, simply, "You've been my good friend." The general's hand is shaking too uncontrollably to pick up a glass once she has left the room.

The play's other snares are differently baited. A young man can neither have the male friends he wants nor quite conclude an "agreement" to marry the resort-keeper's niece, a practical sort born in Europe and given haven after the war; the young man is in thrall to his mother and will—as the no-nonsense grandmother points out—remain there forever. The resort-keeper herself is still clinging to a might-have-been romance with a drudge who has declared himself "out of it" years and years ago and is now content with studying others' mistakes over brandy.

To fuse these mismatched, caught-in-passing lives, Miss Hellman needs a catalyst, and she has, characteristically, fulfilled her dramatist's obligation imaginatively by offering us a catalyst-in-reverse. There appears, with a wife in tow, a once promising painter and eternal charmer who abandoned the community for Paris more than twenty years ago. He hasn't been forgotten and he's eager to see to it that he won't be. Swiftly embarking on what his knowing and very wealthy wife calls "a rampage of good will," he is at once familiarizing himself, generously, with everyone else's problems and—helped along by bear hugs, flirtations, and conspiratorial smiles—pressing his good advice upon one and all.

Except that it is, unfailingly, the worst possible advice. His charm is a mere exercise, quite empty of wisdom, and wherever he meddles he muddies. His wife, growing less tolerant by the moment, points out that once upon a time he'd been satisfied with charming women and children; now he is beginning to lavish his talents on "sirloin steaks, red squirrels and lamp shades." Nor does she mean to be merely amusing; she knows that her husband is dangerous, not only to others but to himself as well, perhaps never more dangerous than when he is being most open ("I'm not a good man"). He must be watched; pain and embarrassment are apt to follow in his wake.

And so they do, with the household aroar and his wife finally determined to leave him. *His* adhesive powers are a shade different from Rose's. First a crooked little smile and a half-admission: "People have hated me, but I don't think anyone's not liked me." (He is entirely willing to overlook the fact that one guest has hurled a wineglass to the floor rather than listen to any more of his cheerfully obtuse do-goodery.) A bolt of clarity overtakes him, though. Is it possible that his *wife* has never quite liked him? She is ruthlessly, if still patiently, telling him now that he hasn't completed a painting in twelve years, that he was always an amateur. Why, then, would she ever have married him? Suddenly, through the blur of early morning, he sees. She is a woman who needs someone to condescend to, to feel superior about. Very well, then. She is still that woman, as he is more than ever that man. "Put up with me a little longer, dear, I'm getting older" is all he says in rejoinder, realizing at last that contempt and kindness can be synonymous and that it is their special inadequacies that have made them inseparable.

The vision is an oblique one, oblique as autumn light, and its people rustle about as though the first leaves had already fallen underfoot. Miss Hellman's play has from the beginning been an honest and a witty one, marred in its original 1951 production by what seemed an inexplicably melodramatic third-act device: the impoverished niece, homesick and anxious to return abroad, resorted to "blackmail" for her passage (the failed artist-charmer had drunkenly fallen asleep in her bed for the night and she seriously threatened to make the most of the scandal).

In Arvin Brown's production, however, and in actress Susan Sharkey's handling of the sequence at the Long Wharf, the difficulty vanished without a trace. Miss Sharkey made it plain that she knew perfectly well what nonsense the "scandal" was, and when she spoke of blackmail she spoke of it with contagious irony. She was, after all, a girl of spirit and considerable independence. She wanted no favors, would accept nothing like charity. Ergo, call the money by some other name ("blackmail" would do), and she would be buying something, giving value for value. The performer was both intelligent and wry; and the painter's wife handed over the check with a full appreciation of the faintly black humor inside the concordat.

If a small puzzle still clings to *The Autumn Garden*, it comes earlier—in the initial relationship between the niece and the mother-ridden young man. We can readily understand the girl's motives in agreeing to a loveless but possibly workable marriage: she is on alien soil, she needs placing. But why the boy, with the world to choose from, should have proposed it remains perplexing: overtones of homosexuality are easily read into the situation now, but there is no substantial evidence in the dialogue that Miss Hellman intended anything more than a silver-cord motif.

And if one performance might have been improved upon in New Haven, it was John McMartin's as the painter. The actor is, as anyone who saw him in Molière's *Don Juan* perfectly well knows, gifted in a half-dozen ways. Here, however, he had—in his loose-limbed, languorous idling about the set, his *leaning* on the play—given us the failure and the meddler in his man before he had bothered to offer us the advertised charm. Surely that was backward; we needed the façade first, needed almost to believe in it, before we began prying into the secrets it concealed. Otherwise we were apt to become as irritated by his intruding upon the private perplexities of his friends as the glass-smashing Josef Sommer did.

But it was difficult to fault either play or production. Carmen Mathews's salty, resilient grandmother (she seemed approximately as much a grandmother as Ina Claire ever had, which was never) adopted Miss Hellman's own challenging, archbacked stance and delivered her haymakers with aplomb; she was rather like the goddess Athena in a snap-brim fedora. The unfailingly expert Mr. Sommer, a bystander eternally in need of a haircut he wasn't going to get, pronounced the evening's valedictory (whatever these autumn people may have become, they wanted it that way) as sensibly and persuasively as he rejected a love that had come too late. Charlotte Moore played Mr. McMartin's wifely baby-sitter and banker with resolutely folded arms and an eye that couldn't be fooled. Joyce Ebert's work as Rose was, in a very real sense, beautiful.

The play itself emerged, at long last, as one of Miss Hellman's very best. Fresh recognition of its qualities had been overdue for some time; in taking such care with the work's nuances, the Long Wharf had arrived at an evening in the theater that was within inches of perfection.

3

The Shutout

Is there a more characteristic Tennessee Williams effect than one that occurs, noisily but helplessly, halfway through the second act of *Cat on a Hot Tin Roof*? In a vast plantation bedroom, with the lush greenery of the finest land "this side of the Valley Nile" barely visible through billowing white lace curtains, a father and son are having a nervous, finally passionate, private conversation.

They have been interrupted, now and again, by a visiting preacher simply searching for a bathroom, by greedy in-laws eager to make their presences felt before father Big Daddy dies of the cancer that is eating away at him. But Big Daddy has roared them all down, banished them to any balcony he could sweep them onto, and then continued to probe at the sore that has made his son Brick an idle, perhaps impotent, drunk. The one who had a right to intrude, and does intrude, is Big Mama, worried mistress of a household that is somehow fetid with evasions, if not downright lies. As she insists on her right to be present she puts the cheeriest possible face on things: what could be so wrong that she ought not to know of it?

Then the effect. Big Daddy will have none of *her*, either ("Hell, I slept with Big Mama till, let's see, five years ago, till I was sixty and she was fifty-eight, and never even liked her, never did!"). Out she must go, out beyond the louvered doors to the hallway, the bolt rammed home in her face. We can still hear her through the louvers, wheedling, demanding, protesting, loving: "Big Daddy? Big Daddy? Oh, Big Daddy!—You didn't mean those things you said to me, did you? Sweetheart? Sweetheart? Big Daddy? You didn't mean those awful things you said to me?—I know you didn't. I know you didn't mean those things in your heart. . . ."

She has been shut out, and a voice or a heart or a suspicion or a truth that has firmly been shut out will at last go away. Or so the self-protective, bound tight in their armor, hope. Williams has very literally used the effect in another play, *Mutilated* (a play I have always hoped he would rework), but whether the plaintive and painful begging at closed doors is literal or figurative, it is nearly always there. *Cat* is almost entirely composed of it, and the guiltiest keeper of the castle tower is not Big Daddy. It is Brick.

For Brick has shut out everyone: father, mother, closest friend, wife Maggie. Maggie is the "cat" of the title, lithe body whipping about the unproductive bedroom like an electric wire that has been loosed in a violent storm and left to thrash snakelike and purposeless on ground that has no use for her. She has felt Brick's detachment from the beginning: it was that very detachment, she sensed, that made him such an accomplished lover in the early years of their marriage. Suspecting that his emotional reserve has something to do with a lingering attachment to Skipper, his one-time fellow hero on the football field, she has meddled. The meddling has brought about Skipper's breakdown, ending in a telephone call to Brick in which Skipper confesses his long-suppressed homosexual feelings. Brick has slammed down the receiver in fury, hastening Skipper's death. And he has ever since refused to bed Maggie, though Big Daddy very clearly wants an heir from his favorite son. Cut off, though we can still hear voices begging to be let in.

Michael Kahn's 1974 production, brought to Broadway after a summer run at the American Shakespeare Festival Theater in Connecticut, did something more than make the isolation of Williams's damaged soul vivid. It displayed the work as something clearer than it had seemed to be in its original and vastly successful Broadway run, clearer and more honest than some of us had at first supposed. An unresolved mystery had always seemed to envelop Brick. Was he or was he not homosexual, did Williams mean him to be but—given the discreet silences of twenty years ago—cautiously refuse to say so?

The answer came exacerbatingly clear—to me, at least—in the new mounting. As Maggie (brilliantly played by Elizabeth Ashley) completed the first long lacerating soliloquy that failed to break down Brick's willful, liquor-laden silence and Big Daddy (astonishingly effective in the hands of Fred Gwynne) took up the task, a pattern of hysteria emerged. Mr. Gwynne, who had seen and bought the world and was unshockable, was prepared to face Brick's possible homosexuality, face it and make no more of it. Brick (Keir Dullea) was not. Writhing in uncontrollable anger, spitting out the word *sodomy* as though to cleanse his mouth of it forever, vehemently insisting that his "real, real, deep, deep friendship" with Skipper had been a "clean, true thing between us," Mr. Dullea all but collapsed into excess, his outrage growing in direct proportion to Mr. Gwynne's tolerance. He was, of course, protesting too much.

Which does not mean that Brick would ever have become a practicing homosexual: as Mr. Williams writes in a stage direction, "*the wide and profound reach of the conventional mores he got from the world that crowned him with early laurel*" embrace and protect him too firmly. That is not what he fears. What he fears, and can never acknowledge, is that he at any time might have *felt* such an attraction. Merely to have felt such an attraction would destroy his self-image, make him an outcast in his own eyes, reduce him from the "god" of the playing field to a failed branch of the species. His need is to see himself as straight, clean, uncorrupted, and even untemptable—and at any cost to those about him.

It is curious how casting, even questionable casting, can sometimes illuminate the darker corners of a play. In the earlier Broadway production, that fine actor Ben Gazzara had taken up his climactic stance in the confrontation with Big Daddy so foursquarely and with such obvious virility that it had been difficult to question his complete sincerity. But evidence given in the play—the friends had a habit of clasping hands at bedtime—pointed in another direction. The issue, in consequence, had seemed blurred. Mr. Dullea, who was not nearly so good as Mr. Gazzara in the hothouse atmosphere of the opening sequences, brought to the key outbursts a near-delirium, an interior terror, that at once demanded further explanation, betrayed its own cause. It was reasonable to ask this Brick, "Why are you so excited?" as Big Daddy did; and we were now forced to look for a reasonable answer, which was there.

It was fascinating to watch a play and its problem come untangled at the ANTA, luring us further and further into the intricate psychological maze that its author intended as "a snare for the truth of human experience." If *Cat on a Hot Tin Roof* still seems to me to be second-rank Williams, it is because our fascination is almost exclusively intellectual, grounded in those psychological twists and turns alone; our emotions are nearly as shut out as Maggie's. There remain imbalances in the play's structure—the first two acts are truly near-soliloquies, allowing Brick's early passivity to become irritating while Maggie and Big Daddy talk him down—and there is a slight falling-off in Williams's magic with idiom (though his southern locutions, as in "Death *commences* so quickly," continue to charm even as they sting).

But the "snare" is a valid one, unrigged, untendentious. No judgment is passed on lying as a form of living, not even on the unwisdom of lying to oneself. Some lies are hurtful, some neutral, some ironically benevolent. When Maggie lifts her face to Big Daddy with a gently luminous smile to tell him that she and Brick are about to give him a grandchild, she, too, is lying—but only partly out of self-interest. There is also in the untruth great pity for a ravaged man. See how subtle life's chess moves are, Mr. Williams suggests, and which lie would you most willingly part with?

4

A Footnote on Williams

While we are speaking of Mr. Williams, and now that so many of his plays are proving successful in revival, we might pause and praise him for a virtue with which he's not normally credited. He is a man unafraid of melodrama, and a man who handles it with extraordinary candor and deftness.

This isn't exactly the party line on Williams. When we acclaim him, it is mainly for his women and his words. Fair enough. His women are the American theater's best, and so are his words. But if we mention the melodrama that marks the plays at all, it is usually to rue it: what's our finest living dramatist doing mucking about with arson, political violence, gunplay in shady roadhouses? We don't need that sort of thing, in an artist, do we?

In point of fact, we do. Something's got to move the play, propel it dynamically toward wide-open, emotionally revealing scenes, and while of course it needn't be, shouldn't be, cheap, it does have to be vigorous. Watching a 1975 production of *Summer and Smoke* at the Roundabout, I was suddenly struck with how swiftly and economically Williams had brushed in the situation that would lead to a shooting. The sequence, as it happened, was awkwardly and too garishly handled in this particular performance; even the costuming seemed to make a B movie out of it But I went back to the text and there, as I suspected, it was smooth as silk, neither florid nor forced, utterly logical given the habits of the young wastrel-hero we'd been following all along.

In *Sweet Bird of Youth* the venal politician and his suavely vicious son were as readily established, plausible in their language first, in their extravagant deeds thereafter. The plotting itself became a kind of poetry as discarded mistresses, ravaged film stars, and end-of-the-road young studs seemed to claw with their nails to keep a grip on a crumbling reality.

And in the relatively short *27 Wagons Full of Cotton* almost the first word spat on a Mississippi plantation is *arson*. No bones about it.

Mr. Williams is certainly not primarily interested in some sort of whodunit or will-he-get-caught, though he'll use the values as the values serve him; he's interested in temperaments, twisted psyches, people probing one another—sadistically or sensually—to see what brain and flesh can be made to yield. But to get to the portraiture, and to get to it in some depth, he's got to have an occasion, a first pressure. And so, in about two seconds flat, he slips it into *27 Wagons* with the ease of a knife blade. Aging, impoverished Jake Meighan has set fire to a syndicate cotton gin so that the syndicate will have to come to him to process its waiting wagon loads. His wife, younger, less than bright but animal-wily, knows what he has done and must be urged to silence: the urging takes the form of brutal, but connubially acceptable, arm-twisting. A battered but pliant girl will be circumspect—or as circumspect as a tongue that outraces thought ever can be.

Pressure applied, we're ready for the play proper. The setup, unblinkingly bold, raw and natural as the Blue Mountain dirt beneath booted feet, has been quickly, quietly arranged. When a young syndicate superintendent comes prying, with caresses for the girl and a riding crop to brush provocatively against her dress, there are both tension and breathing space for the dramatist to play with. We can settle down now, locked into the girl's dilemma, to let an actress (Meryl Streep in the Phoenix Theater's 1976 revival) studiously slap away thoroughly believable mosquitoes, splay her legs like a rag doll, twist an evasive but sinuous toe to keep the porch swing rocking rhythmically, count her thoughts on her fingers, clutch her oversize white purse as she weighs inadvertent betrayal against what is happening to her flesh. Her alternately violent and seductive inquisitor can take his time, too. Intimacy, the interplay of intelligence and sexual heat, becomes the body of the altogether persuasive piece. Mr. Williams has got the truth of devious, vengeful, vulnerable, and calculating human beings out of a situation, an essentially melodramatic situation, faced straightforwardly.

5

Who Is the Poet?

Eugene O'Neill's *A Touch of The Poet* is a good play and a deceptive one. I'm afraid that in its 1978 mounting it deceived director Jose Quintero and his company most sorely.

The final scene played best. Jason Robards, the preening, posturing, self-advertised aristocrat and military hero who had never resigned himself to the fact that he was now nothing more than an impoverished tavernkeeper in the Boston of 1828, had discovered that his daughter wasn't considered good enough to marry into the American *nouveau riche*. Riding off on his prized mare to horsewhip the successful Yankee who had forbidden the betrothal, Mr. Robards was instead clubbed nearly senseless by a waiting band of servants and some eagerly cooperative police.

He returned to his desolate inn bloodied about the mouth and forehead and—this was Mr. Robards's oddest and most telling effect—with his eyes so retracted into his skull that you felt he would never see or laugh or flare in anger again. Certainly he would never again survey his shabby domain, or his drink-stained figure in a mirror, with pride. Whatever trick of the light he had once used to make his person and his past seem romantically imposing had gone out. It would stay out. Reeling to his feet, Mr. Robards deliberately resumed the coarse Irish accent he had long since abandoned, cursed himself for "having lived all his life in a hell of pride," and made his way to the tavern's barroom to become a tosspot among tosspots, a common man among common men. So much for this man's "pipe dream." The turnabout had had some theatrical energy in it; and we were looking at an ending—an awakening—happier than any of those provided the dreaming derelicts of *The Iceman Cometh*.

Or were we? Several contrary strains—faint, but insistent—recurred during the passage. Mr. Robards's wife and daughter, Geraldine Fitzgerald and Kathryn Walker, had small reason to be grateful to the man. He had married beneath him, and then only because a child was coming. He had sneered at the "peasant stock" with which he had embroiled himself, had hurled his wife from his arms simply because she hadn't washed her hair, had mercilessly baited his daughter for having ankles thicker than his mare's. The two women were drudges, body servants to his delusion; one might have expected them to rejoice to find the delusion dead. That wasn't the way of it.

In a rare moment of candor, Miss Fitzgerald had let us know that she had seen through every last pretension of which her husband was capable, seen through it and embraced it. "I'm the only one who doesn't sneer at his dream," she concluded, ending the revelation with tight-lipped satisfaction. When the clearheaded Miss Walker, who had done her share of sneering, heard that Mr. Robards was on his way to give his still-haughtier opponent a thrashing, she was exultant—and not because of her lover or her hopes of marriage. She was exultant for her offended peacock of a father. "Then he's not beaten!" she cried. At the end, once he had been beaten so thoroughly that he could not and would not ever strut again, she was rueful. Staring at his humbled back as he made his way toward his cronies at the bar, she asked herself, most seriously, "Why do I mourn for him?"

In any production these lines, few and fleeting as they are, must be attended to, for they create the rich ambiguity, the internal contradiction, the intellectual tension without which the play becomes a mere parade of pomposities marching toward not much more than a sound thump on the head. What are the lines saying? They're saying that there was something good about the dream, about the aspiration that gave birth to illusion, about the imagination that has gone into the lying, about that "touch of the poet" that—vainly or no—sees glory in the world.

Who has a touch of the poet? O'Neill himself did; he always regretted he hadn't more of it, regretted having to settle for the less he'd been given. In the play, the tavernkeeper does; he is not named Con Melody for nothing. And, again in the play—the complexities turn on themselves now—the young man the daughter dearly loves has it, just a touch. He has separated himself from his worldly family to live in a hut by a pond that is not called Walden but might as well have been, he has become ill, he is being nursed back to health in an upstairs room by the girl who has deliberately enticed him. The girl has planned to make him love her "just enough" so that she can marry him without cheating either of them; instead, at the moment of seduction, she has found herself genuinely adoring. She is, in a very real sense, marrying her father.

For, when the boy's mother comes to visit, it is made abundantly clear that Con Melody's daughter will live out her life with yet another failed artist, victim of his own self-image. As his mother relentlessly points out, the boy comes from a long line of thoroughly Americanized pragmatists, men who have all had their own "touch" of idealism but who have, in their grubbing after money and power, ruthlessly suppressed it. The boy will ultimately abandon any imaginative powers he may possess because the American ethos is hostile to such powers, a theme O'Neill intended to elaborate majestically in the uncompleted *More Stately Mansions*. The destruction of the poetic impulse is universal; it is still with us.

But if all of this is to hold in the theater, the poetic impulse must be constantly present and be recognized for what it is. Those who cling to it may be fools, but they must be ambiguous fools: men with a trace of actual talent, men with color on their tongues, men of ludicrously thwarted aspiration. And it was here that the new production collapsed completely. Until the satisfyingly vigorous final scene, neither Mr. Quintero nor Mr. Robards suggested that there was anything to be salvaged from a fantasist's inventive brain, from a memory of heroism on the battlefield under Wellington, from an ostentatious fondness for Byron's rhythms, for, if you will, an unquenched thirst for blarney.

Mr. Robards *looked* right when he entered, straight-backed in a black frock coat, lace at his throat and wrists. Almost at once, however, he was reduced to an idle popinjay, tyrant to no purpose. Nervously and noisily rattling a whiskey bottle against a glass for his first nip of the morning, he was very nearly a cartoon. The one-dimensional humbuggery continued as he wriggled his fingers high in air like a barnstorming Osric, as he turned from self-adulation in a mirror to arch his eyebrows at the audience in a vaudeville leer, as he adopted stances that constantly seemed to be inviting someone to slap him across the face with a glove. "Thank God," he purred, "I still bear the stamp of an officer and a gentleman." But he didn't, really; he bore the stamp of a fop. When he attempted to flatter the visiting mother by pawing her, the clumsiness of the gesture may have been half right. But surely it should have had another half to it: some echo of the suave gallantry that must have been his as a young man.

Many of the things the skilled Mr. Robards did—he was especially amusing when he was lying, a stogy clamped between his teeth, about the visitor's offer of a kiss—would have served the play well if only the second side to the ambiguity, the truly imaginative and commanding side, had showed its face occasionally. At the very least we needed enough of it to justify the lingering admiration his wife and daughter offered his battered ghost in the play's final lines. But it wasn't there as steady counterpoint and its absence drained the earlier scenes of tension, of now-you-see-it-now-you-don't possibility, of thematic clarity. So long as only one note was sounded, the evening lacked meaning; the actors were left to fidget rather than listen, to do individual "line readings" instead of pursuing a continuity, to grope about in what seemed a peculiarly empty large room.

It is possible to shrivel a play by doing only one aspect of it, and we watched just that happen to *A Touch of the Poet.*

6

Quietus

When, come 1971, we were offered *Waiting for Godot* again—in a production directed by Alan Schneider, who may know more about Samuel Beckett than any man living—it became infinitely clearer why certain purists should have objected so strenuously to the lovely performance given by Bert Lahr in the Broadway mounting fifteen years earlier. Mr. Lahr completed things. Every once in a while, even if only for a little while, something changed for him.

When he had struggled and struggled and strained and strained to get those miserably tight shoes off his feet, and they came off, he sighed. He sighed a sigh that swept out over the auditorium like a sudden, soothing breeze on a hot August night, he sighed a musical sigh, he sighed a sigh you could wade in. Gogo had got what he wanted and, for one unforgettable moment, it was worth it. When he was at last given a carrot instead of one more detested turnip, he didn't leap at it greedily or dispose of it swiftly. He paid homage to it, surrounded it in adoration, made its glory blaze before your eyes. He could be satisfied, he could be content, he could bask as well as cry.

But that, strictly speaking and being completely *serious* about the matter, is neither the point nor the tactic of *Godot*. In Mr. Schneider's off-Broadway production, when Gogo's shoes came off they simply came off, and were forgotten. If anyone remembered them it was Didi, that other tramp who is passing the time with his friend waiting for a Godot who never comes; Didi picked them up, twice, to smell them and to wince. When Gogo exclaimed, "It's a carrot!" the announcement was more nearly a brisk statement of fact than a submission to rapture. And when Didi left the stage to seek relief for a probable prostate condition, he did not return relieved. He seemed, rather, in greater pain than before. The implications of each attempt to gratify desire were very plain. Giving a man what he wants gets him no nearer what he wants.

For *Godot is* a play of waiting, of incompletion, of stirrings aborted and satisfactions withheld. Didi and Gogo, killing time with idle verbal canters and occasional catnaps, speculate on their chances of being rescued, eventually, from death or from hell. The chances are about even, they figure. After all, of the two thieves alongside Jesus on the Cross, one was saved. "That's a reasonable percentage," Didi estimates. Of course, the story of the saved thief appears in only one of the four gospels. That reduces the percentage, doesn't it? No matter. They will wait. And no matter. In this play, which is our house for the evening, Godot will not come.

Beckett builds his play to become his theme. If hope is to be deferred, so must humor be, so must movement in space and time be. He will give us beginnings, but no endings. And so a joke is begun, teasing from us a small smile of expectation. Didi, shaping a battered clown's derby to his graying head, asks, "How do I look?" There are many funny answers to that. Gogo, delivering *his* answer in the rhythm of vaudeville riposte, says, "How would I know?" The expected sally is stillborn, deflected, now and forevermore. There are rumors of humor, and they infect us in anticipation; they must be quashed before we dare laugh openly and take solace from them.

The fact that movement in time and space, toward any conceivable goal, toward an end of the waiting, is utterly impossible is stressed in repeated ironies. "If we all speak at once we'll never get anywhere," Didi insists. We realize on the instant that if they ever so carefully speak one at a time, they will never get anywhere, either.

Can anything they *do* matter? No, that is an illusion, fostered in part by drama and its fondness for action. The illusion must be mocked, the possibility of drama exquisitely insulted. That is why Didi and Gogo spend such thought and such passion on the great dramatic issue of whether they will sit down or stand up. On whether they will or will not lift a satchel. On which of them will dry a slave's tears. The issue is of no moment, either way. "Well, that passed the time," Gogo murmurs, in mild justification. "It would have passed in any case," Didi replies.

Change is brought to a halt, the hope that anything *else* will happen or that anything—even a joke—will be resolved is resolutely curbed. Drama as we have known it is terminated, blandly, deliberately, wryly, a bit maliciously, a bit conspiratorially. "You see?" with a half-smile, is the mood of the empty-handed evening.

Mr. Schneider had been as scrupulous as his author in honoring the method that so suits the meaning. He may have gone a bit far in driving Henderson Forsythe, as Didi, and Paul B. Price, as Gogo, to speak at exactly the same rate and at exactly the same pitch, taking contrast and melody away from them as though these things might contaminate the barrenness. But he had got all good performances. Mr. Forsythe, looking like a frock-coated preacher with his fly open, first spoke of Godot as though he might have been a long-lost bar companion, someone casually known; an unsuitable awe was promptly removed from the proceedings. Anthony Holland, as the near-spastic, sniveling, haltered slave of the burly Pozzo, lifted his feet in a broken dance that seemed the shudder of a lanced cavalry steed, then cranked his rusted vocal apparatus up to the frenzy of his single Joycean cadenza with extraordinary force. A moon rose in each act on a rapid predetermined curve; this moon was not tonight's news but a repetition of yesterday's. The mounting was spare. Its only unforeseen generosity was in the second-act appearance of green buds on every branch of the lone tree, a generosity which, in fact, the text calls for; some productions have allowed us just one bud.

Given the cool immobility, the impotence, the anguish at being lost and the sensation of unmeaning endlessness that define the play, what is the play's hold on us? Why has it, after our first bafflement with it, become *the* representative play—though never the most ardently attended play—of the second half of the twentieth century? Precisely because of those qualities, not in spite of them.

I don't think we learned to accept *Godot* because we were able to find a secret warmth in it. There are small fires to put our hands to, to be sure: those few green buds, the companionship of the clowns, the fact that though there may be no Godot there *is* a messenger who says he has seen him. One can claim to detect in Beckett a regret that his vision is the bleak thing it is. But one has also got to stay with the vision, the word pronounced by the shape of the play: the void, not Godot, is with us.

What happened, I think, is that we had come to see ourselves, or were just ten minutes shy of coming to see ourselves, as immobile, impotent, lost on a planet's surface, deluded about the possibility of arriving at meaningful resolutions in just the way that these defrocked vaudevillians are. The play was ahead of our heads, but not much ahead of our intuitions. Recognition came not in our eyes but in the pits of our stomachs. We had sensed where we were but had not seen it. Beckett made a picture of it. There was no reason why we had to like the picture. Is there anything very likable in it? What we had to do, and have done, is acknowledge it. With a dry taste in our mouths, and still trying to smile, we have nodded yes.

A problem remains. Having refused drama its movement, the stage its habit of occupying us with a happening that may come to something, how can the play sustain our attention the whole time? I don't find that it does. I am bound to confess, with reluctance but with such candor as I can muster, that I am restive in its presence, ready to call the image clear and the evening quits, nearly half of the time.

There is every reason why I should be. My attention is constantly being caught, by a gesture, by a slant of thought, by an alluring line. The moment it is caught it is canceled, turned back, deliberately ripped from its roots in order to make the play's point. After a given number of such severings, my mind catches on, and begins to wander away on its own; I must force it back. The forcing is real because, after all, there is nothing I *must* listen to. When everything that is said is arbitrary and optional, and is meant to be, then I fall under no obligation: I am not obliged to pursue a line where it is not going. Overall, I am aware that the forward thrust of drama has been intercepted so that it can be philosophically denied; it is not surprising, then, that I should no longer respond to that thrust, that I should instead feel an urge to cut loose. I sit in a theater giving substantial assent to an image all the while that I know the image to be saying, among other things, that drama has stopped. To the degree that it succeeds it stills itself.

Godot is the only play I know of that is seminal and terminal at once.

VII

THE
TRAINING GROUND

1

Lions and Lambs

I have just seen the lion lie down with the lamb. Suppose we fantasize for a moment. Let's say that a young, green playwright with a young, green script has been able to see that script—however unpolished it may be—acted out. His audience has been composed of some ordinary, quite amiable and easygoing people, plus a large contingent of those extraordinary, constitutionally suspicious creatures called critics. Next morning, quite early, he has been able to sit on the stage so recently occupied by his actors and directly confront the critics.

He begins the conversation neither arrogantly nor defensively. He speaks of "my doubts *now*," indicating that the previous evening's performance has itself suggested unresolved problems to him—without any help from professional gadflies. He is not fearful, or at all self-conscious, about speaking of his structural search for a "cleanliness and elegance of line." There is nothing pretentious in this. He is serious and means to be taken seriously. He does realize that in rewriting during rehearsals he has "unlocked certain major themes without really dealing with them." These things said, he invites comment.

The critics, all of them professionals, respond courteously but straightforwardly, with no air of passing judgment from on high, with none of that condescension that comes of wishing to be kind. The play's qualities, achievements, possible stumbles, intended and unintended ambiguities are considered, candidly but with great civility; conceivable alternatives are explored; differences of opinion are weighed, calmly, reflectively. The critics are not *telling* the playwright anything; they are asking, talking *about*. Every single thing they say could fairly be called constructive.

The playwright takes notes furiously, sometimes nodding his head rapidly in momentary assent, sometimes raising his chin sharply in fleeting private debate. When the session is pronounced over, he thanks

his critics with an earnestness that must be taken as genuine. He has
been stimulated by the exchange and he is grateful. For a very brief
moment the theater's two arch-enemies—the writer and the reviewer—
have become companions working toward a single end: the making of a
better play for a richer stage.

Do you believe a word of it? I said we were fantasizing, because it's
all so unlikely; but, as it happens, we weren't. In July of 1977 I spent
several days at the Eugene O'Neill Theater Center in Waterford, Connecticut, and I can assure you that Utopia, if what I've been describing
strikes you as Utopia, exists. The process not only functions, under the
presidency of George C. White and the artistic direction of Lloyd
Richards, with an incredible serenity; it produces. Of the twelve plays
mounted and discussed during the previous year's four-week working
season, *eight* had reached New York, at one production level or another, during the ensuing winter, with a ninth waiting in the wings. I
won't even go into the regional and university theater productions that
have followed first exposure at the center, enabling the writer to take
advantage of anything learned during his baptism and providing his
play with its "second step" toward a dreamed-of perfection. It wouldn't
be gross exaggeration to call what is happening in Waterford
miraculous.

But miracles, large or small, don't come easily, and this one certainly didn't. Any gathering of writers and critics is potentially explosive and when, thirteen years before, the O'Neill National Playwrights Conference first tried its wings it was quite badly burned. It
was already finding, and helping to mature, valuable plays during its
beginning years: Ron Cowen's *Summertree*, for instance, was performed
beneath a tree on the lawn in 1967 (the tree has grown taller now but
everyone still calls it the *summertree*). But the volatile mix of authors
and reviewers led, in its original form, to something like disaster. The
practice at the time was to complete the performance and, within ten
minutes, have a handful of professional critics onstage to take the play
apart. *Summertree* was promptly savaged, with one reviewer magisteri-
ally instructing the author to forget the theater altogether and go back
to pumping gas. The battles—and that is what they were—stopped
short of being bloody, but rancor made the cool night air from Long
Island Sound a great deal warmer than it need have been.

In an effort at easing the unhappy tensions, a National Critics
Institute was formed to house a few reviewers from major newspapers
together with a larger group of student-critic "fellows" for the entire
four weeks, and the lot of them were hustled off the stage and into the
"mansion" that serves as headquarters. There they were given type-

writers and asked to write out, with rather more time and more deliberate consideration, their reviews. Unfortunately, these reviews were either posted on a bulletin board the next morning or read aloud at a conference table in the presence of the author. To give you an idea of how this worked out, on one occasion the author arrived at the morning session carrying a briefcase, which he placed firmly on the meeting table at which his probable detractors sat. From the briefcase he solemnly removed a pistol and waited for the reviews to begin. The fact that the weapon was later discovered to be a water pistol only means that the author is still safely at large. It didn't change the atmosphere or put an end to recriminations.

Do you know how the problem was solved, leading to the astonishing harmony that prevails today? In several ways, actually, but in one that was undoubtedly all-important. The Critics Institute, under Ernest Schier's direction, altered its focus. Its principal object was no longer to review the plays. Its purpose, rather, was to review the reviews, with the author absent or present as he chose. Critics assembled to criticize, or at least discuss, one another's criticisms, and this singular act of humility—this facing up to the fact that the reviewers were in every way less than infallible—did the trick. It was now understood that a review might be every bit as flawed as the play under consideration, that it, too, was open to debate; the news got through to the gratified playwrights, a sense of common difficulty and common purpose began to take over, easy interchange replaced what had for so long been contention.

Two other things helped. Four or five well-known critics, with an occasional established playwright thrown in, were invited to stay for the full session to serve as dramaturges, counselors to the playwrights while their plays were in rehearsal. (Prowling through the big red barn on the premises, I was cheered to see Edith Oliver of The New Yorker sitting most casually on the floor alongside her assigned author, checking the manuscript with him while keeping an eye both generous and sharp on the players who were giving life to his lines.) Each dramaturge stays the course until the play is at last performed for the public, venturing suggestions, listening to questions, hand-holding if need be. It is no doubt good for a critic, now and again, to become *involved* in the making of a play; it is surely good for the playwright to deal, however temporarily, with a reviewer who is not so much fiend as friend.

And, in all probability, the O'Neill is now benefiting from what I think of as the Law of Accelerating Returns. It has, by this time, helped give birth to a good many well-known plays: Israel Horovitz's *The Indian Wants the Bronx*, John Guare's *House of Blue Leaves*, Charles

Fuller's *The Brownsville Raid,* Kevin O'Morrison's *Ladyhouse Blues,* Albert Innaurato's *The Transfiguration of Benno Blimpie* among them. As the numbers increase, and the organization's reputation for finding work of quality grows, better and better scripts are going to be submitted for a possible hearing. As it is, Mr. Richards and his staff manage to read eight hundred plays yearly while getting ready for the July plunge, thinning this to eighty "finalists," and then—no doubt with pain—cutting to the feasible twelve. As the submissions *do* grow better (if that little law of mine really operates), reviewers obviously have an easier time of it; the more serious the work, the more seriously it can be taken. One more nudge toward good author-critic relations.

The conference has managed to solve a thorny problem ingeniously. That is not its only achievement. Visitors are asked not to write about the plays they may see for the simple, and sound, reason that the plays are still in work. But I am free to say that the production quality of the piece I saw and heard discussed was, to me, downright unbelievable. There had been less than three days' rehearsal time. The actors were carrying scripts, as is customary. And yet the performances were both vigorous and sensitive, the stage direction was fluid and fully shaped, and the carried scripts seemed to vanish along with the last traces of daylight that filtered through the leaves of a huge copper beech overhead. Not a scene lost its momentum, or its dramatic design, for want of a word or the need to turn a page. The playwright *could* see his play.

Five minutes into the performance a stray voice floated up from the road below, clear in the night air. "What's goin' on up there, huh?" it asked. The audience laughed, but it was a strangely contented laugh. Contented, I think, because it knew the answer to the question. Plenty was going on.

2

Helping the Hand
That Feeds You

There is one thing British actors do that no American actor ever thinks of doing, and that is tend carefully to the nursing of playwrights. To an American actor a playwright's growth and reputation are matters for the playwright himself to take care of. The writer's early struggles, his experimental reaches, are no part of the star performer's business. Let the young fellow learn his trade, fight his battles, rise majestically—and alone—to the top of his form, and *then* the star may very well think of favoring him by appearing in his newest piece. The piece had better be good, and right for the particular star, of course. If, a year later, the writer slips slightly off form, no phone call from him is likely ever to reach the performer again. The performer's obligation, if any, has ceased. This is all rather silly, considering that without the playwright the actor really has nothing to keep his trade alive, but, for the most part, it's the way things are over here.

In England, it's different. The night before I left London in August of 1973, I hied myself off to the Royal Court, a distinguished tryout house that mounts new plays for runs of about four weeks each, after which they may or may not be transferred to the West End for commercial showing. I was drawn to the theater partly because the evening's opening was a new David Storey play: the Royal Court had already introduced five of them, including *The Contractor, Home,* and *The Changing Room,* and I was naturally curious.

But that was only part of the reason I went. I'd also rushed through my scanty dinner—can't bring myself to call it high tea—to make the early curtain because Albert Finney was appearing in Mr. Storey's *Cromwell,* though it had been made abundantly clear in the advance publicity that Mr. Finney's was not a starring, or even an especially important, role. Mr. Finney was simply helping to make sure that a goodly number of picking-and-choosing playgoers would get there, get to see what Mr. Storey was up to this time whether this time was successful or not. He was supporting the man who supports him.

A few months earlier Paul Scofield had done as much for Christopher Hampton, that very promising, very young writer whose elliptically comic *The Philanthropist* made Broadway a bit more cheerful in 1971. Mr. Scofield's role was, theoretically, a starring one; I'll have something to say about that in a moment. But the play was a new kind of trial flight for its probing author, echoing not at all the bizarre humors of his earlier success, and it plainly wanted some assistance if it was going to make a suitable noise. In the upshot, it made enough noise to get itself transferred to the West End, where it was still running. It was called *Savages.*

As it happens, I didn't care much for either play, though that's far from the nub of the matter. Both writers seemed to me to walk into a trap always lying in wait for ardent newcomers who have earned the right to be heard: now that they *will* be heard, they feel free—briefly, it is to be hoped—to pontificate, to unleash all the impulses toward do-goodery that have been churning inside them since they were members of their second-year debating societies. Concern for shape, for tension, for simple dramatic interest gives way to a rush of reforming zeal; the results are apt to seem pretentious or gauche, or both.

Cromwell was simply Mr. Storey's antiwar play. Astonishingly, it promptly became a blend of everyone else's. As a stark black curtain did a filmwipe across the proscenium to reveal an equally stark white platform, strongly raked, we began to meet the oafish common soldiers, those itinerants without weapons or purpose who are so often drawn into battle because battle is where the food is. We met their recruiters, men impassive as boulders; we met their opponents, good at pillage and torture; we met rebel idealists who would start new wars the moment old ones were done; we met the girl who only wanted to remain on her land and till the soil. We never did meet Cromwell because the whole shadowy, often sluggish, business was not about the historical Cromwell but about all wars ever fought.

Into the symbolic, though handsomely staged, jumble went bits and pieces of *Mother Courage,* dramatically lazy echoes of *The Good Soldier Schweik,* the shade of Ibsen's Button Moulder, and, for good measure, the spirit of Edna Ferber's *So Big.* The girl, hands on hips, surveyed her flourishing crops between holocausts and murmured, "What can't be taken away is our joy of labor." The war-weary fellow who settled down with her, really the central figure in the play, knelt in prayer for illumination: "When the goal is clear, the path is straight," he said.

There was no dearth of platitude anywhere: "A brave man makes his life," "No course is greater than its means." At the end of the evening, after the farm had been pillaged once more, the three principal sufferers were seen solemnly marching toward us in mist, announcing, "For the first time there is no turning back." We didn't really know where they were going; pretty certainly, not to the West End.

A perverse case could be made to say that Mr. Finney's presence actually created an imbalance in the evening's emphases. Mr. Finney hadn't become the star he was without growing a magnetism of his own that made the shafts of stage light seem brighter around him. Stomping on brogans big as slapshoes to find a patch of ground he might steal sixty winks on, or sidling up to run his finger along the arm of a girl he'd never be bright enough to make his own, he was good. Just good enough to make it quite a long while before we were able to focus our attention on Brian Cox (a chap who looked a bit like the young Brando and who seemed regrettably to be aping his mutter) and recognize him for the dramatic cornerstone he was meant to be. Still, Mr. Finney was there; it was an occasional comfort.

Paul Scofield was there, too, in *Savages,* though his apparent starring role proved to be nothing of the sort. No American actor of Mr. Scofield's prominence would have touched the part, that's for sure. *Savages* had to do with a British diplomat who was kidnapped by South American revolutionaries, to be held in exchange for twenty-five political prisoners. (Mr. Scofield was marvelously droll in his outrage when so informed: after all, the kidnapee just before him had been exchanged for *forty* prisoners.) The play was, as you immediately suspected, one of those obvious stabs at irony in which the Indians native to the country were regarded as savages while the real savages were, first of all, the imperialists who exploited them, and, after that, the revolutionaries who promised change but were chained to their own ideologies.

Mr. Scofield was a passive figure throughout, from the time that men masked in black stocking caps interrupted his dressing for dinner, taking pains to tie his tie properly before being handcuffed to an iron cot in a dingy cell. The handcuffs were the least of it. Mr. Scofield was really the prisoner of another man's tongue, and had to listen endlessly to the harangues of his young, ruthlessly idealistic, guard.

But when he was out of the cell, via flashbacks, he was listening again: to an anthropologist with theories, to a military fogy who was fond of playing "modern stuff" on the phonograph ("The Black Bottom" was what was being played), to a missionary who had barred his windows against Indians who wouldn't abandon their own rituals ("No coexistence" was his creed). And when the Indians themselves were about, swaying in ceremony or leaping into stylized wrestling matches, Mr. Scofield tended to vanish altogether, appearing only to recite a small legend or two. (One of these, in which the many children of an impoverished family flew into the heavens and became the stars, there to do their parents some good, was rather attractive.)

The fact was that Mr. Scofield had nothing to act, and was therefore required to spend his evening reacting. His silent vocabulary— eyebrows raised in infinite variation, sharp turns of the head, humiliated pursings of the mouth—was astonishing. He was certainly able to do what he was asked to do: create some kind of man out of the verbal lumps he took, the recoil of his shoulders, the helpless protestations of his free hand. And it must have been exhausting for him. Any giving that was going on here was from the actor to the playwright, not vice versa. It was a free gift from a man of great generosity.

Whether such an appearance did Mr. Scofield any good, or Mr. Finney any good, was quite beside the point, just as the failure or relative success of a given production was beside the point. The point is plain. Both plays, whether one thought them good or bad, were the work of men of talent. Talent needs exercise, an open field and an unfettered stride, if it is to discover precisely what it is and where it ought to be going. The exercises must be produced if the playwright is ever to find out whether his thrust has been effective, and they must be presented for long enough, with sufficiently sturdy companies, for an audience to send back a valid verdict.

This done, the playwright can take his *next* step, whatever it may be. But he's never going to ripen if the last try is languishing in a drawer somewhere, or if it ends up in a fringe production so inadequately cast that its failure can be blamed on poor actors. If the best new talent is to become the best mature talent, generosity is dearly wanted: instead of simply capitalizing upon a playwright's high spots, an actor has got to help him over the bad ones. Give the current piece the best that's going, and find out.

British actors, British stars, are willing to do that.

3

Beehives

Let's say you're a tall and attractive young woman with a manuscript under your arm—tall and attractive is fine, but it gets your manuscript nowhere—and you'd just love to find a place in New York to stage it, to see what it looks like and what you can make of it. The manuscript may not be your own; it may be the work of a friend who graduated from Yale when you did. You've already knocked on the door of Terry Schreiber's Studio, where new plays are being given first hearings all the time, but Terry Schreiber's was, at the moment, overloaded. You've also tried the Hudson Guild Theater, where new plays are an exclusive concern; overloaded there, too. In all, there are approximately one hundred different doors you can make your way to around town—off-off-Broadway doors—and of the one hundred perhaps twelve are not one-shot houses, doing whatever single plays can be financed, but rabbit-warren buildings reconstructed from old brownstones or clubs in which every closet and corridor, bathrooms excluded, has some sort of reading, rehearsal, or performance going on.

In 1972 a tall and attractive girl named Lynne Meadow made her way into the cluttered entryway of one of these multi-theater workshops, the Manhattan Theater Club on East Seventy-third, asked if she could find stage space for the play she carried under her arm, and, lo and behold, was told by the then artistic director that she could. A year later *she* was the artistic director, poring daily over an unfathomable wall chart that apportions rooms, pianos, pillows, and stage hours to as many writers, directors, and actors as can be fitted into three dizzyingly staircased floors. She was running, or helping to run, the kind of off-off-Broadway center that is, just now, saving the American theater's neck.

Once off-Broadway had done the saving, providing a display window for the new playwrights, performers, and entrepreneurs who would feed plasma to an anemic Broadway. Then off-Broadway froze

into Broadway. As quality, and a demand for production polish indistin-
guishable from Broadway's, increased, so did costs—of every kind. But
the costs couldn't be met in such smallish houses, and off-Broadway
became as risky a proposition as its big brother had so long been. The
once acclaimed salvage operation had noticeably—even notoriously—
shriveled during the late sixties.

A solution had to be found that would keep immature playwrights
at work inexpensively. Ellen Stewart, lovingly collaring potential
young artists on the streets and hurling them—no questions asked—
onto the available floors of LaMama, paved the way indefatigably.
Joseph Papp's complex at the Public made the concept more stable.
Others followed. If I focus my attention on the Manhattan Theater Club
here it is not necessarily because it has become the best of the lot—
though it has introduced work of promise and even of importance—but
because it may most readily illustrate the two almost contrary principles that govern this new kind of theater-nursing.

On the one hand, it is institutional. It is institutional because it is
run by somebody: Miss Meadow makes the final selection of ventures to
be given temporary houseroom. It is institutional because it solicits
memberships: memberships are slightly different from subscriptions
because they foster a social urge to drop in any old time. It is institutional because memberships, which constitute up to sixty percent of
any given audience, do not at all cover expenses, which means that help
from foundations is necessary, and forthcoming.

On the other hand, it is extraordinarily eclectic, free-wheeling,
uncommitted to any one policy that might invite arthritis. Not just new
plays, though approximately sixty-five percent of those done thus far
have been originals; in one of the three playhouses (not counting the
cabaret) revivals of Williams, Odets, Behrman alternate with the untried. The cabaret offers entertainment the minute the three theaters
drop their curtains. Opera is done as freely as drama; so are poetry
readings. And the doors remain open to those who come manuscript in
hand, open on unusually flexible terms.

That is to say, the club itself may decide to do a play, perhaps as
nothing more than an unstaged reading, perhaps with minimal production on a budget of $200, perhaps with more production on a budget of
$1,000. It is also wide open to coproduction. If Ed Bullins wants to scare
up a part of the financing for a new play by Richard Wesley, the club
will hurry him in and foot the balance. When, after the club had done
its $100 workshop version of Michael Sawyer's most interesting *Naomi
Court,* someone who'd seen it was willing to try it again after revisions,
the club promptly joined him in doing a second, $1,500 staging. And
when that staging attracted considerable attention, the club rented out

space for a full off-Broadway dressing-up that cost its final producers as much as $30,000.

Long runs are in no sense the object; testing is. Indeed, the club's deal with Actors' Equity is a happy one for the purposes. It need pay its actors no salaries, only expenses, so long as no more than twelve performances of each play are given, divided over several weekends. Actors like acting, and are happy. Directors are delighted to have them, writers sometimes ecstatic. No one gets rich, except—looking ahead—the theater itself. All concerned are able to watch and evaluate work in constant progress. Flow is of the essence.

Having spent a day and an evening poking my curious way through the Manhattan Club's labyrinth, I can tell you something about the flow. In the cabaret, when I was there in 1975, librettist-composers Gretchen Cryer and Nancy Ford (fondly remembered for their *Last Sweet Days of Isaac*) were rehearsing an after-hours program of songs, some of which were intended for a new musical. In sweater and slacks, and working over a sore throat, Miss Cryer began quietly, curbing a tendency to tap a toe with the rhythm, singing her honest surprise that "it never crossed my mind, it never crossed my mind" that she'd lose a man, or, having lost him, find another. Two surprises and a charming melody. (As she braced herself for the next number, a lyric recording her astonishment that she should have an album filled with photographs "and not one of them is me," I made the fool reviewer's customary mistake. I blurted out that the song was lovely, only to be informed, most charitably, that it had already appeared in a show I hadn't liked. Served me right.)

What I was hearing was so enchanting I wondered that it needed rehearsal at all. It didn't, for long. As I was slipping out, Miss Ford was asking for a pillow to prop her up on the piano stool (she wasn't getting the audience's eye level right). When I glanced in a few moments later, the two were gone and an operetta melody for a program to be called *Three by Offenbach* was being urgently trilled without lyrics (the lyrics weren't finished yet).

Across the hall a bearded young director was quietly calming two eager but apprehensive young women reading a new play for him—Edward Bond's *The Sea,* which hadn't yet been done in New York—while, two floors above, a new American play, Margie Appleman's *The Best Is Yet to Be,* was finally bringing its author some long-delayed comfort. The play had once been under option to Jules Irving at Lincoln Center, never produced. A writer can't judge *anything* he's written until he hears it, sees it move. The grin on Miss Appleman's face was nearly as wide as the hall that was giving it home.

Three floors below—we're in the basement now—director John

Pleshette was animatedly reshaping a household tempest for resident playwright Jonathan Levy's *The Pornographer's Daughter.* The wealthy pornographer himself, it seemed, had lost interest in everything but *haute cuisine,* and it was taking some doing to awaken his sexually introverted daughter, a lass of thirty-nine still working on her doctoral dissertation though all of her advisers had long since died. With swift professionalism, the company was enjoying making dialogue exchanges become *scenes.*

Midway somewhere—I've lost track myself—William Inge's *Bus Stop* was being given a brushup rehearsal, to replace an actress who hadn't been able to work the final weekend. And I *know* that midway somewhere else I peered through one doorway to overhear the matriarchal Eugenie Leontovich at work, while just across the hall a six-year-old in leotard lifted a trained leg precisely. On the main floor once again, a bar was being torn out and a thrust stage erected; though it looked as if a storm had struck, this may have been the quietest room in the building.

In the evening Joseph Chaikin's production of Chekhov's *The Sea Gull* was being given its second performance. Doing Chekhov, and doing him naturalistically, was actually a first for Mr. Chaikin, who had devoted himself until now to the kind of improvisational, sometimes nonverbal, theater that gave us *The Serpent.* Jean-Claude van Itallie had provided a fresh, gently straightforward adaptation, and for the first three of Chekhov's four acts Mr. Chaikin's sensitivities functioned as superbly here as they had done with experimental forms.

The passionate interplay between a gauche but manly Konstantin and a Nina whose mouth was too inexperienced to suppress laughter and pretend to gravity was lovely, puppyish stuff. The affection between the boy and his uncle, an uncle with fussed hair but composed mind, was wonderfully, unselfconsciously demonstrative, rare warmth in a house with a chill on it. Leueen MacGrath, using her willowy body and tapering fingers to create a provincial Garbo who had surely spent most of her time as an actress arranging stage flowers, was amusingly transparent as she intercepted a handclasp between Konstantin and his Nina while urging them not to be so shy with each other.

Virtually all of the one-to-one confrontations were secure, illuminating. Mr. Chaikin's only difficulty seemed to lie in the business of crossbreeding them; he had trouble keeping the established intimacies alive when the room was crowded, when all were gathered for an idle evening that would end in Konstantin's suicide. The fourth act thus refused to climb, emotionally or otherwise, and we had to fall back on our memories of the private duets. But it was a production Mr. Chaikin not only wished to do, but had a right to do. We were better informed for having seen him explore what was, for him, a new vein.

New veins and old, and both together, had become the unrestricted business of a narrow, jumbled building on Seventy-third Street—ever so appropriately, it had once housed the Bohemian Benevolent Society—as these have become the vital stock-in-trade of similar beehives scattered across town. Our theater is constantly creating crises for itself; and then resolving them.

4

A Small Caution

Now that theatrical workshops have multiplied felicitously and even ferociously, I'd like to offer playwrights approaching them a handy rule of thumb. It's really a double-pronged rule: (a) use the workshop for all it's worth; (b) don't fall in love with it.

The worth of a workshop is by this time obvious, and not only because some embryonic productions have flowered into very profitable operations. Everyone remembers the long run that Lanford Wilson's *Hot L Baltimore* parlayed out of mere weekend beginnings, the nation is at this moment saturated with duplicate productions of *A Chorus Line*, Broadway was quick to open its doors to the Public-born *For Colored Girls*, and so on. What starts in a lab can wind up in the whole world's lap.

Just as important—up to a point—is the twelve-performance try-out that never does go anywhere else, except into the playwright's head for corrections. It's been said often enough that anyone who hopes to write for the theater has got to hear what his work sounds like *in a theater*. The line that he loved on paper may instantly make him cringe as he stands at the back of the auditorium and shares it with—hears it with—a hundred or so other people. The author who has done something in which the assembled audience doesn't believe is, in his own imagination, stripped naked on the spot. He feels abashed, penitent, and in a hurry to go home and set the sorry mishap right.

It's not that the audience needs to groan, titter inappropriately, or otherwise vocalize its dissatisfaction. It can remain entirely silent. The writer will still pick up the verdict, by radar, by extrasensory perception, by the simple fact that he is among his fellows and begins to respond as they do. It's the only satisfactory way to learn, and everyone who hopes that the year after tomorrow there'll be new scripts on producers' desks—scripts worthy of getting off those desks and onto the stage—has got to be grateful for the whole development.

If I issue a partial caution, it's because of two things I've noticed, two things not immediately related. The first is this. On several recent occasions playwrights have *specified* that their plays must be done in workshop situations—even when more completely professional productions were open to them. During a visit to The Performing Garage on Wooster Street, where Steve Gooch's *Female Transport* was being given its first American performance, I was informed that Mr. Gooch, having had some success with his piece in a tiny London house, had turned down offers from commercial producers here and insisted on an intimate, remote, low-risk mounting. Within the same week I came across a casual note in the press indicating that producer Roger L. Stevens, in Washington, was mounting his next play *not* in the Kennedy Center, where he'd like to have put it, but in a miniature house especially leased for the occasion. Again the author had insisted.

Well, good enough. A playwright has got to mature at his idiosyncratic rate, and sometimes it's better to keep small work in small environments, safely away from demands it doesn't mean to meet yet. No writer *has* to tangle with a thousand listeners in a thousand seats, or with the economic pressures that start up the minute a stage (all that scenery) or the auditorium (all that overhead) gets larger. Not until he's ready for it, braced, ripened, reasonably confident.

Mr. Gooch, for instance, was undoubtedly wise to continue circling the fringes for the time being. His *Female Transport* had to do with six shackled women in the sunless hold of a convict ship carrying them to Australia in 1815. Though it contained effectively managed scenes—a newly shipped sailor lad wanting to ask one of the manacled girls for sex but sorely abashed by the eternal presence of five onlookers—it was a virtual catalog of stock slave-ship images: the bloodied lass who had taken twenty-six lashes on her back, the storm at sea that set the lot of them reeling dangerously, the morose member of the group who hanged herself during the night, the impoverished doctor who wished to insist upon more humane treatment but who could be bribed to silence. The play lacked a center of emotional interest, an omission that robbed it of its possible suspense. Any other six women would have done as well. In short, *Female Transport* was wise to retain its workshop standing.

There is, however, a danger in *contenting* oneself with what may be called sheltered productions. A writer can freeze himself at the tryout, or small-audience, or not-quite-developed level, protecting himself from the slings and arrows of larger confrontations, persuading himself that, so long as he is producing material for what finally becomes a coterie audience, he is growing. Undoubtedly he *is* growing, for a given length of time—an indeterminate length of time, since it is bound to be different for each man and woman. The trick is to know when you've hit it, when it's time to get out and go to the mat with more complex materials, with the more varied reactions of great big audiences, with the demands of full-scale, no-allowances-made theater.

I'm stressing the point because we've spent so much time lately asking ourselves whatever happened to the so promising young writers of the fifties and sixties, only a few of whom have hitched up their shoulders, forcibly added cubits to their stature, and resoundingly delivered what was expected of them. In 1976 Eleanor Lester raised the issue again in *The New York Times*, running through possible answers to the mystery—the strongest of which was that Broadway, the "big" theater, had for so long been inhospitable to the relatively experimental work being done by the better-than-beginners.

I think another answer—I count it only one—might be given. Too many of the fifties and sixties people may have lingered too long in the places that gave them birth, nursed them, praised them for partial accomplishment. In time the partial accomplishment that brought them to first attention may have come to seem enough; working in familiar surroundings, with partners as sympathetic to effort as to achievement, before audiences prepared to accept fledgling work and even dedicated to seeking it out, is a great deal more comfortable—and safer—than tackling the possibly hostile unknown. One can tell oneself, after all, that what is done in limited situations for limited audiences is *superior* to the gross commercialism that inevitably attaches itself to any more sizable try. And development can stop right there.

Development comes from constantly increasing the size of the challenge. And though larger theaters, larger audiences, do in fact embroil writers in commercial hazards of many a sort, no writer need take the plunge—nor should he—for the money that *A Chorus Line* is earning. He should do it for the massed people he must face, in their diversity, in their ranging tastes, in their show-me sluggishness and their universal capacity for being electrified. They're only people; there's just a bigger bunch of them, demanding—if all are to be satisfied simultaneously—a bigger play. If our one-time young hopefuls have not produced the "big" plays expected of them, it's possibly because too many of them kept on playing it small, small and secure.

It's true that Broadway was once in no mood for "experiment." Broadway in the sixties was withering on the vine and couldn't even find customers for the commercial materials in which it was supposed to wallow. Since the mid-seventies, that's all changed. With audiences racing back to the theater, with productions being snatched from here, there, and everywhere, with all stage doors open and even the unlikeliest comers welcome, the opportunities for writers to jump in, mingle, and—let us pray—grow are greater today than they have been in many, many years. Seize 'em, I say.

VIII

THE PLAYERS

1

The Top of the Mountain

Irene Worth has become what every young performer of talent and intelligence promises himself he will become, hell and high water notwithstanding. In the process, she has also become hard to find. She doesn't very often come where you are. You must go where she is. As I left the Brooklyn Academy of Music after a performance of Tennessee Williams's *Sweet Bird of Youth* in December of 1975—a performance in which Miss Worth played the ravaged but still diamond-hard movie queen to Christopher Walken's stubborn young stud—I noticed that my companion of the evening, long a conscientious theatergoer, was seething. Virtually stamping his feet in fury on the sidewalk, he exploded. "But this is a great actress! Why haven't I seen her before? Where has she been? Where have *I* been?"

And that's more or less the story. You see, when boys and girls begin their work in the theater they set themselves certain standards. They do mean to become great actors and actresses, they know more or less how to go about realizing their dreams, certainly they're familiar with the lures and the booby traps that will keep them from maturing. They vow never to give in. They won't give in to typecasting, to playing themselves and exploiting their mannerisms over and over again. They won't give in to the long-run system, cuddling up securely in profitable repetition that will leave them automatons after a year or two, half asleep onstage. They won't give in to a prevailing naturalism of style that will effectively prevent their ever attempting *Macbeth* but plan to extend and vary their respective ranges at every opportunity. Of course they won't give in to films or to television, at least not permanently.

They will, they one and all swear to themselves, spend their lives leapfrogging, jumping from Noël Coward to Christopher Marlowe, from Broadway to Hollywood and then right back again, to London perhaps and no doubt Minneapolis, to off-off-Broadway if that is where they should be next, to wherever the beckoning finger of fresh experience summons them. Never mind the big money, never mind adulation. Where can I learn more, add one inch to my stature *as performer?* Greatness comes of growth, and growth comes of getting around, changing one's spots, trading the tried and true for the untried until it, too, becomes true. Everyone knows how it's done.

Alas and of course, hell and high water prevail. Films are exciting and why shouldn't I make three more? Six more? I *know* how to do Neil Simon, why should I risk my reputation trying Congreve? I have a wife and children, how dare I walk out of a hit? If I go off-off-Broadway, won't everyone think I've slipped? Sooner or later, usually quite soon, performers settle, especially if the settlement—like a divorce settlement—is a good one. And they do divorce themselves from their dreams.

Irene Worth has never been so reasonable. She's played on Broadway, all right, which is unsurprising since she's American born. But as soon as she'd "made it" in an out-and-out thriller called *The Two Mrs. Carrolls,* she took flight to London to see what else might be available. And she's been back on Broadway, once with Alec Guinness in T. S. Eliot's *The Cocktail Party,* years later for Lillian Hellman's *Toys in the Attic.* With a little care, though, you could easily have missed her. She's also done time in London's commercial West End, making certain that she could manage the baubles of Ferenc Molnár and Terence Rattigan. But when she wanted the Old Vic, Lady Macbeth, and a low salary, she went to the Old Vic, Lady Macbeth, and a low salary. And when she wanted out, she went out, here, there, anywhere that might challenge her to do what she hadn't done before, to do what she might not be able to do, to chance the impossible. (I have, in fact, seen her master the impossible.) With her antennae constantly alert to the rumor of new risk, she has climbed the mountains of Iran, with Peter Brook's experimental troupe, there to perform for no audience at all in a language that wouldn't have been understood if there had been an audience. No questions asked, except when do we start?

My own introduction to the actress came in Stratford, Ontario, at a time when Stratford, Ontario, seemed as remote and improbable as the mountains of Iran. With Tyrone Guthrie and Alec Guinness, she'd agreed to open the startling new tent playhouse that bequeathed the continent an entirely original stage shape, and to do it in an out-of-the-way hamlet that seemed to most people inaccessible. The small community itself thought the project foolhardy; the family I was lodged with— no hotel space available—confided to me that the whole thing was doomed. It stopped being doomed the evening Miss Worth stepped

forward, charming in her wimple, as a chaste and put-upon but decidedly clever Helena in *All's Well That Ends Well*. I had long supposed the
play, with its improbable love story, unplayable. Glistening with grace,
Miss Worth made the absurd more than palatable; she made it lyrical.

Like my recent companion, I'd never heard of the lady before. That
was twenty-six years ago. If I've been able to follow any part of her
chameleonlike, elusively magnetic, cumulatively stunning career, it's
because I've been lucky enough to be where she was from time to time.
London, with Miss Worth in the company of John Gielgud, Ralph
Richardson, and Sybil Thorndike (*A Day by the Sea*) and belonging
there. Chichester, long after, persuading me with her Hesione Husha-
bye that *Heartbreak House* was—how could we doubt it as she locked
arms about her knees and stared at the dangerous night sky?—Shaw's
best play. Back in New York again, but not on Broadway: at the old
downtown Phoenix doing Schiller's *Mary Stuart,* taking time out to
create a venomously powerful Clytemnestra for television.

In Ontario once more, a proud peony of a Hedda Gabler, spine
ramrod straight as she fired a pistol directly into our faces. And,
somewhere between, at Yale, where she did the impossible. It really
isn't possible, is it, to play Io in Aeschylus' *Prometheus Bound*? Io, as
the *Oxford Companion to Classical Literature* has it, "is a mortal whom
Zeus has loved and Hera's jealousy has turned into a heifer. She is
doomed to long wanderings pursued by a gadfly, and haunted by the
ghost of the myriad-eyed Argos." Try that on for size. Io is a speech, not
a person, a mythological remnant with which we have lost sensitive
contact. Miss Worth, eyes glazed but beginning quietly, moved downstage, made her ravishing by Zeus harrowingly, terrifyingly intimate,
went on to detail her subsequent torments with such tactile intensity
that we found ourselves flinching from each threatened sting. The
performance was a mystery in the old sense: a source of awe, of wonder.

But the wonder could be explained. Miss Worth was able to play
Io—to make her stripped flesh real flesh, and that without loss of
iconographic stature—because she had played all of those other parts
all of those other years. She had climbed, step by step, test by test, to a
mountaintop of her own, where she could turn in any direction and
rearrange the emotional weather to suit her needs. An actress' resources may at last come to seem infinite; but that is because she has
transformed herself so often that she has simply lost count. What is left
is reflex, the result of a thousand and one inventive nights.

Not surprising at all, then, to discover Miss Worth, in *Sweet Bird of
Youth,* making the transition from early morning terrors to grand-
dame wisecracks in a matter of seconds, to see her smeared eyes grow

brighter as she babied her callow stud, to watch her confidence become
a tremor as she suddenly insisted she wasn't quite ready to be left
alone, to listen to her passionately try "to prevent the death of a
lapdog" as she urged the boy to take flight before other men's razors
could get at him, to hear desperation made into sheer music as the
frenzied cadences rose. I should say in passing that Christopher Walken
rose in turn to the challenge Miss Worth presented *him;* this was far
and away his best work since his *Caligula* at Yale. Furthermore, Mr.
Williams's play seemed richer and more complex than it had when it
was first produced; the "permanent" Williams library keeps increasing.

But we're speaking of Miss Worth at the moment, and of the
curious thing she's done. She's kept the promise she made herself
when, like so many thousands of others, she first took the plunge. The
promise, the practice, works. It may brush certain personal rewards
aside: the prominence that comes of standing in one spot until everyone
recognizes you; the money and assorted comforts that follow upon
merchandised "stardom." But it yields what it is meant to yield:
greatness.

2

Growing Up and Up and Up

The tiniest tower of strength on Broadway a year later was Julie Harris, and therein lies a lesson for all who would add invisibly to their natural gifts. Some people are born to be actors and actresses. They just look like that's what their mothers and fathers had in mind. Others have the talent, all right, but in effect it's their secret: they look like mud fences, tame mice, the Monday wash, or—as I believe Miss Harris was once called—an unshelled peanut. In which case they must create themselves in order to let their secret out.

It does happen all the time. When Lynn Fontanne was a youngster in England, she was told by a distinguished producer that she could never become a leading lady: her nose was too long. "Nonsense," she answered, "my chin is too short—I shall see that it grows." Whereupon she began exercising her chin before a mirror until it came into luscious line with her nose, and, lo and behold, she was not only a ravishing leading lady, she was a star to discourage other stars.

Miss Harris's initial problem, I would say, was not her nose but everything. Of course she lacked the sort of physical stature that made Katharine Cornell a presence before she'd bothered to speak. Her features lacked emphasis, did not precisely blossom into a "stage" face: it might have been better if *her* nose *had* been too long. And, worse yet, her voice was a small, rustling, warm but intractably girlish one-note: raise it a decibel and it scratched.

"Would you tell me how to grow?" Miss Harris asked in her one-woman triumph as the custodian of Emily Dickinson's mind, heart, letters, verses, determinations, and disappointments in *The Belle of Amherst*, and the question proved a multiple irony. In the "play" that William Luce had adroitly fashioned for her—and it was so emotionally varied, so cumulatively riveting that it functioned just as a full-fledged play does—she was putting the query to an *Atlantic Monthly* editor who had had the sense and taste to encourage Emily Dickinson's writing but not the courage to publish it. He'd been suggesting, with the horrendous vagueness of many an editor, that she "grow," instead of offering anything like practical criticism. And she knew that he was being absurd. She was really, subliminally, being sassy to him—in a controlled New England way. She'd taken the measure of his mind, and preferred hers. But there was that further, hovering irony: the actress posing the challenge was an actress who'd had, from the beginning, to learn and learn and learn how to grow.

She was first a rumor around the Actors' Studio, then a noticeable bit player in a handful of flops—until she appeared in *The Member of the Wedding*, a play that offered her a role that seemed precisely cut to her pretensions. She was exactly big enough to curl up in Ethel Waters's arms. It seemed as though, if she knew what was good for her, she'd stay there forever, playing children.

Whereupon she next strode onto the old Empire stage in the outlandishly chic, 1930s mod black that Sally Bowles wore, long cigarette holder weaving figure eights in the air about her, to make a success of *I Am a Camera*. What business had she appearing as the ultimate, irresponsible sophisticate in a decadent Berlin? Only her own, only her own. She was doing a part she shouldn't have been doing *because* she shouldn't have been doing it. The only way to *prove* you're an actress is to knock your limitations into a sharply raked beret, risk making a clown of yourself, declare your identity with the blazing effrontery of electric lights.

Of course you have to live up to what you're daring. Miss Harris did, the electric lights went up outside as well as inside the theater, and, at a star-studded party held in the Empire's lobby, she was officially proclaimed a star, too. While the stars were studding, and the punch (I think it was) flowing freely, Miss Harris sat huddled on a balcony stairwell, looking for all the world as though she needed Ethel Waters's arms, in a hurry. Actually, she was probably plotting her next improvement.

Which turned out to be St. Joan, a part the statuesque Miss Cornell, among others, had played. In the process of pulling herself up by her own bootstraps, from child to wanton, from innocent to damned, could she take the next step in actual *boots*? On went the boots and armor for Lillian Hellman's adaptation of Anouilh's *The Lark*, out went the actress into open stage spaces that ought to have overwhelmed her, and guess what got overwhelmed? Yes, the spaces, and the audience, too. Miss Harris could *occupy* more turf than even a spunky kid seemed entitled to.

Still one problem. The voice. When she pushed it for Joan's big speeches, and she had to push it if there was to be heroism tonight, it still scraped, sometimes badly. It was really still as small as she herself had started out to be.

And so. She took care of this little matter—it's curious how many actresses have done the same thing—not by straining at once after further seriousness but by appearing in a stylized French farce, *A Shot in the Dark.* Anything stylized allows for, even begs for, an artificial elevation, and Miss Harris played the clockwork nonsense with all bells ringing. She'd pitched her vocal tones right over her head (which is where the balloons in a comic strip always are) and discovered that she could sing lines serenely that formerly had to be forced. Smooth, mellifluous, oversize, and still conversational. One last limitation bit the dust.

By the time of *Belle of Amherst* she had—to use a phrase that would not have appealed to Emily Dickinson—"got it all together," which is why she could brush her way past desk and piano on the Longacre stage in her faded virginal white with rose sash at the waist and, instantly confiding in us, alert us to the truth of what she was doing (apple pie occupied as much of her life as poetry did, but she knew the difference), call our ears to order as she invented her own psalms ("In the name of the bee and the butterfly and the breeze, Amen"), touch us quickly and deeply over her failures with her parents ("Mother didn't care for thoughts," and thoughts were all she had ever had to offer), make us laugh at the news that she'd been fifteen before she could tell time ("Thank goodness for twilight").

As I looked back, I found *The Belle of Amherst* the most stimulating event of the 1976 season, and not only because I'd long since been persuaded that Emily Dickinson was our finest poet. It might have seemed a form of magic to make Miss Dickinson's most casual lines live so intensely on a stage. But for magic read craft. And for craft— painfully, stubbornly, at last stunningly acquired—read Julie Harris.

3

The Summing-Up
of Alec Guinness

In a sense, all good performances are cumulative performances. That is to say, the actor or actress builds the role at hand from moment to moment, taking on psychic weight as the evening rises in temperature, adding an ounce of sorcery here and a threat of mystery there until—at the end—the figure onstage can take a stance or make a gesture that seems the sum of all its speeches plus the sum of all its silences plus a little something in the way of compound interest left over. Sure. Everybody does it.

But there are some performances that are cumulative in a slightly different sense. These seem not content with adding up the author's handy points for the enterprise but instead reach out and beyond and behind to embrace a whole lifetime of getting older, a whole career of getting wiser, a profound sense of all the damned beauty that's come and gone on a thousand stage floors and had better be remembered tonight—or else. That's the kind of performance Alec Guinness was giving in a trifle of a play, Alan Bennett's *Habeas Corpus,* and it made its ultimate sweeping statement, cocky and graceful and dour and deep, in a final three or four minutes that were as moving as anything the London stage had to offer as surrendered treasure during its thriving 1973 season.

"Alec Guinness wants to dance" I found unaccountably scrawled among my notes from the early part of the evening. Obviously I'd noticed something, without in the least realizing that Mr. Guinness—now *Sir* Alec, though I shall continue to think of him as Saint Alec—had surreptitiously intended I should notice it, certainly without suspecting that he was going to build the whole finale out of just such strange fleeting itches.

What itches? Well, they were odd, especially in this play. Alan Bennett was really doodling out a casual curse upon the body. The human body. No member of an aging doctor's household was content with the flesh he was heir to and stuck with.

Mr. Guinness, head of the family and weary general practitioner, had coped for so long with the only kinds of illnesses there are—those above the belt, those below—that it was *he* who was a constant victim of nausea, not his patients. He was eager to take us all into his confidence while a clergyman stripped in the anteroom—"Shut up!" he snapped when the gentleman of the cloth, who was removing the cloth, attempted to interrupt his raging soliloquy—and his confidence was a bitter one. All these bodies he was forced to stare at, poke at—all, all so much junket. "Is this the image of God?" he cried out.

His wife, fiftyish and more than plump ("She's *enormous!*" exclaimed a former suitor who had thought to renew his quest), had no such attitudes. *She* was unhappy because her body was being put to no use: Mr. Guinness's legs tended to give at the knees now whenever she threatened sex. She was, in her own view, rather like the Taj Mahal lying alone in the wasted moonlight, and she was prepared to rectify the situation with any other body that came to hand.

His sister was still less well off. A virgin of thirty-three, she looked at first sight, or first sigh, like a long brown wrinkle. You assumed that this was because she was wearing a wrinkled brown sweater. Then you realized that the wrinkle was spiritual, and that the sweater could only conform. If Connie had had her way, she'd have said to God, or to someone, "This body doesn't suit me, could I look at something different?" She had to settle for ordering falsies, which arrived and caused no end of trouble.

There was a son, Dennis, who was certain he was going to die in three months and whose estimate, once you glanced at him, seemed overly optimistic. Curled into limpness like a flower that couldn't find the sun, his elbow patches the sturdiest thing about him, he was a creature, as a member of the family remarked, who had somehow or other managed to contract lockjaw all over. And there were other oddities about, including a representative of the landed aristocracy who couldn't bear to have her body touched under any circumstances, and a fellow who was getting rid of his baggage altogether by hanging himself. The play *was* called *Habeas Corpus,* remember. And very witty it was, too—in a freehand, what-shall-we-mock-next way—about the whole scruffy business.

But I said something about dancing. The urge—it was hardly more than that, but it had a teasing shape of its own—began the moment an especially luscious lass dressed in rose walked into Mr. Guinness's office, causing the stage lights to turn thoroughly rose as well. There was clearly something to be said for *this* body—Mr. Guinness's hand trembled noticeably as it dared professional exploration—and even the physician's hard-earned philosophy required instant revision.

Once she was gone again and the doctor was mourning his loss, Mr. Guinness reminded himself that he was not only old enough to have delivered this child at birth but that—and there was a forlorn pause— he might have touched her then. Briefly, he cradled the imaginary, ever so desirable infant in his arms, and it was at this point—of all points—that a very small shuffle, the first whisper of an adagio that would take him in great circles through the air with something feminine in his arms, stirred. As I say, it only stirred, it was just a man's soul coming back and finding the door rather firmly closed, but, against all nature and all reason and out of his very despair, the man did want to dance.

As author Bennett continued making monoplane loop-the-loops around his subject, actor Guinness continued, slyly, to keep the impulse alive even when his anger and frustration were most intense. He had asked himself a question: why should the door be closed, why shouldn't he meet the girl in less clinical surroundings? And he'd made the date, only to be ditched—the girl was actually pregnant, that's what was the matter with *her* body, and she'd latched onto the soon-to-die Dennis as a logical brief husband. Which left our graying doctor standing trench-coated and alone at the end of Brighton Pier. Somehow the furrows in Mr. Guinness's brow, and the wisps of hair that kept falling over his eyes, came to seem one and the same thing.

And the hatred was back. "Filth! Filth!" he screamed as he was confronted on all sides with the flurries of the flesh, stamping his feet as he did so. Curiously, one foot had no sooner stamped than it flipped into a reflexive back-kick. He seemed to be doing the Charleston to express his dismay. And that is how it went through the evening: the more harassed our hero became, the stronger was his instinct to take off, to pick up a beat from the silent-movie organ music that had gurgled through all of the entertainment's transitions and ride away on it.

At the end, it happened. Guinness danced. I am told that the actor had been offered the help of a choreographer when it came time to create a pattern for the rueful lark's final moments. He'd declined, and he was right. It isn't an actor's business to really dance. It's an actor's business to *act* dancing, and that, precisely, is what Mr. Guinness did.

After the girl he yearned for had married the son who would

conveniently expire, and after everyone else had cleared up the various mistaken identities that impertinently substituted for plot, Mr. Guinness was alone once more, this time in a pearl gray top hat. It was, obviously, the hour for Astaire, the top spot on the two-a-day, the moment—if there was ever going to be one—to let loose the insane surge that had lurked behind the fury, the fierce displeasure with the flesh, all along.

There is something about the body that wishes to praise itself in spite of itself, to proclaim its grace in plain sight of the grave. Mr. Guinness, in a vaudeville-sharp circle of white light, stepped out, and off, and took great gliding curves, and dipped gently to come up like a brand-new sea breeze, his walking stick a wand, his free hand free enough to lead the Philharmonic.

Suddenly the spotlight shivered, seemed to crackle; Mr. Guinness's ankles, knuckle joints turned arthritic. Here was the truth, now. But only half the truth, perhaps the unimportant half, and he was on his way again, lighter than mortality, bolder than the cold night, spats leading the way, lined face proud in birdflight. Everyone knew how it would all turn out but in the meantime the body sang.

It was something to see: a man putting everything he knew into a thimbleful of hoofing. Enough to make your heart stop.

4

The Seeing Eye
of George C. Scott

Attention has been paid. In reviving Arthur Miller's *Death of a Salesman* at Circle in the Square, and in taking on the part of the self-doomed but perpetually incurable Willy Loman himself, director-star George C. Scott had first of all behaved not as director or as star but as servant of a play, of a piece of work in the hand. Furthermore, he had not behaved as though he were serving an old play, a familiar play, a play whose ancient echoes were so overwhelming that a kind of fearful obeisance was the best that could be offered it. He had chosen not to remember it, or to remember other people's remembrances of it, but to pay attention to its undeniably powerful, still most affecting, but extraordinarily ambiguous voice. Not what Elia Kazan had once heard in it, not what Lee J. Cobb had once heard in it, perceptive and just as they may have been. But, with one sharp ear cocked, what was it saying *now*?

This was not simply a matter of muting the lines we recall all too well. Mr. Scott had a fascinating trick—it was more than a trick, it was a heartrending trait of character—of burying a phrase like "He's liked, but he's not well liked" by making it part of a compulsive contradiction, hurling it so hot on the heels of a contrary line preceding it that we were forced to take the two in balance and believe neither. We heard him, without transition, pause, or apparent dishonesty, breathlessly bracketing "I'm very well liked, the only thing is people don't take to me" and making both sense and agony of it. Or, glorying in his talent for regaling his New England buyers: "I'm full of jokes, I tell too many jokes," with the savagery of the second thrust seeming to bite off his own braggart head.

There was much savagery in Mr. Scott's performance—he came on like the last bald American eagle dead set for a final reckoning—but it was more than the quite normal savagery of his customary stage deportment, it was a savagery uncovered in the near-manic, electrifying shifts of mood, boast and bile back to back, of Arthur Miller's play. And it completely disrupted my *own* (perhaps faulty) memory of the original production, its original meaning. I remember assuming that Willy Loman had once been a successful salesman, had once done well by his wife and his boys, had once made "a smile and a shoeshine" work for him. That the dream (the American dream of success by backslapping and coming in Number One on all the sales charts) had eventually collapsed of its own essential vacuousness became the pathos of the moment, but the pathos of the moment had been a somewhat recent discovery, a realization, not a permanence recognized from the beginning.

With Mr. Scott it was certainly otherwise. Quite apart from absorbing the catch phrases by which we had come to identify the play into a relentless, run-on "yes-no," Mr. Scott made us hear lines we seemed *never* to have heard before. He was speaking to his outrageously successful brother, Ben, despoiler of the Gold Coast, reaper of fabulous Alaskan harvests. Ben was older than Willy, got started sooner than Willy. Ben even remembered their father, a man who played a flute as he carted the family from state to state across the American landscape.

But the father had died before Willy could quite know him, or know himself in relation to any father. "I still feel a little *temporary* about myself," he said, reflectively, with unconscious regret, to the solid, if almost mythical, brother who had never felt temporary about anything. Mr. Scott's Willy had *always* had to compensate, to inflate his indeterminate place in the scheme of things, to substitute for his sickened hollowness an equally hollow image in which only others— only his adoring sons could possibly have believed. He had been a shell from the beginning, filling himself with borrowed life, life that could be borrowed from successful salesmen he'd admired, life that might be borrowed—on a kind of promissory note—from the envisioned success of his two boys.

This became stunningly clear in a scene almost impossible to contemplate, given Mr. Scott's intensely mesmerizing presence. Willy was to recall a day, early in his career, when he'd listened to a salesman, an eighty-four-year-old master drummer, in his room at the Parker House, making an ample, indestructible living by doing nothing more than reaching for a phone and running up orders by the dozen. He had to make us believe that this one image of success, picked up by eavesdropping, had given him his goal in life, a self-image strong enough to sustain him. And he had to do it while the man he was presently talking to, an employer about to fire him now that he'd reached an exhausted sixty-two, paid him no heed at all, proved incapable of being moved by anything he might say.

To begin with, it was unthinkable that anyone within Mr. Scott's feverish, concentrated range should not have listened to him. And if we could bring ourselves to believe that the man was not listening, then why should we have continued to listen? The essence of the sequence lay in the deaf dismissal of Mr. Scott's dreams. And yet it happened both ways, creating stage magic of the highest order. Our own absorption in Mr. Scott's passionate recollection of things past was total: we saw everything he saw, the room's furnishings, the drummer's posture, the waves of power reaching out to envelop Mr. Scott. At the same time the actor was able to distance himself from his indifferent employer, to isolate himself with *us*, to the point where we heard what no one else could hear, shared what no one else could share. He *obliterated* a rival voice without destroying its message. The doubleness was devastating; I still don't believe it.

And, at the same time that Mr. Scott was alternately drawing his teeth across his lower lip and lifting the corners of his mouth in a mirthless but expansive smile, abruptly shifting from snarl to endearment, Teresa Wright, as his wife, was creating the perfect complement to his instability. Face severely in repose, voice rarely raised, she was both patient and rock-hard in her steadfast coping with home truths. She was not deceived, not even by love. But she did love. And her love had the toughness that would tolerate neither lies nor laments from her failed children. Their father was an ordinary man; they were to find no blame in him for that. Ordinary men become exhausted as surely as great men do; the exhaustion is just as real, no guilt is to be lodged against it. She had heard her husband, letting himself in by night beneath the naked bulb over the back door, sigh as he dropped his satchels; she'd listened as he greeted her encouragingly, then explosively betrayed his own sudden envy of men who have "accomplished something." She knew he had accomplished nothing, hadn't an identity to do it with. The boys were not to say so. "Attention must be paid" to ordinary men, exhausted or no. There was no rhetoric in Miss Wright as she spoke the words, no lumpy quasi-poetry. She was enunciating a harsh truth, harshly. Let the boys be "bums," if that is what they were to be. And let them honor their father, who would have honored them if he had only known how. If we shed tears, and we did, they fell on granite.

Between Mr. Scott and the superb Miss Wright, the 1975 *Death of a Salesman* became a play of persons, not of social prophecy or some archetypal proclamation of an already failed American myth. It was too richly contradictory, too intimately detailed, too ambiguously loving and desperate for mere abstraction; its weaknesses and its toughnesses were tangible, not distantly theoretical. If the work now seemed tantalizing in its implications, the implications were more nearly those that endlessly badgered O'Neill: it is illusions that destroy. "We never told the truth for one minute in this house" was a cry near the end in a house that could not stand; to the last, Willy Loman kept imagining that, somehow or other, the $20,000 in insurance money that would come of his death would guarantee the successful future of his elder, equally emptied-out son. Death went right on dreaming.

Mr. Miller's play held, contained its own complex meaning that was beyond facile ideological analysis, lived and moved and had its being in the mercury of its ravaged, hoping, falsely jovial, forgiving, unforgiving figures. Mr. Scott's staging was as restlessly right as his performance: the man was endlessly on his feet though he knew that his feet would betray him before they could ever see him home.

5

The Other
Katharine Hepburn

Although Katharine Hepburn was both master and mistress of the play she was appearing in, and though the play would neither have moved nor levitated had she not been in it, the actress' 1976 return to Broadway in Enid Bagnold's *A Matter of Gravity* was not—repeat not—a "personal appearance." A "personal appearance" is a condescension to the stage, a visitation of mere flesh so that onlookers can see that it *is* flesh, a display of presence and a parade of mannerisms, and then off, off into the night. Without having truly been there, really, without having worked, without having *acted* anything.

In *A Matter of Gravity* Miss Hepburn was not only acting something, she was acting better than she had ever before in her life. I'm allowing for some fine performances, particularly in films, and rather discounting the sheer loveliness that made gossamer of *The Philadelphia Story* on stage. The loveliness was still with us, ostentatiously older, not as much older as proclaimed. But there was something different here, now. It was as though the feathery bravura and the challenging nasality and the chin held so high that one scarcely dared question the authenticity behind so much panache had all dissolved at last, had been absorbed into simplicity, had come home to roost and rest. Leaving only a clear intention in the eye, an economy of gesture (except for that walking stick the lady dropped twice on opening night, obviously because she had no conceivable use for it), and a directness of address—sometimes forceful, sometimes most quietly bemused—that together bespoke plainly the actress' sincerity. She wasn't decorating; she *meant* every bloody word of it.

When Miss Hepburn came onto the Broadhurst stage to stir a storm of applause that wouldn't die down, crossed the living room and exited promptly into the kitchen to see if *that* would help diminish the reception, we were of course attending to *her*, as a personality, as someone known in a dozen, three dozen, roles but not in this one. As she reentered, though, and the applause did finally give up, we were gently but forcibly asked to meet someone, someone who resembled Hepburn but who was not Hepburn *solus*. We were invited to acquaint ourselves with, and share the not always sequential thoughts of, a Mrs. Basil, wrapped in apron and cardigan, wondering if a kitchen could be tucked into the living room to save steps, not mourning the thirty empty bedrooms above (some of which would be shortly, temporarily filled) but determined to keep intact the mulberry tree in the garden and the richly lacquered walls about her that were dappled with fading light.

Her task was formidable, and wanted wiliness. Disliking "dead ends" as she did—and as she let slip, in an unpremeditated fury, when a homosexual friend of her grandson made a rather spectacular nuisance of himself—she had to be both strong and yielding. Everything was unraveling about her, tradition, family, the very grounds she inhabited, the society she was forced to put up with when her grandson brought his contemporaries home, and only a keen, pragmatic intelligence would keep the single servant in line or guarantee a future for the once rather aristocratic estate. She'd have liked a miracle to arrange it all for her, but "there are no miracles, we are too clever, everything is explained." And so she herself was required to control the habits of her four-foot-square lesbian housekeeper ("What time do you start drinking in the morning?" she asked uncritically, to be given a succinct reply, "At eight") as well as the marital destiny of her grandson. Her grandson, towering above her until she seemed a tot beside him, was much more insecure than she; the social and sexual shapelessness of his generation had left him fearful of women, above all of the pretty young woman from Trinidad he would have liked to marry. She was black (butternut, at the Broadhurst), but that posed no problem either for him or for Mrs. Basil. The girl's candor was the problem: she didn't love the grandson but would marry him for the house.

To which Mrs. Basil, with stipulations, agreed. If there was a penultimate triumph for this far-seeing old lady, and a thundering irony in Miss Bagnold's play, it lurked here. The play, in part, had to do with the breaking up of a privileged world and its thoroughly utilitarian occupation by the once underprivileged. What Mrs. Basil banked on, you see, was human nature: like all the rest of us, what the underprivileged want is *privilege*. And so she disposed of her cherished inheritance by giving it to the black girl who would love it and keep it just as it was. Canny and impertinent, that.

Mrs. Basil's ultimate triumph was that, having made her surrender that was no surrender, she had an unknown, but wide-open and welcome, future ahead of her. As she said, she had *been* modern, liberal-minded, infinitely adaptable. "I got tired of it," she snapped with a wicked trace of a smile. Now she would allow herself, cheerfully, to be "put away" ("I'm a new girl, at the asylum") because she had learned not only to "imagine people" but to look forward, really, to that "terra incognita" that old maps used to label HERE BE DRAGONS. The new would always be new to her; even dead, "I may be talking to the roots of trees for all I know." What could be odder than what we already are, already have? In her stubbornness and her suppleness, in her tartness and her melting laughter, Miss Hepburn was integrity incarnate, piercingly authentic.

Though *A Matter of Gravity* was all at sixes and sevens as a play, willfully untidy, subject to dizzy spells, possessed by a wanderlust that kept urging it to drift off into other possible plays, Miss Bagnold *had* written the part Miss Hepburn was playing. And if she hadn't, in some mysterious way, written it honestly, Miss Hepburn would not have had so much to be honest about. There was simply no doubt that the actress had got hold of something strong, tangible, and real, something apart from herself. She'd had to rummage through a lot of cavalier improvisation to find it; but it was there and she came up with it, held tight in her tenacious fist.

6

Mostel

Watching the 1976 revival of *Fiddler on the Roof,* I was sorely tempted to pronounce Zero Mostel simply unreviewable and let it go at that. What was one to say of him? That he was a magnificent, wholly legitimate, actor capable of tearing your heart out as he bent himself double, brow pouring sweat, over the milk cart he must push on alone? No, you couldn't quite say that, indelible as the image was, because just a few minutes earlier in the same *Fiddler on the Roof* he had been bringing down the house with a cross-eyed grimace—tongue lolling wildly—contorted enough to resurrect vaudeville, burlesque, and possibly the commedia dell'arte in one great swivel of his head. The swivel undercut the sweat, the seriousness of the second image couldn't be taken at face value because of what the man had so recently been doing with his face.

What, then? Did you treat him as a clown, almost as a king among clowns, because the manic impulse to which he so frequently surrendered was, for him, irresistibly real, a seizure rather than a posture, an inspiration from his daimon rather than a reflex acquired during long years of stand-up entertaining? God knows he was one of the four or five funniest men of our time: scarcely a year earlier I'd seen the man do ten minutes at a banquet, ten minutes that left me gasping with admiration whenever I could stop laughing. But in *Fiddler* he was playing Sholom Aleichem's Tevye, Tevye the dairyman with all those daughters he had to marry off sensibly, Tevye the intimate of God with whom he was candid but to whom—as he pointed out—he never complained ("After all, with Your help I'm still poor"). Wryness, yes. But crossed eyes, cap, and bells?

The professional fool intercepted the great actor, the role the actor was playing inhibited the fool—somewhat. And you could, as a reviewer, point out the contradiction, the quarrel of styles. What you would still not have done is account for the effect Mr. Mostel imposed upon the yielding Winter Garden stage, upon the *shtetl* folk around him who lived in designer Boris Aronson's lovely floating spill of houses strung along a backdrop that threatened sunset, upon the audience. It wasn't that he was good, wasn't that he was funny, wasn't that he was one when he ought to have been the other. It was simply that he was there.

Zero Mostel was a mighty presence rather than a completely honest performer, so enormous in his nimble bulk and so violent in his willed impact that he didn't invite judgment, he defied it, successfully. You could measure what he was doing, if you wanted to; but it wasn't going to get you anywhere, he was going to roll right on over you no matter what. And so you surrendered, agreed to let him dictate terms, simply watched him.

You watched him do things that Sholom Aleichem would surely have approved: tilt a sad head toward one weary shoulder not because he had a crick in his neck but because his eyes had opened so wide so often at the world's unexpected ways that they'd grown top-heavy, developed a list; wring out a wet sleeve as though the elements themselves had planned this injustice, while glancing at God to let Him know *he* knew just who had perpetrated the joke; try desperately and helplessly to keep a stern finger pointed at the impoverished young tailor who'd have liked to marry his eldest daughter while that same daughter stroked his beard and begged him to reconsider his wrath. Even this behemoth, properly handled, could be tamed, touchingly.

You watched the actor do things that might have brought a bemused shrug from his original author, since even authors understand that adaptations for the musical stage must be given a little leeway: hold his head during a hangover and then wince mightily as his wife clapped her hands in joy at a piece of welcome news; lapse into unintelligible prayer as a means of silencing the woman he had married long before youngsters were making marriage a matter of love; find himself utterly immobilized because he was standing on his own nightgown. And you watched him, listened to him, engage in familiar routines that hadn't much to do with folkways: nearly strangle on a drink and then pronounce it "Very good!"; camp a bit by rolling his belly during an otherwise charming marriage dance; pursue the intimidated tailor in circles until, losing him, he lifted the tablecloth to see if *that's* where he was hiding.

Whatever was done was done with such almost indifferent authority that it seemed irreversible, like a landslide. One hesitates to raise questions about natural forces. Mr. Mostel was a natural force, going its own predetermined and quite conscienceless way, effortlessly brushing aside such obstacles as presented themselves, using up all the oxygen in the immediate vicinity. The performer never seemed to be contriving effects calculated to please us; he seemed simply to exist, and let who would issue challenge. With the heft of Mt. Rushmore and the wing-spread of a giant condor, the man went by, lifting one finger in acknowledgment of God and the rest of us. No, he didn't go by. He happened.

7

Colleen Dewhurst:
Circe-in-Waiting

Colleen Dewhurst was a beautiful woman giving a beautiful performance in the 1973 revival of Eugene O'Neill's *A Moon for the Misbegotten* (which also just happens to be a beautiful play, possibly O'Neill's best), and I found nothing more fetching about her performance than her witchlike way with an unfinished sentence.

Unfinished sentences can be hell for actors, often because the playwright has had no thought to complete and has simply handed the performer the task of implying one. They can hang there, limp as on a washline, ready to blow any which way a wind happens along. Not in Miss Dewhurst's firmly ruled kingdom, though. In *A Moon for the Misbegotten* she was, in her shanty-Irish father's words, "big and strong as a bull and as vicious and disrespectful," and she was waiting, in the early kerosene-lit moonlight, for a visit from one of her betters. The visitor was to be Jason Robards, member of an acting family, handsomely educated, already half broken by drink. He should have been, in the opinion of a canny father, readily seducible.

In fact, father Ed Flanders (another stunning performance) had the night's course well planned into dawn. He would slip off to a bar and get himself drunk enough to be utterly unable to prevent anything Mr. Robards might have in mind. It was Miss Dewhurst's assigned business to see to it that Mr. Robards's mind took a right turn.

At this point in the conniving, the actress suddenly turned on the aged leprechaun who was whispering goat songs in her ears. Eyes blazing, hair pulled taut from a clear forehead, arm ever ready to take a stick to her mentor, she let him know what she thought of "a father telling his daughter how to—" and there let the sentence die. The special splendor of the moment was that it didn't die. The obvious finish to the line was "to seduce a man," and, if that had been all, it wouldn't have been much. By letting it break where O'Neill broke it, and by reaching out to join her playwright creatively, Miss Dewhurst filled the void with a heartful of contending emotions. What was left over, and unsaid, was that she wanted the love of the man, that she wanted it on her own terms, that she was terribly, terribly afraid she was not going to get it, and that seduction—if she knew anything at all about it—would waste the last ounce of goodness in two malformed lives. That's a lot, but it was all there.

It is generally difficult to take your eyes off Miss Dewhurst, whether she is smiling or in fury. She has a smile that behaves strangely. Most smiles, when they are about to break in dismay, break downward. Hers shatters upward, sustaining the shape of happiness while a tell-tale quaver makes a lie of the crescent corners of her mouth. Her face seems actually to brighten under the hint of pain, a sense of unruly merriment tries hard to assert itself, a vixenish gaiety becomes permanent companion of disaster.

The effect is enormously touching, and it blended ever so easily with the roustabout humors of her donnybrooks with her father. The racy, fork-tongued, rattle-on chaffings between Miss Dewhurst and Mr. Flanders were exhilaratingly designed by director Jose Quintero, and they reminded you, in case you'd forgotten, that when O'Neill wanted to write comedy he had only to pick up an alternate pen and let another kind of theater ink flow, an apparently inexhaustible know-how take over.

But *A Moon for the Misbegotten* is not, in the end, comedy, which is where Miss Dewhurst's unfinished sentences and upsweep dismays, and Jason Robards, came in. Mr. Robards began brilliantly, self-conscious not only about his natty 1923 clothes but about his need for a drink, his need for a woman who would not turn out to be a whore, his need for nothing so much as an impossible forgiveness.

The shaking hand with which he lighted a cigarette as their tryst together was to begin established its outcome; the succulent surrender to a first taste of the drink she brought him outlined precisely the one comfort this doomed man could know. The detail—an uneasy balance on a treacherous planet, fingers at his collar, palms scraping the nap of jacket and trousers as though something dirty could be wiped away—was graphic, conscientiously arrived at, intelligently used.

I had one important reservation about the production and still feel something of an ingrate for bringing it up. But at the performance I attended the terrifying "almost" of the third act—the teasing possibility that against all odds two rattled, emotionally starved, yearning and yet distrustful misfits will somehow find a crooked way to an ultimate meeting—simply didn't happen. We know that it *can't* happen, that it was never in the cards; but that is for the fourth act to say. In the third, with all of the anger and ugliness and awkward groping allowed for, there must be a rhythm that moves toward fusion, toward a coming together of the far ends of the earth. Without it, without its momentary false promise, the play is too much of a piece, each movement reiterating those that have gone before it.

Mr. Robards, possibly out of overconcern that each moment should be technically right, continually aborted that promised rhythm, lurching away in self-disgust and trying to spit from his mouth the venom of lost years so often that the design became fragmented, the contest stalemated. There were times when I wanted to collar the man and order him to stay with the scene, stay with the woman, until O'Neill's play could come as close as it dared to a psychic embrace. *Then* it might be shattered, letting us see the remorse-ridden figure as truly dead. It was the crest of the wave, before it collapsed onto the beach, that was missing, leaving me with slightly fonder memories of the 1968 production at the downtown Circle in the Square.

If I suggest that *Moon for the Misbegotten* just may be O'Neill's richest work for the theater, it is because the free creative impulse is allowed more play here than in the directly autobiographical *Long Day's Journey into Night*. The Robards role is, of course, rooted in O'Neill's older brother. The other figures, however, draw upon, and demand, vast imaginative resources; life is made on the wing rather than painstakingly remembered. It is an honest life and, for O'Neill, an unusually lyric one; the crafty, the damned, and the forgiving breathe.

8

That Channing Creature

In 1973 Carol Channing and *Lorelei* landed exactly where they belonged, at the Palace. If the new/old entertainment—once called *Gentlemen Prefer Blondes*—that had been shaken down by a dozen or so successive hands resembled anything at all, it resembled one of those peacock-fan, aerodrome-portaled "tab" musicals that used to roam the better vaudeville circuits with at least a rhinestone of a star set dead center in a spotlight. In this case, no rhinestone. The real Carol Channing, golden girl, tiger, tiger, burning bright, shinier than her own anklets, bigger than her moist heart, may be the only creature extant who can live up to a Hirschfeld.

Do you know what I mean by living up to a Hirschfeld? Hirschfeld always lives up to the people he draws, but the people he draws don't always live up to him. Don't explode in the same way, like new constellations doing tours jetés in the heavens. Here was the exception: mascara to swim in, nobly tragic mouth, the face of a great mystic about to make a terrible mistake. To get right down to it, do you realize that C.C. may be the *only* entertainer left who can carry a whole show by herself, portal to portal? Or even compete with her own lobby photos? Or stand there with her hands clasped and make you believe she's surprised you like her?

No doubt I think she and her show belonged at the Palace because of something the lady did as the first-act curtain was coming down. She wouldn't quit. Here was this curtain descending, right on top of her, as though some stagehand had been told to lower it exactly at nine no matter what was going on, and she fought it. Tried to hold back the fringe that was engulfing her, battled the batten with her strong right elbow, got to her knees and kept on singing, wound up with no more than a finger keeping in touch with us.

I hadn't seen anybody do anything like that since the days when Rosetta Duncan used to ride up with the asbestos. Never did see Eddie

Foy—if it was Eddie Foy—walk upside down across the proscenium arch. It's a nice kind of thing to see. People playing with the very stage that cradles them, and keeping contact long after more reasonable souls have gone to their dressing rooms to undress.

The contact works, means something. I was further entertained the night I went to see *Lorelei* by the audience, watching it visibly shiver with delight the moment Miss Channing quacked her way into "Little Girl from Little Rock" or "Diamonds Are a Girl's Best Friend." I kept thinking: they *know* this song, they've heard it a hundred times, they've heard Miss Channing herself do it, on stage, on records. But now they shiver. They still want to be there when girl meets intro, two furs to a wrist, two encores on demand. *They* want to keep the curtain up, too.

There is one mistake we must not make and that is to suppose that Miss Channing is something that nature fashioned (to quote a silly old song) by way of spectacular giftwrapping and then left to fend for itself, no real gift under the tinsel. The performer is not only a marvel to look at, she's *equipped*. Again and again during *Lorelei* she took a line that might well have laid there and played arpeggios on it, falsetto to bass, making it come out music, the night music of near-madness.

She only had to mourn the fact that since the sequined 1920s "transatlantic oceanic travel" had deteriorated terribly (leaving a sociable girl with only six hours' flight time to become acquainted with her fellow men, and that unnecessarily complicated by the constant fastening of seat belts) to double up an attentive listener. As wit, "transatlantic oceanic travel" isn't in it with Wilde, but by the time Miss Channing had put those long *a*'s beneath a flatiron, lifted the recurring *ic*'s to the height of radio signal towers, and blended the whole julep-time-in-Old-Heidelberg collision of consonants and vowels together with soothing syrup, Wilde might have been forgiven for wringing his hands in despair.

And she was so soothing, so earnest, so kind. When she said to her friend Dorothy, "Dorothy, it's time you found happiness and stopped having fun," she did indeed rag the scale from initial squeak to ultimate profundo, but it wasn't just the orchestration that made the whole theater happy. It was her deep, deep consideration for Dorothy. And her rectitude! Explaining away a new tiara bigger than the chandelier at the Met ("I bought it with my own borrowed money!") she was an unchallengeable innocent, caught doing right. She does know what she's about, this Channing person.

9

Mr. Burton at Home

Richard Burton had done this thing simply to drive theater-lovers lunatick. (The spelling is Elizabethan, and so, dammit, is he.) Returning to the stage in 1976 after an absence of ten or more years to appear in a play already teeming with ironies, he compounded the ironies of *Equus* to the nth power, overwhelming the audience not with his performance alone but with its implications. Consider some of them.

We are always, always prating of the theater's "live" qualities, especially when we are trying to distinguish it from film. Yet, for all our hearty good will and for all the truth that lies locked somewhere inside our boasting, we haven't the faintest notion of what we are talking about. We don't know what is meant by "live." We don't know because we so rarely see it, above all because we so rarely hear it. The fact of the matter is that, in one strict sense, we hadn't heard it in a Broadway playhouse since the last time Burton came by.

Obviously, I'm not speaking of the "personal appearance" factor, any more than it is necessary to speak of it in discussing Katharine Hepburn's *A Matter of Gravity*. Oh, curiosity, the desire to see a film shadow fleshed, plays a part in the experience. How can it not? Even Burton's tabloid-fodder romances, his self-advertised boozing, the over-size spectacle he has made of himself as an important actor cavalierly squandering himself on unimportant materials all have something to do with the fact that audiences began buying out the Plymouth before he'd appeared and certainly before anything was known of the quality of his performance. In fact, one would have expected the audience to be concentrating so intensely on Burton the man up there—sitting to one side, staring past his psychiatrist's notebook into infinite space, his crowded blue eyes and deeply creased cheeks registering a fevered exhaustion from the outset—that it would have been virtually unable to see him in the *part*, in the *play*.

All of that nonsense vanished five minutes after he had begun, and the only reason it took five minutes for us to surrender our preoccupation with the man and attend freshly to the tormented character Peter Shaffer had created was that Burton rattled off the opening speculative monologue as though he were eager to be rid of himself alone on the stage and get on to his deep and desperate engagement with others. Once he had begun an exchange with Marian Seldes as the magistrate who has brought him a stableboy so disturbed that he has inexplicably blinded six horses, the hum and buzz began, the battery could be heard recharging itself: in Burton's head, in his sometimes shaking hands (he looked at them with such surprise), in the itch to move faster, and faster, and faster.

The performance was very physical, and it was there that we began, but only began, to sense what "liveness" is. It isn't simple physical presence. It's physical presence radiating more than the sum of its own known energies, working on a scale greater than it is, pacing space on an arc more sweeping than is properly natural, more alive than "live." It scarcely seemed necessary to ask this sort of physical dynamism from Burton in *Equus*: the play already has quite enough of that in the brilliantly staged midnight flight of boy and horse turned centaur, in the growing hysteria of the boy as he comes nearer telling the truth about himself, in the final physical, religious, sexual, mythical violence of a spike driven home.

Yet the sense of pursuit that overtook Burton early was enormously restless, an alert and ready-to-leap edginess that informed his most casual postures and questions, rising in intensity until he seemed to be whipping the past into place, its participants into an angry dance of candor. When he affected relaxation, there was a whiplash in his stance; and once he had begun to envy the boy his imaginative freedom, to resent the bit he had put into his own mouth by way of leading a "normal" life, he could stand absolutely rigid in his naked arena with every muscle visibly throbbing as it discharged fury into the very floorboards. Crying out against his own lack of passion, he was at his most passionate.

But physical was only the half of it, if that. Mr. Burton happens to possess a vocal instrument that, we suddenly remembered, is exactly what we expect to hear, and almost never do hear, on going to the theater. The sounds produced in the living theater are not meant to be the sounds produced in day-to-day life, though that is what actors have been giving us for years on end. We look again for a "liveness" that has been intensified, as it is so often intensified in the control rooms of recording studios. Mr. Burton was his own control room, sending out sounds that swept the walls of the theater clean with an apparently effortless power, magnifying the "natural" until we were caught up in its gale, left stunned and breathless. And yes, we said to ourselves, this is precisely the penetrating resonance all actors should possess, if the tonalities of the stage are to be differentiated from those of film. Not everyone, to be sure, can be born in Wales. But the sound, with all of its nuances and its pressures, can be acquired, as Irene Worth has acquired it. It is thrilling when heard, and the thrill is what playhouses are for.

Yet—I spoke of ironies—Mr. Burton had kept this sound from the stage for a decade, he was present now for only a limited engagement, and—I also spoke of ironies compounded—he had, according to report, accepted this engagement as a warm-up for the projected film version, where he would not use the special equipment at all. Ye gods. It is one thing for Katharine Hepburn to flit back and forth between stage and film, with an emphasis on film. The majority of Miss Hepburn's finest performances *have* been given on film, although, with *A Matter of Gravity*, it was clear she had mastered the stage as well. She is an evening glory, too.

But Mr. Burton owns powers that are *exclusively* theatrical powers, and it is just plain unthinkable that he should not use them in the one place that has use for them. Let us pray. I should say, if I have not already intimated it sufficiently, that the actor's performance in *Equus* seemed to me the best work of his life.

10

On Such a Night

Ethel Merman was the bonfire and Mary Martin was the smoke. They went very nicely together, if you were in a mood to burn up the town.

At least that's the way they struck me—I think they did strike me, I was still reeling days later—on a Sunday night in 1977 at the Broadway, where the "two first ladies of the theater" (as Mayor Abe Beame called them while presenting them with identical crown-shaped trophies) did what was called a benefit for The Friends of the Theater and Music Collection of the Museum of the City of New York. But it wasn't a benefit, really. It was a blessing, as any good warm blaze in this old cold world of ours is bound to be. Scorched you a bit sometimes, too.

The scorcher, as you scarcely need to be told, was Merman, too hot for Fahrenheit to measure, too bright to be stared at without a pair of those goggles riveters wear. (Do they wear something for their eardrums as well?) The pair came on together, bursting through circus hoops as Mama Rose and Nellie Forbush respectively, and they sang "Send in the Clowns" (which belongs to neither of them, professionally) like a prayer, demurely, devoutly, disarmingly. But it was Ethel the Everready who opened up first (and second, and third, and after that I lost count).

I always think of her as standing still and belting, I don't know why. I'm pretty sure she did stand still once, when she was first singing "Let's Be Buddies" in whatever triumphant show that may have been. But at the Broadway she was an itch that couldn't be scratched, a brush fire claiming a whole mountainside, a pop and a snap and a crackle that kept rocking from side to side like a metronome on wheels, slipping without warning into a fiercely infectious jigstep for "Doin' What Comes Natur'lly," throwing her substantial but untamable body around as easily as she tossed breathtaking keyshifts to the winds, and—I guess I still don't believe it—unleashing "Everything's Coming Up Roses" like a freshly tapped gusher, with the sound soaring high in the air, straight up and off into eternity. Incredible.

Speaking of eternity, there is an afterlife. During one of her subsequent appearances, Miss Merman was momentarily interrupted by the appearance of a trumpeter, choosing to play Gabriel in the song featuring that archangel's name. The trumpeter ripped off a few calls, judgment-day calls. "Do you hear that playing?" Miss Merman asked with an instant pickup, and in earnest. Gabriel's stand-in kept blowing. Miss Merman began caroling. Guess who won? The thing is, with Gabriel now definitely outclassed, they're going to need her up there. And if they need her, when they get her, she'll oblige, so we're all set.

Okay. Miss Martin. I think of her as smoke not just because everything about her curls, like her apricot smile and the peach-tinted fringe of auburn hair that sneaked out from under her sailor cap like seafoam. It's a matter of elusiveness. Smoke is always changing shape, so that you can't be sure from moment to moment just what it most resembles; heaven knows you can't catch it.

There was a moment, for instance, when master of ceremonies Cyril Ritchard—impeccable in white tails, splendidly imperious of tongue—began to speak of Miss Martin's past adventures in the theater while simultaneously draping himself in Captain Hook's wicked black wig. As he did so, for a few seconds, there was a flicker of moving light along one side wall of the auditorium, a flicker that then leaped clear across stage to flare into a full spotlight circling Miss Martin herself. But before anyone had seen her, they'd applauded that delicate, teasing, evanescent flicker of light, quite as though it was Tinker Bell she'd once played instead of Peter. But I guess that's the point about her. She's both, and neither, and just you try to nail her down while she's vaporizing, silkily and conspiratorially, with a wink and a kiss and a crow and a cackle, before your eyes.

On this particular Sunday night she teed off with a slight vocal mishap: seated on a piano and running through a medley of songs she'd done in cabarets before fame found her out (songs not identified with her), she somehow slipped off-pitch and stayed there until her next time around. Next time around, though, she knew where she was: down at the footlights, subtly weaving magical patterns made of near-whispers and visual slipperiness. You see, she starts off like a stray feather rising unbidden from the floor to undulate gently in midair, lazily doing the bidding of any breezes that happen to be around, and then just as you've got used to her easygoing, little-girl charms, you notice what a very dirty sound the lady manages to produce during one of the breaks in "My Heart Belongs to Daddy." At which point you realize that you've got a much more complex proposition on your hands than you'd thought. Meantime, she's up and taken off like a hummingbird gone ice skating. And opened her throat, as well as her arms, to skip deliriously as ever through "Wonderful Guy." At least, that's what she did that night. I keep imagining the two of them still there, captives of the theater they've captivated.

They work together most remarkably, without sentimentality or undue deference. Obviously each has a healthy respect for the other, obviously the strains of "Friendship" that floated from the pit during the overture weren't inappropriate. But no goo, and who needs nostalgia? They're pros, they can either do it or they can't, and they were up there to show that they can. Not even a "Hello, Dolly!" with two crimson Dollys descending two mauve staircases—and with a chorus line that waggishly included Joel Grey, Yul Brynner, Burgess Meredith, and the like—got out of hand. Sleek, sure, robust, finally riproaring. Ditto with a duo-medley of "I" songs, with the pair harmonizing on "Red, Red Robin" and doing counterpoint with "Indian Love Song" and "Tea for Two" (Martin yodeling, Merman munching on the fox trot).

It's Tuesday as I write. I hear music and there's no one there. . . .

11

Robert Preston:
The Scoundrel as Innocent

It would take a very brave man to say that Robert Preston played *Sly Fox* better than George C. Scott did. I am a very brave man. Robert Preston played *Sly Fox* better than George C. Scott did.

I was a surprised man, too, but we must always square our shoulders and face facts. Larry Gelbart's *Sly Fox*, purloined with fiendish delight from Ben Jonson's *Volpone*, had been an entertaining evening in the theater from the time of its 1976 premiere, though when it first opened its zanier values seemed oddly distributed: most of the fun went to the splendid supporting clowns—Bob Dishy, Jack Gilford, Hector Elizondo—while the stalwart Scott was left with the task of pumping air into the plot. Shouldn't he have been funny too? As funny as they were, and maybe funnier? As an actor, George C. Scott had certainly long since devoured, and savored with his satisfied twitch of a smile, just about every comic style known to man: he'd been superciliously convulsing in *Children of Darkness*, farcically uproarious in the third act of *Plaza Suite*, and satirically murderous in *Dr. Strangelove*, to name the barest few. Furthermore, hadn't he been perfectly cast as the greedy, cunning, lecherous Volpone—renamed for the occasion Foxwell J. Sly—who so cynically exploits in other people the vices he most relishes in himself?

I think that may have been the little hitch. He was *too* perfectly cast. With that blaze of his eyes, that lick of his lips, that whiplash intensity that signals danger a half-mile off, he may have brought us too close to total belief in the whole business. And total belief can be fatal to *Volpone*, for *Volpone*—under any name—is an exceedingly peculiar play. It is bleak, its vision unyielding. The fact that it is also no doubt entirely correct about human nature simply makes matters

worse. Played as Jonson wrote it, it doesn't provoke laughter line by
line; not even Paul Scofield and John Gielgud, who were loyally serving
the original at the British National Theater the very same season,
could make it do that. It's far more likely to produce a bilious attack.
And Mr. Scott's own native and magnificent biliousness may easily
have given us too much of a fierce thing. We often speak of "comedy
relief" and know exactly what we mean by the phrase. Did Mr. Scott,
following Jonson rather than Gelbart, take some of the relief out of the
comedy relief?

Mr. Preston, following in the role during 1977, was another matter
and a merrier one. He didn't really alter the story's jaundiced implications as he set about robbing an entire Barbary Coast population of its
gold plate, diamond rings, inheritances, and even wives; the dirty work
got done, ardently, devilishly. And Mr. Preston carried with him his
own kind of supercharge: his vocal cords could turn to throbbing banjo
strings, his restless, slippered feet carried him three ways at once, his
fingers flexed and splayed as though he'd recently been struck by
lightning and simply absorbed it. Dynamic in Scott's way, almost.

Two differences. No menace in the eyes. Quick, almost feverish,
contact, yes; but no menace. He didn't really hold contact long enough
to burn a hole through anybody or anything. He bounced off, rico-
cheted, behaved rather like those pool balls he'd once so piously condemned in *The Music Man*. He was too quick-triggered to stay long, too
interested in the next idea that occurred to him to dally over the last
one, too riddled with interesting impulses to attach any very great
importance to a particular tic. He was a jack-in-the box constantly out
of the box; the second the lid was fastened, he'd blown it again.

One result of all this was that he never got stuck with a joke
because (a) he was already three feet past it, and (b) he'd never placed
that much stress on it. He'd believed in it while he was saying it, all
right, but life is short and what were we settling down for? Thus if he
murmured, en route to the canopied bed in which he would feign
mortal illness, "I've got a fever bright enough to read by," he didn't
work hard to land a laugh with it. It was just an interesting way of
putting things that had popped into his head while he was moving, and
he'd tossed it over his shoulder to drop where it might, eventually
joining the litter of such baubles—toys, really—behind him on the
floor. You could have called it a form of vocal deadpan, and then
comfortably listened to him announce, with the same swift solemnity,
"It's time for my morning suffering" as he tugged the bedclothes about
him. What you heard inside all the conniving was sheer playfulness,
crookedness for the pure fun of the thing, a rollicking amoral innocence.

Which turned him into a very grown-up, very virile, very intelligent child. It's children who do things for the uncorrupted love of it, without pausing in their exhilarating hurry to ask whether such things *should* be done, and Mr. Preston found himself loose, unleashed, in a world that proved a wonderland. No matter that half that world was composed of idiots, the other half of people clever enough to take indecent advantage of them. If the wonderland was all wickedness, so be it. That was the way the wind blew, it went with the territory, and it was certainly nothing to be taken the least bit seriously. Make a game of it, make a dream of it, make a song of it. Mr. Preston did very nearly make a song of it as he dwelt on the charm of the virtuous woman he was arranging to seduce. "Ah, yes," he crooned, stretching the syllables like taffy and seeming to spin them lariatlike about his half-closed eyes. "I mean to have her." There was no grabbiness in the phrase, not even any determination. It was a moonstruck lullaby, it suggested that the good lady would appear magically and voluntarily the moment he wished, and the drowsily contented smile that was slowly spreading across the actor's face made it clear that the wish was not very far off.

If Mr. Preston's predator was crooked, which he most exuberantly was, he was a crooked Boy Scout. You could almost see him standing in his merit badges—or am I thinking of his Canadian Mounted uniform—as he asked his loyal manservant a question, adding, briskly and ever so earnestly, "Now be brutally honest, I can take a compliment." Mr. Preston didn't kid around with a line like that. He was *sincere*. And where was this dynamic playfulness, this nobility of stance (if of nothing else), this quick-witted boyishness leading us? To a Foxwell J. Sly who, upon getting out of bed, was bound to bang his head into the open door of a chest and who, upon ringmastering the world to his nefarious purposes, was bound to trip over the ring. That's to say, there was a certain logical vulnerability about him, a degree of absent-mindedness that brought him closer to the rest of us. He was far more interested in breaking the rules for the *fun* of breaking the rules than in the profit he could get out of it (though profit he got); and we dared like him—and laugh at him—for that.

12

Yes, Virginia,
Some Cows Are Sacred

When the Uris Theater opened in 1972, inscribed on one of its interior walls was a Theater Hall of Fame, a roster of distinguished performers, writers, directors, and producers whose individual careers, one way or another, had spanned a period of twenty-five years. A committee had been formed earlier to winnow out the presumed greats from the presumed near-greats; it had come up with a list of ninety-five, a list which, needless to say, satisfied no one.

Further ballots were sent out to correct such oversights as might exist, with a promise that ten additional nominees would be added to the opening display. I received one of those ballots, and it was a nailbiter, I can tell you. You couldn't try to slip George S. Kaufman in without also inviting Moss Hart—or, rather, you *could*, since the original list seems to have included Howard Lindsay but not Russel Crouse, obviously a crime against nature—and, since playwrights as a group were howlingly underrepresented, you were torn between trying to wedge in Sidney Howard and Thornton Wilder at the expense of Philip Barry, George Kelly, Clifford Odets, and Robert Sherwood. What *do* you do?

The original list, you see, included Tallulah Bankhead but not Florence Reed, Charles Frohman but not Arthur Hopkins, Elsie Janis but not Ethel Merman, Ruth Chatterton but not Jeanne Eagels, Victor Moore but not Bert Lahr, Henry Hull but not Walter Huston, Marilyn Miller but not Mary Martin, David Belasco but not George Abbott, De Wolf Hopper but not Bobby Clark. Mae West made the first team, though, which is a credit to somebody's heart. Only to his heart, perhaps; but that's something. And obviously it must have been real torment trying to decide between Charlotte Greenwood (on) and Josephine Hull (off).

Even as I tangled with the unwieldy lists, though, I could hear an unpleasant question just over my shoulder: "Who cares?" Inevitably, people whose careers managed to last out a full twenty-five years are most of them gone now; and in today's theater the gone are well gone, relics as they are of a past we have more or less junked. And those that still survive fall into a very special category: they are, by this time, what the people who write me letters like to call "sacred cows."

Whenever a long-established performer turns up onstage, and whenever I chance to throw a little praise in his or her direction, I invariably get the "sacred cow" letter. It points out that so-and-so *always* gets good notices simply because he or she has been around so long, that critics confronted with such a phenomenon are terrified of telling the truth, that talent has ceased to matter and only sentiment remains.

Well, factually that isn't quite so. Tallulah Bankhead, for instance, who was always an event if never precisely a sacred cow, got some of the worst notices of her life toward the very end of her life. And has everyone already forgotten the reviews that Eugene O'Neill's last, posthumously produced, play got? I won't mention Mae West's *Catherine Was Great*, or, for that matter, *any* review that Mrs. Leslie Carter (on the list) ever received.

But there is a certain spiritual truth to the charge, one that I would like to accept with open arms and, in a pitched battle, defend. Yes, there are sacred cows, and yes, I think there should be. It works like this.

No performer, unless it is his first time out, comes onto the stage truly naked. You have seen him before and you remember—with pleasure or displeasure. He carries his last aura with him. The fifth time you see him he has got four auras going and if, by any chance, he has been interesting or provocative or even wonderful those first four times, that nimbus is beginning to look like a halo. Like the Saturday-night ghost, it walks; wherever he goes, it keeps him company, and you don't need a follow spot to pick him out because the follow spot is already in your head.

A performer's past isn't something confined to a scrapbook. He wears it. He breathes it, laughs it, looks it, rolls around in it. He can't shake it, because it is something he *did*—did with those very same limbs and eyes and vocal cords. (No one ever seems to have forgotten Ethel Barrymore's "That's all there is, there isn't any more" and do you think it didn't hover like an echo over everything she said thereafter, adding a resonance she might not even be bothering to use tonight?) The past, early or recent, is written in indelible ink all over the image onstage, and the new performance, so far from standing alone, comes *through* it.

You must know that you, too, laughed more readily at Walter Matthau in *The Odd Couple* for having seen him in *A Shot in the Dark*; the baggage tags along, custom-free. Things got to a point, after a while, where Beatrice Lillie could come on from the wings and, before she did *anything*, the audience laughed. Were they wrong to do so? They'd have been mad not to. There stood the neon sign that blinked nothing but LAUGHTER because that was what the lady's deportment, her composure, her very *presence* now spelt. It always had; who could erase it? The laughter was an earned response, not a bestowed one.

No matter what part I see George C. Scott play, he will always be part Jaques to me (that ironically melancholy fellow in *As You Like It*) because, something like twenty-four years ago, I saw him play it to checkmate. I don't want to banish the overlay from his present performance; if, in his present performance, he shows me an entirely new facet, I see it all the more clearly for the contrast with what I know. Tonight's performance is simply the richer for the variety that is stored up in my mind's eye; the labors of twenty-four years exist simultaneously now, a dimension of days is contained in each gesture.

To deny that our mind's eyes are at work would be simply to lie. And so, when a current performance is not quite as good as it might be, we don't leap at the man's throat, or the lady's. That throat is still quivering from having said "All the world's a stage" or "Maude, you're rotten to the core." We may regret a little lapse; but we do not abandon the radiations that enter with the performer, stage left, and keep clown or tragedian phosphorescent company straight through to that exit at up right. It's not a matter of mere gratitude; it's a matter of multiple vision.

Of course, performers occasionally do fall off. Sometimes the decline is steady, ultimately irreversible. But, if the performer has honestly won or impressed us over an extended period of time, it cannot be precipitous. For the glow fades slowly. It must be taken away as it was built, a millimeter at a time. Certainly we must keep our wits about us and notice that it is going; but there is no sense in rushing it, not even any real possibility of rushing it unless we are willing to perform lobotomies on ourselves. You can't wipe out *your* lifetime quickly, no matter how eager you may be to wipe out a star's.

And so I salute and thank the sacred cows; their sanctity rests on merit. When they sin, I hope I shall notice; but there is no potion that can turn them into Mr. Hydes overnight.

IX

FROM THE
MUSICAL LIBRARY

1

Choreography in Crisis

Choreographers have been having identity crises ever since *Okla-homa!* Once musical-comedy dancing had ceased being an irrele-vant, slapdash, one-two-three-kick precision affair and opened up into the sensually free and psychologically expressive patterns of near-ballet (or ballet itself), the men and women who'd been responsible for the changeover began to wonder just who and what they were.

Were they still hired hands, brought in to bolster a song by sending twenty-four trained bodies soaring through space to its rhythms or to rescue a libretto by taking over the tough spots in the story line and making them emotionally dynamic, visually lyrical? Or were they really the master weavers of the occasion, creators of a show's, any show's, most expansive, all-encompassing images, the real begetters of its climaxes, the true dictators of its style, frame, tone?

There was nothing particularly egocentric about this, it was just a matter of answering a question about function and structure, a practi-cal question that had to be answered whenever a new show was being put together. After Agnes de Mille's unforgettable first dances, and with Jerome Robbins following in her footsteps to see how interestingly he could change them, people spoke of musical-comedy dance as at last having been "integrated." But which way was the integration flowing? Were the dances being logically incorporated into the book, or was the book now being consciously shaped to show off—to serve—the dances?

Though no one made a public announcement of the fact, the latter question was the one being answered in the affirmative. Musical com-edy was moving in the direction of *West Side Story*, a show dramatized by its dancing, dominated by its dancing. And why not? Librettos had never dominated anything; music had. And dance was more than music's best friend; it was its ultimate, most graphic extension, its explosion from a handful of sung notes to an entire stage filled with orchestrated sight and sound, massively emphatic, totally exhilarating.

The choreographer's takeover became obvious enough as the man or woman doing the dances ceased being a collaborator and became the sole ringmaster, staging not only the "big moments" reserved for dance but the book and the song numbers as well. De Mille and Robbins now staged complete shows, as, a bit later, Gower Champion and Michael Kidd and Bob Fosse would do. Let it all flow together, and who better than a choreographer—instinctively a creature of flow from toes to fingertips—to handle the unified task?

One thing bothered me after a while, and it wasn't the usurpation of jobs formerly assigned to other people. I noticed, after a certain number of masterworks in which book, song, and dance did indeed sweep through the theater like an all-of-a-piece gale, that as the choreographer-director became more and more preoccupied with his secondary chores, we began to get less and less dancing. Understandable enough. There's only so much creative energy on tap at any one time, and as portions of this were siphoned off in other directions the choreographer found himself with less and less time, less and less leftover inventiveness, for the one thing he or she had always done best. As I watched Mr. Robbins devote more of himself to the atmosphere of, say, *Fiddler on the Roof* than to its principal ballet, or Gower Champion spend his entire evening with the constricted two-character opportunities of *I Do! I Do!*, I might admire what *was* accomplished. But I did miss the headlong, full-bodied buoyancy of the lift and swirl and demonic intensity these men had displayed when they had nothing but dance on their minds. It may be a law for genuinely gifted choreographers: don't mire yourself in the book, nor even in the undanced production numbers.

Perhaps it was out of a sense of the gradual diminishment of dancing since dance directors have taken on other burdens that Bob Fosse did what he did in his 1978 *Dancin'.* In *Dancin',* he reversed field entirely. Almost as though he were mortally fearful of succumbing to alien temptations, warding off evil by putting a hex and a pox on all that might distract him from his best talents, he banished the libretto entirely, banished numbers that were simply sung, banished everything—or almost everything—but the rush and stomp and pat and pistonlike thrust of hands and feet, the glide and spin and sinuous self-assertion of bodies.

The bodies were bathed in red light, with intermittent flashes of lightning blue, as they writhed, coupled, detached themselves with Olympian grace until, picking up the shock of a rock beat, they burst into a flaring, knee-jerk restlessness. They floated in slow-motion as a derelict, in clown costume, remembered all that he could of his idol, Bojangles, while the spirit of Bojangles hovered rhythmically over him. They responded instantly, and with infinite variation, to every sort of percussion, hiking their shoulders and cocking knees at right angles like so many Walt Disney skeletons, dropping heads between their knees to bid us farewell like just as many *Mummenschanz* spiders.

They slipped quietly into line clothed in the ice-cream suits, bow ties, and straw hats of *I Wanna Be a Dancin' Man* (the music was from here, there, and everywhere) to count out a bit of very soft stop-time, they fastened their white shoes to the floor so that they could do an undulating dance in luminous-paint leotards without ever moving their feet, they picked up the smoky or sneaky or bleating sound of solo instruments to mirror their distinctive qualities evocatively (Ann Reinking was particularly brilliant whipping the air with her hair as she shattered space with the same piercing force as her trumpeter), they turned a finale composed of Americana from Cohan to Sousa into a medley that mocked, whispered, and did strangely yearning things to march tempos that once had been brisk. The men and women whose bodies were put through the dizzying three-act drill were one and all exemplary. Every move that was made was accomplished.

And this solution to the problem didn't really work, either. Dance can stand by itself when it aspires to, and achieves, the interior integrity, the long spiritual spine, of ballet. But this was mainly *show* dancing, these were the steps that had distinguished and/or set fire to *Sweet Charity* and *Cabaret* and *Pippin*. Some, with their Disney echoes, were less than that. But at their best they were not intended for independent statement; they were decorative, illustrative, meant for reinforcing something else. They wanted a book, if only a book to fight with.

Some kind of challenge was needed here, to push the often brilliant Mr. Fosse to maximum freshness, to beginning middle-end completeness. I think we all understand that musical-comedy books, feeble though they often are, accomplish something. They press the evening's characters toward crises, toward moments so urgent that some sort of detonation's in order. The situation's going to splinter and the splinters are going to fly off in the air. Which is what the dancers are for: to fly off into the air. The poor libretto's never going to manage anything quite that spectacular; so dance takes over.

But in *Dancin'* there was nothing that *required* the dancing, no stepping-off place, no trigger, no cry for immediate help. And that meant that each of its numbers had to start from the floor, had to generate its own need and build to its own satisfaction of that need. Since most of them were short, it was a tall order. They tended to become fragments and, because each fragment was forced to begin all over again, both the pattern and the individual steps came to seem repetitive.

Another hazard from the same source. Musical-comedy books are about people. The people may be rather thin and they may sometimes be downright silly. But we develop a nodding acquaintance with them, adopt a formalized sympathy for them. The familiarity and the sympathy carry over into the eruptive dance, personalizing it. Here, of necessity, the postures and phrasings were depersonalized, rendering them somewhat abstract, remote, unfelt. Ingenious as Mr. Fosse is—he has few peers in his field—he could not, given his essentially supportive dance vocabulary, overcome the relative coolness.

A degree of anxiety showed. Mr. Fosse had felt it necessary to use spoken introductions and dialogue snatches, after all; these were awkward in the situation and generally weak in themselves ("Oh, you're beautiful without the glasses," said a girl, having removed the spectacles from her male partner). Neon signs repeating the show's title dropped in from the heavens now and then; smoke machines and luminous confetti were called upon for assistance; singers carrying mikes climbed proscenium-arch ladders to no particular purpose; the incidental comedy got right down to bosom-peeking (shades of Willie Howard!). And, most curiously, Willa Kim's costumes were so covered with curlicues, polka dots, outer-space antennae, and whorls of contrasting color that very often the dancers' body lines were seriously obscured. The gimmickry suggested a lack of confidence in the evening's premise: that dancing was enough.

But musical-comedy dancing, in isolation, isn't really enough; I came away respecting the effort but feeling decidedly underfed. Came away wishing, in fact, that we could put musical comedy together again, with all of its parts most cheerfully in proportion.

2

The Sturdiness
of Mama Rose

The special genius of American musical comedy doesn't lie in its stars, though God knows that Ethel Merman and Mary Martin and Bobby Clark and Victor Moore have had a thumping great deal to do with it. It doesn't even lie in its songs, for all that the American musical stage has fired off Gershwin and Kern and Rodgers and Berlin scores like rockets around the world. We are well aware that it rarely lies in its librettos; librettos are most often necessary nuisances to be smothered as swiftly as possible by half a dozen more glittering values, except on those occasions when a Kaufman or a Hammerstein or a Burrows is in top form. Everything's important, to be sure. But one thing is more important than the whole bundle of others when an unforgettable musical is born. The fit.

I marveled at *Gypsy* the first time I saw it, partly because Ethel Merman was having not only the singing but the acting triumph of her life, partly because Arthur Laurents's libretto had overnight joined the theater's own program of Great Books, partly because composer Jule Styne and lyricist Stephen Sondheim had been not only lively but literate, not only rousing but intelligent.

And I marveled all over again in 1974 as I watched Angela Lansbury step not into Ethel Merman's shoes—Miss Merman's are sturdy, nailed into space, while Miss Lansbury's are feverishly elusive—but into those cobbled so craftily for Mama Rose, mother of Gypsy Rose Lee and "Baby June" Havoc, self-sacrificing tigress, secret seeker of the spotlight, a creature demonic and doting in each savage embrace. Miss Lansbury is not really to be compared to Miss Merman: there's no way of doing it. Miss Merman is a natural force, like the Colorado River (I have never seen the Colorado River; I don't feel the need to, having seen Miss Merman). Miss Lansbury is half fine actress, half ferocious personality, admirable because she works so hard and, in working so hard, works so honestly. Divorce the two in your mind. The stars these stars were born under come from entirely different constellations.

But, fascinated as I was with what Miss Lansbury could do with the character complexities waiting for her around treacherous corners, what I was really marveling at the whole time was the expertise with which a potentially seedy show-biz saga, ripe for raucous and campy treatment, had been ever so gently nursed into something infinitely richer, fragment by fragment, lamb by lamb. (You may have forgotten the lamb; wait a minute.)

Keep clock on the show and you may be stunned by the deviously cunning progress it makes. Early sequence: Mama Rose is determined to get her two nestlings into vaudeville, imagining them stars by the time they hit the ripe age of ten, and she is on the road in a cutout revue-sketch automobile, stopping just long enough in her chugging from portal to portal to snatch up any underage supporting talent she can filch along the way. She simply plucks a singing Boy Scout from his unwary troop, without so much as a by-your-leave steals any lass or lad who can do a dance step, tucks the rapidly accumulating company into the rear of the car. Now that's broad, very broad. Watching *Gypsy* we don't mind in the least—because it's funny, and because, for all we know, the whole evening is going to be as quickly cartooned as that.

It's not. The inspired conspirators who put the mysteriously perfect venture together and made it so durable had something stronger, deeper, more dimensional, and finally downright moving in mind, and they begin their subtle structural conniving early. We've been dealing with happy caricature thus far, razzmatazz on the wing. Before the mold can harden, Mama Rose, most garishly outlined of the bunch, just happens to fall in with a tough-minded but soft-hearted former agent who may be able to help them. Sitting at a table, surprised that any sort of guardian angel should ever drift her way and quieted by gratitude into lazy reflection, she begins to sing "Funny . . . you're a stranger who's come here, come from another town. . . . Funny . . ." The song is called "Small World (Isn't It?)", its reeds ripple very demurely by way of intro, its open spaces leave time for an early May mood to set in, a gargoyle of a woman is turning into a human being a stranger might not only love but might, given her increasing dimension, do emotional battle with. The show's grounding has grown warmer with the weather, a trace of amber can be seen filtering through the bold primary colors of the initial pinwheel.

The pinwheel, incidentally, is actually there, and used to accomplish, ingeniously, one of the show's most important and difficult transitions. Baby June and her vaudeville colleagues are sprinting, locomotive style, through their act under a spinning spotlight. They have begun their back-and-forth strides as tots. By the time they have finished the number before our flicker-blinded eyes, they are one and all transformed into budding men and women. An ordinary stage effect, introduced as corn, has—of all things—pushed the narrative line, and its threat of new emotions, miles ahead.

Back to Feydeau farce set to music, with Mama Rose attempting to conceal her vast brood beneath the flying bedclothes of an undersize hotel room and bellowing "Rape!" when the hotel's manager dares pursue her into the somewhat oversupplied sleeping quarters. George Abbott and the Marx Brothers have been here. What comes next as a brass-happy march segues into drowsy strings? The lamb. Young Louise (who will, many graceful dissolves later, become Gypsy Rose) is alone with her pet in her arms, asking it wistfully, "Little lamb/When will I know how old I am?" Until now, Baby June has been the focus of Mama Rose's act and our interest; Louise is the leftover, straining to do splits in spangles and top hat but plain and pigtailed in the shadows. We begin to take *her* measure, too, and we see that it is something more than the insubstantial line-drawing routine musicals permit.

The crucial sequence—the moment when we *do* understand that *Gypsy* is capable of unexpected but apparently limitless dramatic expansion—probably comes in an alleyway, outside a stage door, while Louise sits with desperate eyes fixed on a male dancer. The dancer is in the process of building his own act (composer Styne has done him a fine variant on that stock period hymn to silk vests and striped ties, ending with the notion that "all I need now is a girl"). The girl who would like to *be* the girl is right there, her taut tomboy's face composed, her sense of neglect wholly without self-pity. (As the quite remarkable Zan Charisse played her, she seemed to have had the braces removed from her teeth just yesterday, to be as sexless and as patiently pensive as a Rouault clown.) Without the boy's noticing, she is at last impulsively on her feet behind him and joining him exuberantly in a "flash finish." But, dancing perfectly, she doesn't *look* like his partner. For one thing, she is still wearing the brown felt trousers assigned to her in Baby June's act: she plays the hind legs of a cow. When we learn, a scene later, that the boy she has matched step for step has promptly run off with Baby June, we realize—through our quite genuine dismay—how perfectly we've been set up for the fall. Playwright, composer, and librettist have, for us, glued two people together in a number, then ripped them apart. After that, we can expect almost any degree of substance they care to give us in the second act.

We get it. In Mama Rose's puritanical dismay at having the act booked into a burlesque house, a dismay quickly canceled by the mat-ter-of-fact greed that overtakes her when Gypsy Rose is offered star-dom. In Mama Rose's edgy, despairing uselessness when the star is at last born and her own work done. In the terrible manic downbeat—in the pit and in her fists—of Mama Rose's final thrust at nonexistent glory, "Rose's Turn." In the legitimate, yet always in rhythm, vehe-mence of the agent's abandonment of the woman who had once wel-comed him softly but has no real place for him in her starstruck heart. And, in and around and perfectly meshed with these things, the still outsize comedy of life among the strippers, horn-toting Amazons and all. It's the weave, so securely leading us to an ultimate emotional haymaker rare in musicals, that is so astonishing. Many cooks concoct-ed a superlative broth.

I am informed that Boston University, in conjunction with the University of Hamburg, has established a well-staffed academy in Germany to teach "the art of the American musical theater" there. After another look at *Gypsy*, I'm not surprised. After fifteen years the show, as entertainment and as craftsmanship, remains as dazzling as it was on the day it was so felicitously born.

3

Getting *Candide* Right

Candide may at last have stumbled into the best of all possible productions. I take back "stumbled," instantly. For there was nothing at all inadvertent about the magician's pass director Harold Prince made in 1973 at the song-and-dance celebration of Voltaire's calculated insult to "the best of all possible worlds." Mr. Prince had looked at the materials, long, hard, and lovingly, decided what kind and degree of theatrical impudence was called for, got himself a new and free-floating libretto by Hugh Wheeler, and then simply rebuilt a theater to suit Leonard Bernstein's sweetly irreverent score.

Ever since *Candide* was first attempted, unsuccessfully, on Broadway in 1956—there was book trouble, production trouble, tone trouble then—everybody and his brother had come up with ideas about salvaging the glittering, grinning Bernstein melodies and the muted ironies of certain of Richard Wilbur's lyrics. But no one—before Mr. Prince—had thought of making the entire event spin just as Voltaire's novel spins, dizzily from rape to earthquake, restlessly from Lisbon to Constantinople, feverishly and foolishly from luscious dreams of "breast of peacock, apple pie" to syphilis and pox and the poisoned darts of aborigines. Voltaire's text is short, breathless, cantankerous, and cavalier. Mr. Prince had decided to throw words, notes, and players at us with the same windswept effrontery.

As we found our seats on the staggered benches at the Chelsea Theater Center in Brooklyn we looked down on what was normally the acting area and wondered where on earth the acting was going to be done. Almost everything we saw was audience, facing this way and that, a jigsaw puzzle eddying outward from a space just large enough to contain a postage-stamp-size fourposter on which Voltaire lay, paper and quill tossed aside, asleep. No room for roundelays, let alone heel-kicking romps, there.

Then, in a flash, we got the picture. The orchestra that launched into an exhilarating overture was split: a gold-braided conductor, a bass viol, some trumpeters in guards' helmets commanded a perch at one far wall, a matching complement sent back rich sonorities from the other. Living stereo: we were encased in the music. Simultaneously with the last note of the overture, the first drawbridge slapped down to connect one rim of the house with its center.

The place, it turned out, was—like Voltaire's world—booby-trapped. What seemed no more than shower curtains flew upward to reveal perfectly workable nooks for whole families, ramps flopped forward to help the shipwrecked to shore, a tiny stage opened its drapes to display the likes of a dozen Carmen Mirandas singing sassy tribute to the New World, and when there was no other way for an actor to get from the Inquisition to Eldorado he simply reached for a pulley and glided gleefully over our heads.

The show was now a carousel and we were on it, quite safely. Though the actors were working in and about us—a rifleman shot a brigand dead within inches of my nose—the design of the unending chase was so firm, the performers were so secure in their climbing and tumbling and round-the-earth footwork, that we were able to join the journey and still *see* it with the detachment that Voltaire prescribes. Which only proves, once again, that detachment is more nearly a psychological than a physical matter.

Now all of this proved most important for a couple of fairly transparent reasons. The philosophical premises of *Candide* are pretty readily grasped: Dr. Pangloss teaches his pupils—the happy bastard Candide, the adoring and cunning Cunegonde, the vain Maximillian, and the extremely available Paquette—that everything that happens in God's universe must necessarily happen for the best. (The lunacy of the proposition is delectably, and exhaustively, established in the first three of Mr. Bernstein's tunes, "Life Is Happiness Indeed," "The Best of All Possible Worlds," and "Oh, Happy We.")

Thereafter the perverse universe can only contradict the premise steadily, visiting holocaust after holocaust on victims who are determined to see virtue in snakes, wars, lost buttocks, and being hanged. The pattern is necessarily repetitive and, when it is forced into a proscenium frame with that frame's implications of cause-and-effect logic, its point can become labored.

Labor went out the window here. Librettist Wheeler didn't have to explain anything, certainly never at length: if towers were going to topple in Lisbon or the captive Cunegonde was going to have to share her favors with a rich Jew and a Grand Inquisitor, Mr. Wheeler simply had to toss out a dialogue line to say that the universe was behaving capriciously again and Mr. Prince could swiftly take it from there. On into songs sung by stained-glass windows, on into a whirling worklight that miraculously took care of a volcanic eruption, on into ships' rigging flung in a trice over the auditorium, on into green streamers unsnarling from the ceiling to provide a jungle. The glee wasn't in what was happening—that was all foreseen, anyway—but in how swiftly and inventively it could be made to happen, almost before we'd noticed.

The sheer expedition of it all helped in two other ways. Though there was obviously no great open space for dancing, choreographer Patricia Birch had discovered that by distributing her cavorting figures over bridge and ramp, hill and dale, she could give us the effect of being buoyantly borne aloft on steps that were, taken by themselves, quite simple. And the speed cut the dross away so that we could arrive at another melody all the sooner (the version ran for an hour and forty-five minutes, without intermission, and seemed very close to Bernstein uninterrupted). It did more than save time for music, it established tone for music.

There was a perfect passage, for instance, in which Maureen Brennan, as the ringed and ringleted Cunegonde, plucked jewels to her heart while mourning the shabbiness of it all. The mock aria was itself enchanting, always had been. But Mr. Prince had seen fit to provide Cunegonde with a kind of catatonic alter ego, a lass buried in the floor wearing a vast white wig laced with diamonds and steadfastly playing a pianoforte. Cunegonde not only purloined the necklaces as she pursued coloratura figures, she didn't mind whacking the lass in the head, with her foot, to be supplied with a last delicacy, blue garters. We were ready for the outrageousness of the song because we had been, were being, so happily outraged all along.

Not everything was *quite* perfect. Lewis J Stadlen played Voltaire, Pangloss, and an assortment of other masterminds; he was particularly funny as an ancient sage peeling answers to philosophical questions from a desk spindle. I did wish, however, that he'd been permitted to do one or another role in natural voice; too much of his energy went into assumed quavers. And one large-scale production number, "Auto Da Fé (What a Day)," went mysteriously sober, and soberingly flat, after a cruelly jolly beginning. We were ready to make the most of combining a fiesta with public torture, but ironic balance was lost and the celebration turned merely moody; perhaps poor Candide's flogging wasn't sufficiently stylized to keep us on keel.

But these were minor quibbles about a most satisfying resurrection. Mark Baker's Candide, guileless in lederhosen and seraphic even when tied up in a sack, was splendid, he and Miss Brennan did blissful justice to the open-throated surges and delicate retreats of "You Were Dead, You Know," and June Gable was very funny as a kind of Polish-Yiddish Mother Courage who had been, as she sang, "easily assimilated." Eugene and Franne Lee had designed the functional and revealing snake pit Mr. Prince had demanded of them, and done it ingeniously. Result: a thoroughly iconoclastic evening of enormous charm.

4

Noël Coward, Neat

Oh Coward! was an island of entertainment in the sea of our troubles. And a tight little island it was. Tightness was its quality, its special merit, the key to its merriment. A glazed gentleman with pale eyes named Roderick Cook, whose hauteur had the quality of talcum powder on ice, had carefully scanned every note Noël Coward ever wrote, plucked fifty or more of the very best tunes from the lot, made certain that he and two companion performers could not only remember the lyrics but could pitter-patter them at us as though their tongues were typewriter keys, and had then frozen them in space, imperturbably, impeccably.

Every director in town should have rushed to see the miniature revue at once. For Mr. Cook, arranging, staging, and then appearing in his own 1972 collage, had shown precisely what could be done with fifty numbers and three people if you didn't want the fifty or the three to wear out their welcomes. The economy with which he worked was in itself a thing of joy. Would you have supposed that the entire stage business for a song might consist of nothing more than letting one man's shoulder sag very slightly on one line while another man's shoulder rose just as slightly on the next? It worked. By husbanding his effects, by letting soloists stand virtually transfixed straight through a familiar but freshly mesmerizing ballad, by refusing every kind of vocal and visual extravagance, Mr. Cook had got surprise after surprise out of small catches of breath.

Of course, the Coward lyrics are often written that way. When Coward writes that intelligent people, caught in the midday sun, "put their scotch or rye down/And lie down," the short second line owes its leap of pleasure to the little gasp that comes on the open beat just before "and lie down" and to the abruptness with which the whole structure then stops. The inhalation is prim, and the sudden cutoff is curt. Give Mr. Cook and his talented friends, Barbara Cason and Jamie Ross, a small sputter like that and they could make it sound as though syncopation had just been invented, or as though they'd swallowed the first row of customers in one gulp.

Ingenious and very funny. The infinite reserve—a glance to say that one of course knew who the "Right People" were, the measured lowering of a feathered fan to say that yes, the lady would dance and oh my God wasn't it tragic—made every light inflection or frugal gesture seem a beneficence. And it left room, astonishing room, for an effect emphatic enough to get the intermission curtain down. Because everything had been so tidy, and because these modest magpies had been so decent about the appalling things that go on in the world, they were able to turn their attention to Mrs. Worthington, who wants to put her daughter on the stage, and, after pointing out more or less politely that "the width of her seat/Would surely defeat/Her chances of success," permitted themselves to become angry. In a final, and I would say hilarious, chorus, they turned on the lady and her daughter with a rage that remained controlled but that was nearing apoplexy on the inside. We didn't quite expect fury from these folk who had been bucking for triple-A in Deportment, and it was all the more soul-satisfying when it came.

The intelligence of the occasion was nowhere better demonstrated than in Mr. Cook's own handling of "I've Been to a Marvelous Party." The song belongs, in most of our memories, to Beatrice Lillie. Wise Step Number One: it was here assigned to a man. Scratch the past. Wise Step Number Two: the man was ruefully, though not elaborately, hung-over. So far from wishing to run on in ecstatic trills about the fete he'd been to, gleefully awash in the latest gossip, he could barely remove his palm from his deadened temple. As he bit out the information that he'd attended such a marvelous party, you realized that, if he could help it, he was never going to a party again. The song had, in effect, had its face lifted; we seemed to have known it forever and, mysteriously, it looked new. Nor was Mr. Cook through. Sipping on the hair of the dog that had done such damage to him, he imperceptibly warmed to his task, flaring one nostril occasionally, until at the end he was chattering with us like a maddened dummy. Mr. Cook should have been put under glass, unless he was already there.

It all went to prove that taste is practically everything. It also suggested that Noël Coward, "born into a world that took light music seriously," wrote light music that we might as well begin to take seriously. It lingers.

5

Spontaneous Combustion

What I liked best about *A Chorus Line* was that it was a hit that was made by the public (and at the Public Theater, just to add to the felicity). Long before any reviewers, who must normally function as huff-and-puff-artists blowing laggard theatergoers stageward, were permitted to come near the entertainment, word had got about: something was brewing in one of Joseph Papp's downtown houses, the previews going on were as exciting as any opening night could hope to be, ticket buyers were lining up at the Lafayette Street box office terrified that they might not be able to see the show before they were told to. *A Chorus Line* was selling out before any sales pitch had been made by anybody, a theatrical event had gained momentum on word-of-mouth alone.

What, being a reviewer, do I like about that? For one thing, it fits, very snugly, my own ideal but rarely realized notion of what the audience-reviewer relationship ought to be. It ought to be a conversation about something *both* have seen, not a peremptory command to get going or keep out. I realize, of course, that no one who wishes to write about the theater can possibly wait until absolutely everybody's beat him to it, but if the audience has already claimed the show as its own, if there's a consensus in the air that suggests more and more spectators are determined to attend no matter what *anybody* says, then the reviewer is relieved of his burden of functioning as a shopping service and is free to chat, to compare notes—the audience having already proclaimed its own freedom.

That's part of it. The other is the evidence that the audience has acquired *energy* again. In the theater's dull periods, audiences are notoriously, somewhat understandably, sluggish and need prodding. When they really want to go to the theater, though, want to go badly enough to do some potluck experimenting of their own, things are obviously looking up. Theater's become a lure rather than an obligation once more, a magnet instead of a maybe. And that in turn suggests that the Broadway upsurge of the mid-1970s is no temporary phenomenon, no accident. The groundswell may have greater proportions than we'd quite dared to hope.

The next best thing I liked about *A Chorus Line* was the lightning-stroke severity, the percussive yet infinitely varied discipline creator-choreographer Michael Bennett had imposed upon his open, scenically empty stage. Except for revolving mirrors against the back wall and five or six cheval glasses that could be whipped into place to reflect a spinning Donna McKechnie as she tried to discover and proclaim her identity as a dancer, the space was bare. To fill it, sharply outlined slivers of light darted from the heavens to pick out faces trained to grin, faces quivering in fear, bodies contorted in rhythmic ecstasy or in private humiliation and terror.

Suddenly green and red footlights were given back to us through the dizzily meshing mirrors and we were able to see, as prancing units, four or eight or all two dozen of the chorus boys and girls who were offering their superbly trained feet, torsos, tossed heads to a director for a job. The applicants would have to be cut to eight before the leaps and fast taps were done, and we knew that. More than half of these avid dervishes would be dismissed, disconsolate, when the tryout session was done. Yet Mr. Bennett had been able to isolate them, individualize them, in their sassy or embarrassed or overeager idiosyncrasies (a girl parking her chewing gum, a boy unable to keep his eyes from following his own feet) by his extraordinary skill as a chessboard tactician, by his kaleidoscopic use of Tharon Musser's lighting, by the clues he had given to "librettists" James Kirkwood and Nicholas Dante when each applicant was asked for a fragment of his life history ("What do I want to be when I grow up? Young!" purred the iconoclastically seductive Carole Bishop).

Restless orchestration, expletives drowning music whenever a mis-step occurred, linked bodies cross-kicking forward as rhythms climbed to crescendo, all gave the sense of a word, a sung note, a sprung dance, an entire show being born on the spot, taking shape as we watched. Mr. Bennett *had* actually developed *A Chorus Line* out of six months' improvisation in 1975, teasing its myriad pieces into an ultimately miraculous pattern. The accomplishment was brilliant.

What I liked least about *A Chorus Line* was the ordinariness—no doubt an inevitable ordinariness—of its life histories. These occupied a fair portion of the evening's center; on the not entirely persuasive pretext that we wished to hear the dancers' speaking voices in the event that they should also be given lines to read, Robert LuPone (as the choreographer who would hire and fire) retired to a godlike perch at the rear of the auditorium and wheedled out of the brassy and the giggly, the pleading and the nonchalant, snippets of their pasts.

These began amusingly: some had been culled from the performers' own experiences and then shaped by director and librettists. One aspirant was willing to say that he came from a family that "had money but no taste"; he'd spent part of his childhood breaking into other people's houses, not to steal but to rearrange the furniture. Another boy had spent Father's Day limping in honor of his dad; the old man had been so dismayed by his son's indifference to sports that he'd intimated to friends the boy was a polio victim. Yet another, from Buffalo, had so hated Buffalo he'd thought of killing himself; the catch, he explained, was that in Buffalo suicide is redundant.

But rather too many were familiar and thin: the girl who'd been born just to keep a marriage together (no dice); the girl who'd compensated for a dreary life by dancing because "everyone is beautiful in ballet"; the girl whose breasts had been too small until silicone saved her (am I wrong, or is silicone no longer regarded as a satisfactory solution to the problem?). Early homosexual experiences were obvious and repeated themselves, with a good bit of self-pity creeping in. And a few were simply irrelevant: a boy's alarmed misunderstanding of his first "wet dream" didn't really add anything to the evening's focus, to our understanding of the drives that kept young men and women feverishly toeing that long white "chorus line" (plainly painted on the stage floor) in spite of the fact that nothing but age and disillusion were likely to come of all their labors.

Having said so much, I must now point out that ordinariness, and the disillusion that comes of it, were unmistakably on Mr. Bennett's mind. He wanted us to feel the happiness that overtook these nonentities so long as they slapped the ground or flew in the air—at the same time that we recognized the essential hopelessness of their lot. When a dancer was injured and carried away—it was a knee injury that could write finis to everything he'd worked for—the others fell into silent small groups, scattered numbly about the stage, reflecting on their own probably nonexistent futures. The tableau was not unworthy of Degas, though the rehearsal clothes were different (Theoni V. Aldredge had stunningly designed realistically slapdash rehearsal wear that nonetheless fused line and color to serve Mr. Bennett's most varied purposes), and we were as sobered as those who remained. When the applicants were called back to the long white line again, we saw now that it was sadly symbolic: for almost all of them, the line was a cutoff point; they could go this far, no farther. You were certain, I think, to find yourself very much moved when the final selection was made and the last eight rejects, shrugging their separate shrugs, moved on to seek other jobs they would not get.

There was thornier matter still. Miss McKechnie, whose lashes seemed to graze her eyes as though there were quiet tears to be attended to, played a dancer who had once escaped the line to become a star, or near-star. In time, there'd been no more jobs. Too good for the anonymity of a precision routine, she hadn't been good enough to make stardom stick. Now she was *still* too accomplished to return to the line, she no longer fit neatly into its limited uses; what hope for her? Here a real show-biz tragedy—that of the in-betweener—was touched on, freshly and with honest concern. If it was only touched on, and not ultimately illustrated, it was because when Miss McKechnie went into her spectacular solo work ("The Music and the Mirror"), riveting us with her multiplied arabesques, the number was required—for the climactic needs of *this* show—to give off stardust. It did. The issue was ambiguous, then, a verbal statement given the lie by visual excitement, but it was candid and considerate of Mr. Bennett to have brought it up.

Marvin Hamlisch's score was, for the entertainment's purposes, perfect. Filled with echoes—"A Man and a Woman," his own rag arrangements for *The Sting*—it summarized, from the opening stock vamp, the entire lives of youngsters trained in dance studios, kept waiting in wings, auditioning to aged pianos, moving a step up from Radio City to the St. James, riding at last on the standing ovation of a successful first night, going home down the alleyway unrecognized. The sounds that rang in their ears became ours, relentlessly, elatedly. The life histories themselves fared better when they were fashioned into songs by Mr. Hamlisch and lyricist Edward Kleban, providing the wry and fetching Priscilla Lopez with a pertinent and funny account of what it was like, at a "method" school of acting, to feel nothing, nothing at all.

Because the company as a whole had lived straight through the building of *A Chorus Line,* it inhabited its own domain with a dynamic sense of possession that was both rare and irresistible. How could audiences help feeling deeply for the breathless, ebullient, slaving, smiling, all-too-knowing innocents who would never cross the painted line?

6

Maxims
from Miss de Mille

It was a matter of catching wisdom on the wing—wisdom and tart-ness and hauteur and a sudden blunt intimacy that made your head snap back. I'm speaking of a single evening offered in 1977 at City Center, an evening sponsored by the Joffrey Ballet along with Agnes de Mille's American Heritage Theater and an evening devoted to dance in general and de Mille in particular.

Never mind the dancing, though some of it was stunning, above all a set of Martha Graham exercises that somehow resembled a cobra giving birth to itself, and after that—though not *far* after—an unbeliev-ably liquid transition from a standard, stiff-legged Irish jig to the melted-butter downbeat and the floor-gentling taps that American blacks made of it. This last not only took your breath away, for once in a lifetime it took Miss de Mille's away. Seated at a lectern at the side of the stage, she started to say something analytical about the miraculous metamorphosis we'd been looking at and then simply threw her hands into the air with an "I'm sorry," and let it go at that. Words were not going to improve *that* music, any more than they were going to help explain a tap-dancer named Honi Coles. Mr. Coles, as I remember it, performed in midair. The ground came up and touched him.

But the occasion belonged to Miss de Mille, a woman who does not start things she can't finish. She'd started this particular evening a couple of years earlier and had been interrupted, backstage before curtain time, by an impertinent stroke. Miss de Mille has never been one to be put off by impertinence—she rather admires it, being incorri-gibly saucy herself—and, having given rest its due (in a manner of speaking; I believe she wrote a book abed), she'd now returned to fulfill her commitment to her followers and also, I suspect, to show who's boss.

She did spend the two hours or so seated, but, like most dancers, she has other means of achieving elevation. A certain loftiness of spirit, for instance, the sort that led her to dismiss a very cute dancer doing very cute little nothings with the brusque confidence "She's only entertainment." On to higher things. Not that Miss de Mille meant to be snooty about entertainment. She's not. As the woman who really revolutionized dancing in American musical comedy (she passes the credit back to Jack Cole), she had only one piece of advice to hand on to choreographers tangling with the form. Her rule of thumb is simple but all-encompassing: "You must not bore."

But she had more extensive things in mind for the occasion: a quick, straightforward, almost dizzying rundown of dancing from its origins in tom-tom beats and fencing postures to all of the serious and frivolous things we do with its free flights today. So she was curt about some things—she had a habit of tossing off a maxim, sliding the glasses down the bridge of her imperious nose, looking directly at us over the rims, and snapping out, "Got that?"—and extensively rhapsodic about others.

I jotted down a few things *I* got, and on the theory that Miss de Mille might have forgotten to incorporate one or another of them in her assorted fine books I'll pass them along here as possibly useful notes:

"A tacit in music is not a silence, it's a suspension." Hear, hear. And I do wish that actors and directors in the legitimate theater would do some of the hearing. In a play, that tacit is called a pause. And all too often, God knows, the pause in question is a dead, dulling silence, a break in the continuity, a gap, an onstage nap, empty air. Unless a pause *can* be made a tension, it's sheer dereliction of duty.

"There never was a bad folk dance." Interesting. What people do when they're enjoying *themselves* will always be formalized to a degree so that they won't bump into each other but will not be formalized in the same way that they are for onlookers, mere spectators. You can sham a lot, prettify, do all sorts of deceiving and useless things when you're trying to catch the eye of a nonparticipant. But when everybody present is in on the get-together, "whatever doesn't work is instantly discarded." The pragmatic can be purer than the too artfully designed.

"Man is the only animal that dances." I'm still thinking about the implications of that one.

"You don't have to bare the whole fang to show disdain." Miss de Mille was speaking here of the control, the reserve, dancers must maintain if they are not to destroy line, shape, proportion with unseemly facial display, and I must say she is the best living example of her own proposition. You know there is disdain in her, but no fang ever shows. A faint tilt of the nose, perhaps. You might detect the intimation, but only the intimation, of a sniff. Then a smart clap of the hands and just the least trace of irony as she gives instructions for doing it better, or doing less of it. Humor runs along underneath, also barely showing.

Let me add two bits of information, not instruction, and have done. It would seem, if we are to trust the lady with the silver hair and firm spine, that Edwin Booth always had a hornpipe performed between the fourth and fifth acts of *Hamlet*. I *knew* there was something missing from the *Hamlet*s I've seen.

And work on this one, if you've a mind to. When group dancing began in Europe, its patterns always moved clockwise. But by the time the first great waves of immigrants had arrived in America, the newcomers had done a turnabout and were skipping to their Lous counterclockwise. A sea change in midocean? An early declaration of independence? Perhaps the new nation was just putting its right foot forward.

I hope I have made it clear that, whatever conundrums she may have left us with, the lady did not bore.

7

The Candor
of George Gershwin

The jokes are legion about George Gershwin's egocentricity—he was an egocentric, of course, of the most generous sort, being perfectly willing to play his tunes for anybody, any place, any time—but the joke, in the end, is on us, on music, on opera, on the world he took by the tail and snapped to his bidding. For it is his very arrogance, supreme confidence, relentless self-assertion that leave us with an actual opera, *Porgy and Bess*, today.

Most people didn't want to call *Porgy and Bess* an opera when it was written—pretentious of the musical-comedy man, wasn't it, to try to elbow his way into the company of the immortals?—and, as I suppose everyone remembers, the houses regularly devoted to *Traviata* refused to touch it. When the Theater Guild finally summoned up sufficient nerve to mount it, it presented it as a sort-of opera, with much of the recitative (which means much of the actual music and, in fact, the entire musical ambience) cut, and with constant stress on the melodies most likely to succeed.

But no sneering at the Theater Guild. It *did* get *Porgy and Bess* on, it did so in a 1935 production so opulent that it had to lose money even at capacity, and I'd be betraying my youth if I didn't stand at attention before the memory of Rouben Mamoulian's staging, above all the empty courtyard of Catfish Row with an empty rocking chair slightly to left of center—a rocking chair that, after the sultry lift and fall of *Summertime* had grown insistent enough in the pit, began to rock back and forth all by itself. This irresistible image—imitated so often since, in musicals, films, even animated cartoons—may seem *Oklahoma*-ish now (do I think that because *Oklahoma!* was also directed by Mamoulian?), a bit of atmospheric quaintness suited to operetta at best, but it was breathtaking at the time. And as time went on it was the musical-comedy appeals, the insinuating glide of "It Ain't Necessarily So," the bouncing-ball buoyancy of "I Got Plenty o' Nuttin'," that were stressed in revivals of the work. But we knew all that, just as we knew that the production courageously mounted by the Houston Grand Opera Company in 1976 had at last unabashedly put the piece on the stage approximately as its composer envisioned it. What did *Porgy and Bess*, whole, turn out to be?

It was opera, all right, and it was opera because Gershwin was stubborn, cocky, unintimidated. I think you might almost say that it was opera now because it hadn't been then, that it survived (or emerged) with its independent character intact precisely because Gershwin had not got on his knees before the notion of "opera" but stood on his own two feet and, if he felt like it, tapped them. Specifically, he hadn't made Scott Joplin's mistake in *Treemonisha*, going to endless trouble to make himself socially acceptable at La Scala or the Met by suppressing his instincts and aping the standard repertory. That's always death, because the standards weren't standards when they entered, or were forced into, the repertory; the forcing usually came when, after spectacular initial failure on the order of *Carmen*'s, the public simply gave orders that could not be contravened. I can continue to be attracted by the sweetness of *Treemonisha* whether it is characteristic Joplin or not (it's not); but I know I'm not going to be seeing it scheduled, yearly, somewhere between *La Boheme* and *Turandot*. On the other hand, I'm just as certain that any minute now the major repertory houses are going to have to assimilate *Porgy and Bess*. A costly proposition, I know, maintaining a large black company as well as a large white one; perhaps the breakthrough can come by establishing a house in which the black company simply sings *everything*.

The Houston company's restoration was just plain thrilling in part because it was so brilliantly sung (above all by the tall, willowy, musically and dramatically astonishing Clamma Dale) and in part because we could see now that Gershwin had made no bones about the bones he was putting rhythmic flesh on. It was all there in the overture when, after the massive chords and extended structural line that would ultimately embrace gale winds of every kind had been established, jazz piano took over, boldly. (We saw as well as heard it: a honky-tonk piano materialized behind a scrim.) What was happening, so early, even before the completely sung narrative had taken its first deep breath? Gershwin was declaring *himself*, insisting upon his origins, not only scrawling a signature in sound but daring to put a date to it as well. No operas are born timeless. They become timeless by acknowledging, musically, what time of day it was when they were written, by making airs of the air they inhaled-exhaled daily, and then by expanding—heart and lungs—until they've rounded the clock.

So we hear the clock ticking, ticking off a particular century and even a particular decade in that century; and if that involves some ricky-tick, so be it. Identity established, the work moves effortlessly into the plaintive, elongated, breathlessly sustained strains of "Summertime," opening the spectrum wide and paving the way for the impassioned chorales, the counterpointed laments, the fiercely descriptive cries of Catfish Row that accompany dice games, knife fights, green-sky hurricanes, emotional surrenders and betrayals. There is no back-and-forth to it, from pop to "opera" (with a single exception, readily correctable). It's a vast seam, permitting Gershwin to segue—directly, openly, candidly—from the piercing pain of a widow mourning the corpse at her feet into the familiar twenties beat of "Leavin' for the Promis' Lan'."

Again and again it's done, again and again it interferes not at all with what must be intensely dramatic in the so-called "grand" manner. We've no sooner done with Sportin' Life's "Scatty wah! Yeah!" as he slides in his two-toned shoes down the hillock that supports a blasted tree than we're face to face with the fugitive Crown's savage seduction of Porgy's Bess. If anything, the ebullience of "It Ain't Necessarily So" makes the violently contrasted emotion of what follows more ample: in performance, Miss Dale struggled tooth and nail to free herself of her attacker, then signaled her submission by working her way toward him on her knees, exactly—ironically—as she had done earlier with the gentle, crippled Porgy. She had been honoring Porgy; she was matching lusts with Crown. The same movement can be made to serve two dramatic purposes. The same score can be made to serve a "Scatty wah!" period vivacity and the violent passions that rule, against her will, a weak woman. The strict beat gives way to a raging, unpredictable heartbeat; that is all.

I mentioned one exception and it is trivial. When Porgy slips into the first notes of "I Got Plenty o' Nuttin'," the short "pop" phrases we know so well do seem, for a brief moment, an interpolation, something alien to the weave. I think that is because it takes off from dead air; there has been a brief musical silence, and the song has no tonal environment from which it can emerge, detaching itself gradually. Hearing it alone we are reminded of how it is, how it has been, all the times we *have* heard it alone; it wants, I think, some surrounding sound to launch it. The 1976 production did not find that sound.

But that's a small reservation to be voicing about a project that proved so much. Gershwin took on stature with *Porgy and Bess* not because it was an opera but because it was *his* opera; he had seen to that, and he was right. Now that we were hearing *all* he wrote for these happy and unhappy waterfront folk, women fanning themselves at the latticed windows, men drying their fishnets in the sun, children darting in and out beneath wrought-iron stairways belonging to some aristocratic past, the characters themselves took on a stature—a size and a splendor—we had never seen before. The music that had been so long missing lifted them up; they stood astride it like giants, long-suffering but secure now, conscious of power, eager to share a sound that was entire.

Curiously, I found myself asking: shouldn't our straight plays, when they touch their points of genuine passion, offer us something like music? There's got to be an equivalent, at the top; there's got to be.

8

St. Matthew
in Clown White

Early in the fidgety, color-splattered, and jubilant off-Broadway rock musical *Godspell*, a quotation from Buckminster Fuller popped up that sounded as though it might have a great deal to do with the unleashed energies that are bit by bit remaking the contemporary theater.

The quotation, spoken by a young man standing severely alone beneath a harsh white light bulb, went something like this: "I seem to be a verb—not a noun, not a category, not a thing." Within a few seconds after it was spoken, the stage was suddenly aswarm with tumbling, teetering, never-still clown children busy making a verb, not a weary noun, out of the Gospel of St. Matthew. (Have you ever noticed, by the way, that in circuses the clowns are always middle-aged, or elderly, men, never children? 'Twas high time we had them.)

Why make St. Matthew dance? Specifically, why make St. Matthew St. Vitus dance? Well, surely, for the obvious reason that after all these years of hearing and rehearing, of exegesis and apologia and conceptualization, we needed some sense of a man—whether Matthew or Jesus—who'd once moved, who'd put his feet against the earth with a push, who'd known wheat as wheat and not as a noun in a parable, who'd taken pleasure in the tangible, the muscular, the rhythmic, even in the giddy. Did no one in Galilee ever hum a little song to himself, snap his fingers, as he walked the roads?

I mustn't make the show sound self-important, or woozily prophetic, things it almost never was (not until the last fifteen minutes). But composer Stephen Schwartz and adapter-director John-Michael Tebelak, in conceiving of the return of the Prodigal Son as the occasion for a maddened polka determined to turn itself into a cakewalk, in cockily arranging an exultant "Let's hear it for the master!" when the mas-ter—in a patter-song parable—remitted a debt due him from a servant, in using ventriloquists' dummies and magicians' exploding flowers and vaudevillians' sandpaper slitherings to underscore beatitudes, were restlessly on the prowl for a visual vocabulary, and a scatter shot of sound, that would make the too familiar become active again, alive on its toes and happy to be up there.

Jesus, a red heart painted between his eyebrows and a modest but genuine grin spreading wide beneath a red-tipped nose, was surrounded by girls in pantalettes and patches, pom-poms and appliquéd ice cream cones. Starting them off on a question to which they would certainly know the answer ("If a man asks you for his shirt . . . ?"), Jesus whipped them all into that word game, known to my generation simply as The Game, that quickly becomes a forest fire of fingers. What does the provident man in Matthew fill his storehouse with? Why, with popcorn and tuna-surprise, of course (this to the accompaniment of a wheezy concertina with occasional sharp accent from guitars, cymbals, organ, drums).

The 1971 carnival was innocent, busy, and, above all, an uprush of *doing* (remember that verb we were talking about). Good seed being choked by weeds became a girl really getting it in the neck; the division of two sons' patrimony was quickly a plank snapped in half in midair; a moment of terror was mock Mack Sennett, hands flailing overhead as bodies hurtled backward around a fenced-off space. As director, Mr. Tebelak was never at a loss for a pantomime trick that would separate the sheep from the goats; he became a slapdash cross between Paul Sills and Peter Brook, maybe with bells on. And what he did was fun, neither reverent nor irreverent, just fun; it suggested that somewhere in the gospels there was meant to be some good news.

True, the Jesus of the revel was a bit too sweet, too naïve. Every once in a while you began to yearn for the toughness in Matthew that Pier Paolo Pasolini got into his film. When you were given this, though, at the end of the evening's second half, it wasn't good. The occasion became serious for the Last Supper (with paper cups) and the Crucifix-ion, and the seriousness was simply straight, with some of the lightning streaks wiped off the clowns' faces. The trouble here was that the seriousness had no stylization of its own, was not formally related in any way to the antic puppetry of what had gone before. *Godspell* wasn't *Jesus Christ Superstar*, a much more ambitious, musically complex piece of work. It couldn't change its spots—or the tips of its noses—at the last moment without becoming awkward. But until that last mo-ment it had made good its premise and its promise. The verb danced.

9

Quality Camped

The title page of the program for *Jesus Christ Superstar* as done in New York in 1971 stressed that Tom O'Horgan had not only directed the production but had "conceived" it. It was not an immaculate conception.

Before discussing Mr. O'Horgan's contribution to an entertainment that scarcely asked for such alms, however, I'd best say what I find good about the materials themselves—at least as I have heard them on records and as I was occasionally able to get a glimpse of them through the hallucinatory gyrations on stage. Lyricist Tim Rice has found for the rock musical a personal, and I think persuasive, tone of voice. The tone of voice is not merely mod or pop or jauntily idiomatic in an opportunistic way. It sheathes an attitude. It speaks, over and over again, of the inadequate, though forgivable, responses ordinary men always do make when confronted by mystery.

Jesus has passed through a crowd. He has been hailed, derided. The buzz is uncertain, mixed, agitated. Afterward some members of the crowd sing out cheerily to one another, "Did you see I waved?" They are more interested in what they have done than in what is going on before them.

The apostles, drowsy with wine on a Thursday evening and unaware of the mounting tensions between Jesus and Judas, comfortably carol to one another, "When we retire we can write the gospels, so we'll be remembered when we die."

When the cause is lost and Jesus is condemned, it is no tragedy. It is at once a sensation for the gossips and the newsmongers, to be translated swiftly into journalese, into the ready-made explanations for success or failure by means of which all of us try to grasp and pigeonhole events. Did Jesus think he got the breaks? "What would you say were your big mistakes?"

Mary Magdalene and a few friends, sensing the approach of the end, wonder if it wouldn't be better to go back and start over again in some other, safer way. "Don't you think you've made your point?" they ask Jesus, looking in anguish for a copout.

These are blunt, rude, purposefully unlyrical lyrics, not meant to coat any one historical period with a little literary flavoring but to catch hold of thought processes—venal, obtuse, human. Delivered in the jargon we more or less live by, they become woefully and ironically recognizable.

Andrew Lloyd Webber's score seems to me to function well, too, using rock as a frame rather than an obsession. The beat and blare establish an angle of hearing, telling us to cock our ears for the jumpy directness of the lyrics. Inside the frame, though, we're going to hear the genuine sweetness of Mary Magdalene's "Everthing's going to be all right," the ragtime insult of Herod's clog dance around and about his captive, the college-bowl exultation of "hosanna, heysanna" for Palm Sunday—that is to say, all, or nearly all, of the convenient sounds people reach for when they want to sorrow or celebrate. The music is unselfconscious in its borrowings from the melodious and the common-place; it wants to say that the world was commonplace then, as it is now, in the presence of what it could not, cannot, fathom. If it is young work, and work for the young, it has the consistency of innocence, of stumbling upon familiar things with surprise and reacting instantly in slang. *Jesus Christ Superstar* is a pop opera about pop attitudes, and for me it works.

All that needed to be done with it was put it on a stage baldly—baldness is very much of its essence—and, after establishing a few simple traffic directions, let it sing for itself. Instead, Mr. O'Horgan had adorned it. Oh, my God, how he had adorned it. Christ first appeared, flaxen-haired and willowy, rising from a huge goblet or chalice, draped in a silver sequined gown that could be spread to circus-tent propor-tions. He looked like Dolores in the *Ziegfeld Follies of 1924*.

Judas would have been easier to look at, if he'd ever been alone. He was never alone. He had as companions four purple creatures who strongly resembled those Goodyear tire men made of rubber rings that appeared in billboard advertisements when I was a boy, and their main fuction seemed that of intercepting Judas and tossing him about madly whenever he was in danger of getting a lyric across to an audience. Mr. O'Horgan was so determined never to illustrate a lyric—much too square a thing to do—that he almost always wound up obscuring it. If Mary Magdalene was finishing her charming "I Don't Know How to Love Him," she was not permitted to finish it in peace, hers or ours;

Jesus had to be dragged away from her, by four to six stalwart intruders, on what seemed a large slice of eggplant so that the song's ending would be characteristically blurred.

Even before we had met these three principal figures, Mr. O'Horgan had firmly asserted himself. What at first seemed a front curtain turned out to be more nearly a drawbridge; as it was lowered away from us a gaggle of loinclothed creepy-crawlers, virtually the O'Horgan trademark since *Futz* and *Hair* and *Lenny*, came scrambling over the top of it like lice on the loose. They served no purpose. They were simply there to let us know that Mr. O'Horgan was there, inventive fellow that he is.

The "Hosanna" procession began handsomely, stately figures clashing cymbals, white-robed girls raising silvered tambourines; it was then embellished by a gentleman carrying an enormous set of false teeth. A giant cornucopia, with what seemed a lizard's tongue dangling from it, was bandied about the stage while Pilate was attempting to get something done; mammoth caterpillars snaked in from the wings as the evening approached the Crucifixion, only to be instantly covered by a fog from smoke pots and retired before they had acquired any conceivable significance.

It wasn't simply that Mr. O'Horgan's impositions were irrelevant, though they were that (it remains a deep mystery to me how this man was able to identify himself with a counter-culture that prided itself on "relevance"). The worst—or next to worst—of it was that they deliberately interfered. In both the most obvious and the subtlest of ways, Mr. O'Horgan was eternally bent on cutting across what was good, or might have been good, severing head from body.

Take two small matters of rhythm. One of the most surprising, and satisfying, moments in the record album comes when Judas, now in torment over what he has been destined to do, moves without warning from his thrashing agony to the very simple line of Mary Magdalene's song, asking how he, too, should love Jesus. It was spoiled in performance because Mr. O'Horgan knew the shift was there and wantonly broke the orchestral movement to call attention to it. The link, the soft surprise, was killed.

Again, when Herod steps off into his show-biz buck-and-wing in the process of taunting Christ, the new tempo is meant to steal in and, in its stealth, be funny. Mr. O'Horgan took an ostentatious pause and then clumped into it, robbing it of its impertinent pleasure. He had, additionally, equipped Herod with built-up sandals which made it close to impossible for the performer to move in rhythm, just as he had costumed and painted him to seem a drag queen seated upon an amusement-park throne. A more or less traditional Herod doing a kick-step would have been abrasively amusing. This one was camp through and through. The interior contrast disappeared, the comment went flat.

But there was a worse problem to be dealt with, and it lay in the unbelievable vulgarity of Mr. O'Horgan's imagination. Not content with giving us a second spurious resurrection in which Jesus was pumped high into the air swathed in a cloak the size of *two* circus tents, he went on to a Crucifixion that began, rear stage, in a snail-shaped enclosure that might have been the Eye of God and then moved toward us—with the Cross gradually projecting itself from its traveling background—while all about tongues of fire darted like pinwheels into outer space. It was Death in 3-D, and Hollywood at its coarsest has never come up with the like.

I never did see any of the concert versions that were simultaneously touring the country, but I suspect that—having less money to spend and perhaps no O'Horgan of their own—they may very well have been, in their enforced austerity, much better.

10

Forever Fair

In a way, Robert Coote was the dare. I don't plan to spend much time here on the expansive, expostulating, enchantingly slow-on-the-uptake Mr. Coote, though paragraphs could be written—no, sonnets should be written, he deserves better than prose—on the manly pride he took in serving as dressmaker's dummy for Eliza Doolittle's first fancy-ball gown, or on the resolute manner in which he twitched his mustache in order to stimulate his thinking processes while calling Scotland Yard. But when in 1976 producer Herman Levin decided upon a full-scale revival of *My Fair Lady* just twenty years after its first breathtaking opening, and when he decided to recast Mr. Coote in the role he had created to begin with, he was both symbolizing and adding to the risk he knew he was taking: the risk of jogging memory. Everyone was already asking if it wasn't a bit too soon to be renewing our acquaintance with a musical-comedy masterpiece that had run so long so recently, already wondering if we'd be able to erase the likes of Rex Harrison and Julie Andrews from our heads. And wouldn't putting Mr. Coote back in his old place, surrounded by new faces, serve to *accent* what was different, what was missing, what was lost?

Uh-uh. All that happened was that Mr. Coote was twenty years funnier. While all that happened to *My Fair Lady* was that it proved twenty years stronger, a show so dazzlingly melodic and visually rich in its first act that it scarcely needed a second—and so emotionally binding in its second that you wondered why you were merely dazzled by the first. Structurally sound of wind and limb, skipping like springtime and living out its winters on wit, *My Fair Lady* isn't an entertainment that *requires* certain performers to bring off the Bernard Shaw–based libretto, the leaping Alan Jay Lerner lyrics, the sweeping Frederick Loewe score; it's an entertainment that *invites* any and all performers to simply lift the lid from its treasure chest and avail themselves of its glistening baubles.

Which brings me to Ian Richardson. Mr. Richardson is what is known as a gamut. His range is so great as to border upon the ridiculous; he should be parceled out among four or five lesser folk to make them independently wealthy for life. He has a singing voice, one that was appropriately held in reserve as he rapped out the rapid-fire speaking-on-tone that had been devised for Rex Harrison but that was eternally present nonetheless: you heard it behind the cantankerous Henry Higgins scoldings, you found yourself floating on it with every briefly held end note, you knew that it was going to do something radical to you sooner or later. At the same time, the actor moved dynamically, as though he'd been driven by a conductor's baton the whole of his life, whipping onto wing chairs with one foot planted on an arm as though he were Balboa sighting the Pacific and discovering himself mightily displeased with it, scaling staircases like a long-distance runner who didn't care whether he was lonely or not, fusing the beat from the pit with the lash of his tongue to flagellate the poor Liza he was going to turn from Cockney flower girl into princess without past or future.

Behind all of this, bless us, lay his Shakespearean background, which he was going to use to amuse us when opportunity arose. Opportunity arose. When it became necessary to frighten his spunkily rebellious pupil with ghastly visions of what would happen if she didn't submit with a sweet meekness to his round-the-clock strictures, he promised soulfully and sonorously that she would be clapped into the Tower of London, to be beheaded while hovering angels wept. The organ stops came out now, tremolos ferociously included, and, in his majestic mockery, he might have been any Richard (possibly II and III put together) prepared to wreak havoc in what was incontestably his realm.

Mr. Richardson was drawing upon resources that would have got him through a tragedy, though he was kidding both the resources and the tragedy while mesmerizing his victim. Nor was his comedy confined to playing jolly tricks with equipment few musical-comedy men have ever possessed. He was as sly and as nimble as a dyed-in-the-woolsack farceur when it came to disposing of dropped sugar lumps or avoiding the extremely powerful breath of Eliza's dustman father, a breath that quite threatened to extinguish the match with which he was trying to light his pipe. The man could do vaudeville, in an honest sort of way.

And we still haven't exhausted his readily tapped powers; it's a wonder he didn't exhaust us. Perhaps the very best thing he did was to call a halt to all the foolery, to pull up short before a thought he'd never had before or an emotion he really wanted no part of. He didn't make a jolt of it; he made a quiet revelation of it, so stunning to him that his pulse seemed to stop while he gave the thought all his gravity, so surprising to us that we were touched though we hadn't meant to stop laughing. Once he had had his triumph with Eliza, and granted her no part of the credit for it, he was first caught off-balance by her fury, then haughtily offended as she returned her finery and stomped doorward to pack her bag. He saw the sense of it instantly; he was of course a most logical man. The job was done, after all; what else was there for her here? Agreed, all agreed, however testily—"though," he added in sudden piercing reflection, "I hadn't realized you were going away."

The realization was that and no more; sentiment did not enter into it. He would miss her as he would have missed the wing chair if it'd vanished. The obtuseness of Henry Higgins was thoroughly protected, respected. Yet the sobriety, the intellectual earnestness, the sense of a man waking in the morning to remember that something had gone wrong the night before though he couldn't yet make out what, was so swiftly powerful that *we* picked up an emotional echo and held it for future reference. In the end these very small, very serious inflections came rushing to join all the élan, the bite, the up-and-down-the-scale humors to make of Henry Higgins's final song, "I've Grown Accustomed to Her Face," a simple, cumulative masterpiece. A number could not have summarized a performance, a character, and a show with more authority, more at last unleashed warmth, more grace.

Mr. Richardson would surely have overpowered Christine Andreas's Liza altogether if it hadn't been for the songs Frederick Loewe long ago bothered to bless her with. I confess to having had some difficulty with Miss Andreas's broad, quick Cockney in the early scenes, and found myself glowing with relief once Higgins's promised miracle had been accomplished and the rain in Spain had begun coming down plainly. (And *there's* a number that's also a genuine piece of drama for you!) When, in his profligacy, Mr. Loewe immediately followed with the lovely lyric openness of "I Could Have Danced All Night," permitting the actress' smile to become as broad as her heart beat high, Miss Andreas's work turned as expansive as it had hitherto been busily animated—and we all soared. This Liza was also especially fetching in a take-turns duet that I'd somehow let myself forget but that is surreptitiously most important to the play's shape: "Without You." As she nerved herself, moving enticingly, to the problem of getting along on her own, of acknowledging that spring would come again anyhow and she could surely make the best of it, she gave the evening the penultimate little lift it needed before going all out with Mr. Richardson's bravura climax. No reason why *My Fair Lady* shouldn't be revived and revived as long as there's justice, and a thirst for lilting bewitchment, in the world.

11

The March
of the Microphones

Liza, Liza, skies are gray. . . ." Hummed it, mournfully, all the way home.

I didn't mind so much that the various people, some careless, some nightclub knowledgeable, who'd put together *The Act* in 1977 had been opportunistic enough to keep Liza Minnelli onstage, singing and singing and dancing and dancing, throwing back her head and crooking her knee in that chanticleer stance we all know so well, the whole night long. If it was necessary that she perform so uninterruptedly that she hadn't time for a sip of water, a nibble on a sandwich, or an unflustered costume change (some were made onstage by ripping her apart or basting her together in more or less full view), she could still get something out of that.

She could get at least two show-stoppers and an occasional "bravo" from left field (at which she grinned, conspiratorially), though that wasn't exactly a monumental reward for the monumental work she'd been doing (twelve numbers by my count, not including reprises). She could manage a fast and brittle patter song about Hollywood gossip right along with the best of them (sailing blithely past some dated and unfunny Fred Ebb lyrics on the order of "When she smiles not only do her earlobes curl/She looks like Milton Berle"). She could snap suspenders and interlock legs with the athletically zany Roger Minami during an eruption called "Arthur in the Afternoon," she could ride aloft on crossbars and turntables to shiver her timbers and shoot an index finger at the sky, she could swiftly adopt the prance of a prize-winning pony to high-step it in and out of hoops that happened also to be tambourines.

And she could belt till her voice went broke. Coming straight on at us, snapping the brim of her white fedora much as mother Judy used to snap the brim of her black one, she attacked with a bold and regular and don't-say-no-to-me beat. Or, for occasional respite, she pulled all the way back, lingering at the proscenium perhaps, seeming to brush her hushed tones with her fingertips as she yearned for a man who'd be there when he was wanted. She was skilled, she was indefatigable, she was likable at every angular twist and turn, and she was wasting her best talents.

That's what I minded. With all the proficiency she's acquired, with all the power she brought to a downbeat (heavily miked), with all the magnetism she exerted in the thrust of an elbow or the lift of an ankle, singing and dancing weren't and aren't her truest gifts, which is probably why all the dances in *The Act* came to seem the same dance, all the John Kander songs the same song. Down deep, she's an actress, capable of nuance rather than force, vulnerability rather than sheer drive, mysteriously touching comedy rather than wide-eyed vaudeville "takes" (and if you don't believe me take another look at her film *The Sterile Cuckoo*). But it was precisely these qualities that weren't used, or were downright abused, in the Las Vegas ripoff we were offered.

Abused because the show had a book of sorts, a book requiring Miss Minnelli to interrupt her clockwork spins quite frequently so that she could fill you in on her forlorn backstage love affairs, her loneliness, her lost baby, her unhappy relationship with a stepdaughter, her mourning over a "gay" mentor who'd fallen dead onto the piano keys. Though these gloomy interludes were credited to the able George Furth, they were so cursory as to leave Miss Minnelli no time at all to develop a mood before she'd gone past it: she had to try being rueful ("What will we do with the baby clothes?") before she could squeeze out a teardrop, she had to try meaning "I need you" before she or the rest of us had felt anything stirring between her and the man she needed. (Barry Nelson was the man she needed; he was expert as always, but eternally rushing onstage to rush off. Breezing by, he was burdened with some exceedingly hoary jokes, blurting out "I've always wanted to make you—meet you, I mean" and then pretending embarrassment. Or was he pretending?)

The star was left, then, going through the motions of emotion before she'd been able to create any, and we were relieved, finally, when she got back into one or another of her sequined red, blue, and purple gowns to show off her legs again and earn her living on high kicks. But that was backward for Miss Minnelli, and *The Act* amounted to a present betrayal and a bad omen for the future. If she continues in mere floor shows, she can only turn into a mechanical doll. There's got to be a film script or a play lying fallow somewhere, one that will tease into life once more the actress' finest natural equipment. Liza, please look for it.

And what *about* this business of prerecording song numbers so that an entertainer onstage need only synchronize his or her lip movements to a tape played offstage and all is well? Or ill?

When it was disclosed during the run of *The Act* that Miss Minnelli had managed to save a little of the energy she needed to get through those twelve numbers by lip-synching three spots in the show, a small flap ensued. It promised to be a rather larger flap than that for the first few minutes—were people who were paying $25 to hear Liza in person really hearing Liza in person or were they under the thumb of a stage manager who was merely pressing buttons on a control panel?—but the instinctive outrage soon subsided. Nerves were soothed by assurances from the Shuberts, who had presented the stand-up song parade on Broadway, that no more than two brief moments and one longer spot had been so treated, and then only because no human being could possibly sing and dance so persistently and so feverishly as Liza did and still breathe. We do want our performers to breathe, don't we? And *Variety* followed up with a substantial editorial defending the practice, mentioning in passing that *A Chorus Line* and, very probably, certain other of our folk festivals haven't hesitated to back up their hard-working personnel with mechanical support. If the audience is none the wiser, or doesn't really care all that much, why not?

I say there's a very good reason why not, but I'm bound to make certain allowances first. The audience, it would seem, doesn't care very much. Or not for very long. Our stages have been miked, one way or another and finally one way *and* another, for years. Once footlights had been done away with and their little troughs left empty, it occurred to some bright soul that that minimum strip of downstage space might be used for another purpose: microphones could be distributed straight across the area to pick up and amplify voices so that they might be better heard throughout the house, above all— rather literally—in the balcony. There were initial protests against *that*. The theater, "purists" claimed, was meant to be live, just as actors were supposed to be trained to project. But the protests weren't going to get very far. Too many people profited from the change. Patrons who'd spent years all but falling over the balcony railings in their efforts to hear, or who'd been fretting in the "dead spots" that pop up here and there on the orchestra floor, were going to settle for the new dispensation. They could relax a little. Producers were relieved to be relieved of the complaints they'd always got from these same underprivileged theatergoers: no more letters, or not quite so many, going on and on about all the money they'd paid for a seat from which they "couldn't hear a single word." And the actors were content enough, temporarily anyway: they didn't have to work so hard. What's easiest for everyone has a way of winning out.

True, there were a few difficulties. The footlight microphones were more or less evenly spaced but they didn't really cover the entire territory, which meant that if an actor wandered off into the areas between them or—God forbid—got too far away from them by staking out an upstage position, he'd probably sound less commanding, not to mention distinct, than he had just a moment before. The difference wasn't marked enough to make him sound like Enrico Caruso downstage and Minnie Mouse upstage, but a certain undulation was detectable; and unless you really were Ethel Merman you weren't going to get any reputation as a belter unless you were standing smack over the orchestra pit, feet firmly planted on both sides of the source of all amplification.

To eliminate the unevenness, one or another electronics expert came up with what amounted to an actor's security blanket: the body mike. Concealed beneath his clothing, the performer carrried Western Electric with him, assuring him that he could now stray anywhere and remain in touch with his fellow man. Hitches here, too. One of the funniest effects I ever ran across was inadvertently achieved during a performance of Shakespeare in Central Park; doing Shakespeare, the actors naturally raised their voices a bit anyway, with the result that one actor's voice would penetrate another actor's body mike until you scarcely knew which was Hamlet, which Horatio, and which Edgar Bergen trying to quiet Charlie McCarthy. (The play wasn't really *Hamlet*, I've forgotten what it was; but whatever it was, it presented us with schizophrenia rampant.) Less funny was what some overzealous producer or director did to two fine performers, Barry Nelson and Tammy Grimes, in a perfectly straight Broadway play, not a musical. Though the setting was a small motel room and the mood of the evening intimate, he'd body-miked them to a fare-thee-well; not only did they *not* seem to be inhabiting the same building we were, they seemed to have commandeered bullhorns somewhere and to be calling the play in from Shea Stadium.

You'll notice that this was, and is, a creeping situation. The new body mikes didn't displace the footlight mikes; they just doubled them. If, as in *The Act*, a stand-up microphone was added because the numbers were supposed to be part of a Las Vegas floor show, the event could be considered triple-miked; and, for those brief moments when first aid was being piped in from the wings, urban electrification achieved heights hitherto undreamed of—quadruple miking. *A Chorus Line*, by the way, took decided exception to *Variety*'s listing it among the lip-synched, or quadruple-miked, breed, and rightly enough. The show didn't lip-sync, it just put actual singers around a supporting microphone in the wings to enlarge the sound onstage. That qualified as a retrenchment, and a gesture toward humanism; at least the added volume was coming from throats open on the premises. But any sort of retrenchment is rare. Over the years I have heard of only one singing actress principled enough, and stubborn enough, to refuse to wear a body mike when so instructed. Her name was Inga Swenson and she put her first starring role in a Broadway musical on the line rather than give in to a producer's orders to hook her up. She seems to have had no successors. It's not the name of the game. Where amplification is concerned, it's onward and upward and can't-we-computerize-it-all? Spreads like rice, you know. Once started, no turning it back.

And that's the rub. It's a long-term rub, sure enough; no one's going to start pulling plugs at any time in the near future so far as I can see, certainly not when Broadway's thriving and patently unthreatened by the mechanization it's embracing. But time may tell a somewhat different story. Logic has its own rights and sooner or later makes itself felt.

What is wrong with the miking of legitimate theaters, even *with* the interim assent of the public itself, is that what happens in those theaters will in time cease to be legitimate. Night by night and inch by inch, the specific character of the theater will be eroded—until, one miserable day, it will have no distinguishable identity at all. You will have heard this argument before, or portions of it anyway, but let's replay it briefly—and then go on to its unhappier implications.

When you go to "live" theater to see and hear a performer in the flesh, you expect to see and hear that performer in the flesh. Miked, you don't. You see the proper body up there, all right, but it's a body that's taken some leave of its vocal equipment. The voice does not make direct contact with you. It goes first into an electronic receiver and then travels around a triangle—from receiver to backstage controls to the amplification system hung on the walls or proscenium arch—before you pick it up. No time lapse, of course. Just a spirit lapse, a personal lapse, a fragmenting of contact. The body is physically with you, the sounds it produces have been artificially recorded and relayed. You're coping with the half-"live," which is not quite what has been advertised.

Unimportant? No. Contact is either total or it's not contact. You're looking at a physical and vocal presence that is an entity, a unit, an organism. The personality of the performer is related to, and helps produce, the quality of sound that comes from the muscles of the performer's diaphragm and throat. In life—and the theater is described as living—no part of any person is piped in. The person is known intimately and as a whole, in the interaction of sound and smile, the unbroken bond between recoil and scream. Character is deduced from the immediacy, the simultaneity of what can be described as a double response—physical, vocal—but is actually a single one. If, for instance, the scream is a small one compared to the physical contortions accompanying it, we know that the scream is fishy. We instantly distrust it; someone's trying to deceive us. (Comedy is made of this discrepancy in Vanbrugh's *The Relapse*: a woman who's being carried off to be ravaged puts up a considerable show of physical resistance but utters only very tiny cries of "Help! Help!") But no scream, no challenge, no lyric is ever going to be quite that small when amplified. In fact, amplification won't let us know precisely what relationship the scream bears to the movement; we can't be sure of our judgment in the matter. And so a little bit of truth is lost, a lie of indeterminate size creeps in.

The breakdown of the organism is much more clearly seen in certain films, where there *is* a time lapse between the shooting of a scene and the dubbing of voices. Suddenly we notice that the actor's throat muscles and even shoulder muscles aren't in proper proportion to what we're hearing—and we disbelieve. In fact, the first time the film audience discovered that something had been dubbed—Richard Barthelmess's singing voice in an early Warners sound film called *Weary River*—there was a much greater outcry than anything we've heard along Broadway. The cheating became a scandal and for a time it seemed that Mr. Barthelmess's career might not survive it. The protest died down, of course, as it usually does—audiences give in, for a while, if they're enamored of the experience in general—and film *was* a mechanical medium, wasn't it? In due time virtually everything was being put together piecemeal inside studios—faked backgrounds as well as faked voices—and, though the process made a liar of the camera (whose proudest boast had been that it could not lie), it was tolerated. You'll notice, however, that there are no big assembly-line studios any longer. A dozen reasons can be given for their disappearance; ultimate disillusion has got to be one of them.

But that's another story. The theater can never be entirely dishonest, unless they start sending in robots to do the night's work, and its deceptions can be considered minimal alongside what went on in Hollywood. But, as I've said, these deceptions tend to multiply as microphones have already multiplied, and a bare three minutes of lip-synching today can tomorrow spread to cover every sizable production number in a show. Something trivial can become something massive, if no alarm is ever sounded, no serious thought given to ultimate consequences.

What consequences? Three. Even at its least offensive—let's say simple footlight miking—amplification robs live performers of a degree of naturalness. Relayed sound isn't natural, not in the strict sense. It's artificial, and it artificializes what reaches our ears. Of course, we're accustomed to this loss of absolute fidelity. We hear it all the time, accept it in films, on television, even in the finest of recordings. Test this by noticing the sound that greets you with the initial blare of music at the beginning of a film. Compared to live sound, there's a faint underwater quality to the opening swell, almost an earthquake groan as the ground shifts beneath your feet and you realize, fleetingly, that you're leaving one perceived world (the natural world) and entering another (the mechanically reproduced world). This impression quickly dissolves because we have for so long adapted ourselves to it. And film really has no choice but to give us this less than perfectly faithful substitute. But the stage? The stage *can* be perfectly natural.

Amplification's second victim, if the dubbing that's now begun makes further inroads, must be spontaneity. Lip-synching locks a performer in. Voice prerecorded, the entertainer is required to make faces exactly matching a sound he's not producing at the moment, to vary his performance not an inch, not a split second. He can't rephrase, he can't hold a note longer than the control panel dictates, above all he can't respond to an improvisational impulse, an inspiration that's just hit him. *Certainly* he can't engage in any give-and-take with an audience. One of the theater's greatest virtues is the fact that audience and entertainer literally do play with each other, responding freely and freshly and adjusting a joint rhythm from moment to moment. A laugh may be bigger on Saturday than it was on Monday; the actor can wait for it, so as not to destroy his next line. Indeed, the whole work of a performer lies in feeling out his audience bit by bit, testing reactions, tossing out bait and judging just when it's been taken, tugging the caught spectator in at precisely the right moment—a different moment each night. The theater's special miracle is the fusion that can come about when the two parties, mutually parrying, finally meet, feel secure in each other's company, shake hands on the deal and go forward together. But this is something that has to be worked out anew at every performance—the audience is new at every performance—and it can't be done at all if there's no room for maneuvering, if the players are in any way blocked. Tamper with this at your peril.

And the third of amplification's threats is that it weakens the

theater's ability to compete by making it sound exactly like the competition—producing the sounds that films and television make and nothing more. If a medium is to compete for any length of time it must
stress what is unique about it, what it possesses that competing forms
do not possess. Film has its infinite range of place, time, and angle of
vision to secure its distinction; the stage can't hope to manage all that.
Television *is* film nowadays; one of the things that's been going on
during the past twenty years is a battle to death between film in public
on a large screen and film at home on a small one. For the stage to
enter this particular battle by appropriating any part of its rivals'
equipment or effect is a suicidal business: power—money and access to
the mass audience—are all on the opponents' side.

The only way the theater can hold onto all the new patrons it's
acquired during the mid-seventies, and even add to them as the love
affair intensifies (if it does), is by consistently creating for them an
experience they cannot have anywhere else: which means an experience of uncorrupted liveness, genuine intimacy, and integrated naturalness, bubbling spontaneity, honest-to-god give-and-take.

X

AND
A SIDE-GLANCE
AT FILM

1

Why I Hate Paddy Chayefsky

In April of 1972 I spent at least a week hating Paddy Chayefsky. Hating Paddy Chayefsky because he had just dumped a whole tubful of hard-driving, candid, scratchily sophisticated dialogue into a film when the film didn't need it all and our stage is still starved to death for it. In times like these, you've got to hate a man for that.

There I was, on one of those rare nights when the off-Broadway theater wasn't offering a revival of *Rain*, slipping away to a movie just to get the stage off my mind for a while, sitting comfortably before what I thought would simply be a *movie*. (A movie is something you relax with; a film is the same movie after it has been approved by five critics.) The critics had been this way and that about *The Hospital*, mainly because it went through one identity crisis after another ("What kind of little film *am* I?" it seemed to ask itself every so often), but George C. Scott was in it and that seemed a decent enough excuse for dropping by.

And then the language began to hit the amplifier. Blunt language (not blunt in the sense of Ed Bullins's favorite twelve-letter epithet dropped twice into every line but blunt in the sense of naming things that were on the minds of the people in the film), agitated language (George C. Scott screaming at length in an open doorway, racing to get his rancor out before it throttled him), meaningful language (the people kept talking until they'd found out what they *did* want), informed language (the people seemed to live on the planet and not to have been processed in some rehearsal studio). By the time that Mr. Scott, brilliant as ever and thinking matters through freshly scene by scene, got around to a blistering, self-mocking, society-baiting harangue capped by a clenched fist and a savagely impertinent slogan ("I'm impotent. I'm proud of it. Impotence is beautiful!"), I was in a state of despair.

Instead of enjoying the movie (though I secretly was), I was writhing. Why is this sort of speech so rarely heard on the stage anymore, when it is obviously and properly and by birthright stage speech? Compared to what I was hearing, almost all stage dialogue nowadays— with rare exceptions—is polite, plasticized, timid, studied, self-conscious, and, God help us, naïve. It walks on the stage like a stork, spindly and stand-offish.

I don't mean to say that Mr. Chayefsky is Mr. William Shakespeare, lost to the fleshpots. But no one has to be William Shakespeare to write a line that lunges long enough, plunges deep enough, to give an actor (a stage actor) like Mr. Scott a chance to heave, snarl, snort, perspire, and grin ferociously before he's got the whole thing out. And this sort of opportunity is traditionally a stage opportunity: the tirade, the soliloquy, the verbal breaking of the dam. *The Hospital* could have been made with half its words, film's verbal requirements are so minimal. Too many tend to clot the screen; it's on stage that they're free to flow openly, like a cut vein. And yet, and yet. The film had them, the stage didn't.

Neither is this an appeal for Mr. Chayefsky to go back to the theater. He's been there, and doesn't like it anymore, for reasons of his own: he'll tell you his reasons, I'm sure, any four hours of the day or night. (Interestingly, the formal uncertainties of *The Hospital* have not only turned up in Mr. Chayefsky's stage work, they have sometimes been made part of its strength: *The Tenth Man*, for instance, was a very odd combination of neighborhood naturalism and a zany use of the occult.) The loss is not a matter of any one man, any one tongue. It's a matter of near-universal hesitancy, inhibition, a tendency to regard the stage as a medium so artificial that its most obvious gestures must be overexplained (hence the comparative naïveté), its verbal footwork be done cautiously across broken glass (hence the holdback rhythm, the gingerly stride). The stage has become persuaded that it must do its work in baby talk.

Of course I'd admittedly had a bad week in the theater. A musical of staggering ineptitude called *The Selling of the President* had opened and then thoughtfully closed. Dedicated to satirizing the hard sell that makes our presidential candidates palatable, it began by casting the clearly palatable Pat Hingle in the leading role, making the hard sell superfluous. It then removed the hard sell, settling for small, cloying jingles. Its dialogue, which seemed to have been copied from a *Little Golden Book of the World of Politics* by a child short on reading skills, rarely bothered to pretend to wit or even to a wistful wryness. When it did, it got this far: the candidate's wife complained that their new sauna "must be broken, it's so hot." What *is* the theater that it can open its backstage doors to a television comic's refuse?

And there had been a revival of *Rain*. You thought I was kidding. There had not only been *Rain*, there had been rain, enough of it sloshing down from pipes in the ceiling to spray the entire first four rows of the auditorium, causing one woman in the opening-night audience to put up her umbrella.

The production had been unusual in a number of ways. For one thing, the house lights kept flickering on and off during the performance, and so did the exit lights. Hinting, I suppose. More than that, the evening had been cruel and inhuman, above all to a performer named Madeleine Le Roux, who had been rather noticeable in the nude in *The Dirtiest Show in Town*. Someone had had the notion of clothing Miss Le Roux this time, specifically in the finery—fluffy pink feathers, high-button boots, a parasol that seemed fringed with spinach—of Sadie Thompson. Clothed, she lacked equipment. With a frozen upper lip and a voice like a baseball bat, she instantly became a parody of Donald Duck doing Mae West. Nor did James Cahill, as the Reverend Davidson, run her a poor second. Wigged like the Wicked Witch on furlough from Oz, Mr. Cahill clutched onto his own hands as though fearful that one of them would fly away and boomed the play's dialogue with the nuances of a bullhorn.

The dialogue of *Rain* is elderly now, but it is in some ways instructive. One can feel tenderly about it as a doctor's wife enters a totally deserted Pago Pago house of all trades, stands looking for a couple of minutes, and then murmurs, "No one seems to be about." It's a bit harder to keep a straight face when Sadie sashays around a table announcing, "Oh, no, Mr. Davidson, your God and me could never be shipmates" or when the minister's wife, alarmed by his long absence, exclaims, "It's been raining for four days, the air is full of poison from rotting plants!"

But you can say a couple of things about it. You know when a curtain's coming down. When the minister's wife stands center stage and says, "All I know is that I wouldn't be in that girl's shoes for anything in the world!" a curtain is coming down. And when Sadie decides to haul off and tell Davidson exactly what she thinks of him, or when Davidson decides to make an all-out pitch for a bad girl's soul, there are speeches, long, loud speeches. They remain the speeches of 1922, but any actor who *is* an actor could still make some use of them to discharge his energies. Mr. Scott could play Davidson today, without a hitch.

Well, *Rain* can't save us now. But we are in an odd situation. The times are harsh, each of us knows what it is to be roiled, there are unspent furies all over the place, we have our tongues. And yet words turn up on a screen, while the stage makes little clucking noises, laying-in its exposition chastely, keeping cool over drinks, clipping off the ends of sentences lest they seem pushy, taking ever so much care not to disturb the neighbors. You might almost say that a lot of today's theater goes out of its way to avoid scenes.

2

In the Center Ring,
Bette Davis

One evening in 1977 we sat down to our television sets to watch Bette Davis receive from the American Film Institute—hell, we could imagine her practically snatching it out of their hands—the annual Life Achievement Award that had thus far been bestowed only upon John Ford, James Cagney, William Wyler, and Orson Welles. Heady company, heavyweights all, suitable predecessors for the lady who had pumped lead into her lover at the very beginning of *The Letter* and made you believe that the power hadn't come from the pistol but from the thrust of her shoulders, the arch of her back, the blaze of her oversize eyes. Suitable predecessors, too, for the wench who'd been willing to execute any number of Warner Brothers, if the need arose, in order to earn the right to execute Errol Flynn, whack Humphrey Bogart across the face, spit at that nice Leslie Howard. Anyone with a taste for fantasy had probably already visualized her, at the ceremonies, clutching the trophy to her breast for a moment before turning aside to hang up her boxing gloves, tuck away her horsewhip, and file down her fingernails to a gentle, no longer lethal, curve. After all, she'd won, hadn't she? She was the champ, wasn't she? And that's what she'd wanted from the beginning, right?

Wrong, I say, now that I've looked back at an assortment of her films ranging from her very first clinker, *Bad Sister*, to the twilight-of-a-career masterwork, *All About Eve*, in which she played—to a fare-thee-well—not the person she was but the legend she'd become, and passing en route what seems to me the definitive Bette Davis vehicle, *Now, Voyager*. These Davis landmarks contradict one another crazily, but what emerges is not a creature who wished to become Kid Goliath, daughter of White Fang. What she wanted to be was a lovely loser, shy, pliant, docile, and long-suffering, an eternal ingenue eternally shedding warm tears of gratitude on a strong man's shoulder. The only problem was that she had to beat the living daylights out of Hollywood to prove how vulnerable she was.

You probably don't believe a word of this, and you certainly won't have seen many of the earlier films lately—I have a feeling they wouldn't even *allow Bad Sister* on television, it's so primitive-grisly— which means I'd better try to explain. In *Bad Sister*, the Universal sub-jewel that brought her to Hollywood from a beginning career on Broadway, she isn't the bad sister. She's the good one, and a real mess. As she waits around and waits around, closing doors regretfully and drooping through the portieres while her wicked brunette sibling, Sidney Fox, keeps both Conrad Nagel and Humphrey Bogart on the string, Miss Davis seems to have wandered in from Bela Lugosi's set—Universal had a lot of vampires around in those days—looking for a Bloodmobile. Everything about her is white: dress, skin, eyelids, hair. If she'd had a trace of prettiness in her, you couldn't possibly have known: no emphasis. She looks like a flag of surrender.

Clearly the cameraman was embarrassed by her. He dwells suspiciously on her back, once he obscures her face entirely by plunking down a baby carriage in front of it, and when city-slicker Bogart comes to a family dinner—he has a *lot* more hair than Conrad Nagel, nicely parted in the middle—the festivities are half over before we discover that Miss Davis is at the table. In spite of the cameraman's efforts, our heroine was noticed by *The New York Times* reviewer: "Miss Davis' interpretation of Laura," he wrote, "is too lugubrious and tends to destroy the sympathy the audience is expected to feel for the young woman."

The actress Fay Bainter once told me that the *only* thing a celebrated director said to her during the entire out-of-town tryout of a faltering new play was "You're not going to play it *that* way, are you, Fay?" If *Bad Sister* proved anything at all, it was that Bette Davis was an ingenue in appearance and in spirit, all right, but that she just couldn't play it that way. She didn't dare ask for pity outright: too sickly, going on terminal. In the next year or so she managed to squeak in two more films at Universal, then another three at lesser lots, but she was plainly going to be swept up along with the other autumn leaves.

At which point George Arliss happened. Miss Davis hasn't done everything for herself down the years; sometimes she had luck. Mr. Arliss, after what seems to have been no more than a cursory interview, took her on for his true love in *The Man Who Played God*. Mr.

Arliss may have seemed a bit old for her, but that was part of the plot. He was a concert pianist, she his protégée, in love with him out of awe, loyal to him even after he'd lost his hearing, loyal to him even after she'd fallen for Donald Cook. The part called for some determination, a bit of spunk. It also called for a couple of other things: she had to be a "good-looker" if she wasn't to make a liar of the script, and she had to live up to a line that described her as wearing "all the latest California-style clothes." The transformation doesn't seem as startling now as it did to me when I was a lad of nineteen, but from our very first glimpse of her it's there: the dresses aren't at all slinky yet but they give her body enough shape to keep it from blurring into her face; the cloche hat frames her features so that they can be distinguished from her hair; she's acquired lips and eyelashes, courtesy of the Warner Brothers make-up department. Streamlined, on the smart side, speaking up for herself gallantly—albeit with a characteristic urge to self-sacrifice. She is only kept from giving up Cook by Mr. Arliss's deep wisdom—Mr. Arliss was very deep, very wise—in an exchange which contains one of my favorite lines of 1932: "You've behaved like a gentleman, Grace, and perhaps I admire you more than I could ever have loved you." Good boy.

Mr. Arliss may have done her one other favor, though not everyone thought it a favor at the time. The actor's tightly compressed lips were never expressive in themselves. He used them for getting the words out, swiftly and precisely, depending upon his eyes to carry the emotion of the moment. Did she learn the trick from him, firing off a clatter of words at typewriter pace while she invited you to look elsewhere for what she was thinking and feeling? Crisp tongue but dissolving pools just a few inches above. The *Times* reviewer was put off: "Bette Davis, who plays Grace, often speaks too rapidly for the microphone." This became the microphone's problem, not hers. Let technology catch up as best it could, Miss Davis was now fully, sleekly equipped to play magazine editors.

Which is, in effect, what she did for the next fifteen films. Audiences had been alerted to her, Warners had signed her to a contract, she was available to play anything Glenda Farrell or Joan Blondell wasn't already doing. The Davis legend always has her clawing her way steadily to the top, ferociously bearding Jack Warner in the Warners' den, issuing ultimatums about better parts Or Else. Can't be so, no matter what little things she may have said to the management from time to time. *Any* woman, *any* actress of hidden resources, who could have obediently, and even zestfully, plowed her way through those fifteen nondescript films *has* to have been one of the most docile, cooperative, gamely long-suffering, patient, pliable, and probably prompt workhorses ever to visit the planet.

You often did feel she was visiting in the films, partly because the plots might lose her once they really got started, partly because of her own bright and breathless "I can only stay a moment" tempo. But if she seemed in slightly sharper focus than most of the folk around her, as though she had a party to go to the minute she finished work and was already tingling with anticipation, she also made herself appear to be having fun. No doubt it *was* fun to be a part of that Warners stock company so fondly remembered by film buffs today: in the James Cagney starring film, *Jimmy the Gent,* she had Allen Jenkins and Alan Dinehart for company, in *The Bureau of Missing Persons* she had Pat O'Brien, Ruth Donnelly, and Hugh Herbert, in *The Dark Horse*—in which she *played* the Glenda Farrell part—Frank McHugh, Guy Kibbee, and Sam Hardy were around. But of course the whole point about a stock company is that it's a revolving operation: few of the people in it are going anywhere, except into a slight variation of the same part next week or next month. She'd been given a new look and a new career; and she was on a treadmill. She wasn't going to become a star.

Everyone knows that the breakthrough came with the heartless, cheaply artful, greedy, and vituperative Cockney waitress of *Of Human Bondage*, and there's no need here to go back over the electrifying performance that—to Hollywood's eternal embarrassment—didn't get an Academy Award. Except perhaps to note one thing: that this particular actress, given her particular equipment, had had to ask for neither sympathy nor admiration in order to get both. Was that a clue to something? Curious. But we mustn't leap ahead too quickly, because Warner Brothers didn't. What most people don't know or don't remember is that after *Of Human Bondage*, made on loan-out to RKO, the actress returned to her own studio to slave, dutifully, through nine more films, all but two of which—*Dangerous* and *The Petrified Forest*—were almost spectacularly mediocre. It was as though nothing had happened: no acclaim for *Of Human Bondage*, no belated, bad-conscience Academy Award a year later for *Dangerous*. Anyone surprised that at this point the lady blew up? We haven't been dealing with much of a rebel; more like The Mouse That at Long Last Roared.

The blowup was spectacular while it lasted, with flights to England, refusals to work, injunctions against working elsewhere, suits and countersuits. Miss Davis lost, legally; she could go back to Inhuman Bondage or get out of films altogether. Back she went only to discover, possibly to her great surprise, that in losing she'd won: the direct result of her temper tantrum was sweetness and light. By showing her teeth, she'd earned the right to be treated not necessarily as an ingenue—even an ingenue must come of age after thirty-one films—but at least as a lady. Three things promptly happened:

(1) The Brothers Warner fell all over themselves spending money on her films: for dialogue that would unleash the intelligence behind that tricky tongue of hers, for supporting companies with a bit of class about them, for settings that no longer looked as though someone were saving money on the electric bills, for directors who hadn't been hanging around the lot since Dolores and Helene Costello were tots. The cigarettes alone must have cost them a fortune: Miss Davis soon took up smoking with a vengeance, miraculously managing to snatch six or seven quick drags per sentence and often puffing up such a billowing aura about her that the enhanced production values were all but obscured. William Wyler was called in to direct *Jezebel*, the first film to make the most of the family reunion, and he not only trained our attention on her delectable deviousness—she is something to see as she spins a parasol faster than Japanese acrobats can, or as she keeps half a nervous eye on the walking stick with which Henry Fonda means to thrash her while taming him with a little-girl smile—but he photographed a film that remains stunning for its camera placements alone. She was mistress of the manse now, marching to Max Steiner.

(2) The legend jelled. Add the vixen of *Jezebel* to the jinx of *Dangerous* to the trollop of *Of Human Bondage* and you've arrived at the image that would demand she play *The Letter* as a mere way-stop to *The Little Foxes*. In fact, it scarcely became necessary to motivate her behavior: neither *Dangerous* nor *Jezebel* bothers to offer an initial rationale for her unruly conduct. In *Dangerous* she is dangerous simply because she is Bette Davis; in *Jezebel* she is a jezebel for exactly the same reason, that and no more. An electricity crackled about her now that sent out its own warnings, she entered a room as though she were slicing it in half with a knife, disaster areas blossomed where her stride had stirred a breeze. Audiences identified her with a malicious dynamism—for good and sufficient reason, to be sure; and critics would have her no other way. *The New York Times* reviewer objected sternly to Miss Davis's reform at the conclusion of *Jezebel*, sure that she ought to have "remained unregenerate to the end." He only liked her when she was being "hateful" and thought it "a shame to temper that gift for feminine spite."

(3) *Because* this became the Davis iconography, *because* we knew she carried fury inside her and could unleash it whenever she chose, Miss Davis could go back to being a good girl again. Safely. This is the part we forget, even when we remember the films in which she made

the trip back home. Ever see *The Great Lie*? She looks like a pale little schoolgirl, with a white flower in her hair, alongside that towering brute of a brunette, Mary Astor. Miss Astor's the heel here—and dandy, as ever. Miss Davis is the unlucky-in-love slavey who cares for her and cares for her, asking for nothing in return but the right to rear another woman's child. O most noble soul! Of course you recall *Dark Victory*, with our girl realizing that she is at last going blind and rising from the flowers she's been planting in the garden to go to her deathbed with dignity, uncomplaining, alone. Films of this kind appeared at least as regularly as the Wicked Witch films in the twenty-four she made between *Jezebel* and *All About Eve*, and there seems to have been only one precaution they had to take. Each had to display the steel in her spine at least once. Having briefly reminded us of her mettle, she was free to melt as gracefully as she liked into the lemon meringue she was made of.

That's why *Now, Voyager* is irresistible even now. Do you know what it is, really? Cinderella, the Ugly Duckling, the Evil Stepmother, *The Wild Child*, and *Brief Encounter* incredibly, effortlessly, immaculately tucked into one another like a clap-shut telescope. All this and Claude Rains, too. Miss Davis has to have believed in fairy tales, from Goody Two-Shoes on up, to have appeared as she first does in the film: rimless glasses, hair flattened down hopelessly and then braided across the top of her head, dowdy print dress to make her shapeless again, shoes that seem to have been designed for Mr. Howard's clubfoot in *Of Human Bondage* except that she is wearing *two* of them, too inhibited to keep a teacup from rattling against its saucer, utterly incapable of saying boo to a goose. She is the victim incarnate, victim of a wealthy Boston mother so domineering that only Gladys Cooper could possibly have persuaded an audience that such an ogre might exist. No venom in Miss Davis; Miss Cooper's cornered the market.

Temporarily rescued by psychiatrist Rains, playing the Good God ever so cheerfully, the lady undergoes a decided transformation: next time we see her, descending from shipboard, she's ineffably sleek, the curved brim of an enormous hat proclaiming her new-found sophistication. It's as though the washout of *Bad Sister* had turned into a magazine editor all over again. But only on the outside. Inside, she's the same quivering waif, unable to believe a man could conceivably love her, unable, for that matter, to light her own cigarettes—which is how Paul Henreid became celebrated for his romantic little trick of lighting two at once, and then sharing. Mr. Henreid's married, of course, but love is love and in due time the astonished girl is shedding tears of gratitude all over his manly lapels.

No descent into soup, though. Spine-time. Surrendering Mr. Henreid to his wife, and not for the last time, Miss Davis returns home with just enough fresh confidence to do battle, toe to toe, with Mother Cooper, who is still bent on possessing, and even redowdyizing, her chick. We know who's going to win this time, and Miss Cooper winds up dead as a Boston cod. Of natural causes, I hasten to add; Miss Davis no longer requires anything more lethal than her unyielding will. Having given us what we demand of her—proof that an ever-so-shy girl can have guts, too—she is at liberty to devote the rest of the film to loving-kindness, saving Mr. Henreid's own ugly-duckling fourteen-year-old from neurotic despair, returning him to his obligations once more while she contents herself—chin tilted, honey-colored hair sweeping upward from the nape of her neck—with the stars. The film's last line is a sentimental horror; everything else about *Now, Voyager*, so far as Bette Davis is concerned, is Honest Injun.

For this is what she was, no doubt is. A girl who had to become heavyweight champ in order to get permission to play water boy. A girl who had to become shameless as an actress, savagely let herself go, in order to persuade us of her ingenue decency. A not really pretty girl, and for far too long a much too patient one, who had to let us see her tough and had to let us see her cheap before we'd take her on her own terms, neither tough nor cheap but quickly warm and pliant. A girl who had to exercise demonic power in order to exorcise the demon of her blandness, and who was then able to say to another ugly duckling—Mr. Henreid's decidedly unpretty offspring—"There's something else you can have if you earn it, a kind of beauty." And say it not soppily but with unselfconscious conviction. TNT became her trademark, and she used TNT often; cunning pro that she was, she used it to make herself fragile and to make up like her that way.

Good girl.

3

The Visual Verb

Whether you thought John Bishop's 1977 *The Trip Back Down* a most promising piece of work, as I did, or whether you found it a less than vigorous showcase for the bravura talents of actor John Cullum, there was one rap the play shouldn't have had to take. Again and again I came across the suggestion—even the judicial pronouncement—that *The Trip Back Down* didn't belong on a stage, or to the theater, at all. Why? Because it was about stock-car racers, a subject only films could possibly hope to cope with.

At first blush, and blush it should be, there seems some sense in the proposition. As the battered racers straggled into barrooms to drown themselves in beers and compare notes on how bad it had been "driving on walls," as the chap with one arm in a sling managed to sign an autograph no matter what, as the drivers relieved their own tensions by gleefully remembering a time when a car had spun completely around and plunged the wrong way against the whole raging field, it was plain enough that if we'd been able to go to the track with the drivers instead of picking them up after the day's harrowing work was done, there'd have been something to see.

Film could certainly have made the most of that—and has, about twenty thousand times. When one of the bruised contenders brushed back his Stetson to insist that ninety-four percent of stock-car fans came only to see the wrecks, he was probably right. He was also summoning up familiar film images, with all of those wildly spinning wheels tumbling over and over in midair to land, explosively, dead in the path of four more oncoming cars. Maybe ninety-four percent of the people who go to *movies* go to see the wrecks, too.

But, the argument ran, since film can show these things and the stage can't hope to, playwrights should forget about the material altogether, surrendering to the competition whole areas of subject matter. I object. I object on about seventeen grounds, of which I will give you no more than two.

(1) I can see no reason why the theater should surrender any subject whatsoever to any other form, because the theater has its own means of achieving the special effects demanded by a particular narrative. It always has had. After all, some pretty nasty things happen to a speeding chariot in Racine's *Phedre*, and the event has, since 1677, provided the play with one of its most powerful passages. The event isn't shown, of course. It's reported, in a handy little medium called language, and in Robert Lowell's faithfully rhymed translation a fragment of it runs like this:

> ...*and then the horses, terror-struck, stampeded.*
> *Their master's whip and shouting went unheeded,*
> *they dragged his breathless body to the spray.*
> *Their red mouths bit the bloody surf, men say*
> *Poseidon stood beside them, that the god*
> *was stabbing at their bellies with a goad.*
> *Their terror drove them crashing on a cliff,*
> *the chariot crashed in two, they ran as if*
> *the Furies screamed and crackled in their manes,*
> *their fallen hero tangled in the reins. . . .*

That's just ten lines. The complete description requires seventy-five. And a vivid, chilling seventy-five lines they are, too, providing the play with both the graphic illustration and the dramatic shock it requires. All that is essential is accomplished, without stunt men and/or process shots. Need I mention Shakespeare's shipwrecks, which are rather frequent? Of course, neither Racine nor Shakespeare had film to compete with, and could set about their tasks unselfconsciously; they, poor souls, were just doing the best they could. So suppose we come closer to home. Does anyone really think that David Storey oughtn't to have written *The Changing Room* because he couldn't *show* the rugby game upon which everything else in his play depended?

In point of fact, Mr. Bishop's *The Trip Back Down* took care of its own needs handily. Early in the second act, while hero John Cullum was mournfully contemplating the fact that he'd never be anything but third-rate, a younger man who had once seen him win devoted a moment to remembering that triumph. More than a moment. Four or five minutes by the clock. Needless to say, Mr. Bishop hadn't written the passage in verse; he'd used the prosy, colloquial speech patterns that the contemporary theater has long since adopted as "natural." But as Charles Brant, playing the hero-worshipper, launched into his self-hypnotized account of the flying dirt, swerving cars, and breakneck finish of that day, the audience fell silent, as mesmerized as he. When he was through and sank into his chair, eyes glazed with exhaustion that was also exhilaration, there was instant, solid applause. The theater was doing the theater's work the theater's way all over again.

(2) *The Trip Back Down* wasn't a play about stock-car *racing*, as, say, *Downhill Racer* was pretty much a straightforward film about skiing. It was a play about stock-car *racers*, which meant that it was primarily concerned with psychology, not spectacle. Its business was to let us know how human beings feel *after* they've climbed out of those dizzyingly sideswiped shells, wrecked or otherwise. And how other human beings feel about *them*.

On this score, Mr. Bishop had hit most of his targets but missed the main one. The real defect in his play as it stood was that he had given Mr. Cullum no psychological movement from beginning to end: this once ambitious man knew from the outset that he was through as a serious contender; he returned to the home, wife, and child he had exchanged for a promise of glory with that certain knowledge in his eyes; he ended by abruptly returning to the races still carrying the canker with him. Even so able an actor as Mr. Cullum could do little more with his helplessly static situation than find new expressions for registering pain while he listened to the real scenes being played about him.

The real scenes were all given to the sideliners, and they were uniformly arresting. A tired sister-in-law, steadily sipping beer as she did the family laundering, confessed that she had loved him since high school but had been too much in awe of him to show it; now, perhaps, they might do something about it? A father, reliving the lost euphoria of his return from Bataan, yearned for the days when he and his buddies had been "resourceful, wiry, dangerous, wild young animals coming out of the jungle." A wife behaved as decently as she could with a man who'd deserted her for a daydream. A racing friend froze his upper lip into a smile and went on making jokes of the ultimate disaster all were due for. Under Terry Schreiber's direction, the surrounding performances were as thoughtful as they were energetic; though they revolved about a ghost, the parts had been substantially written.

Having accomplished so much, Mr. Bishop should be encouraged to stay with us. He's got a grasp of the territory. And there was never any need to send him packing off to films, even if a film was due to be made of *The Trip Back Down*. We *can* have it both ways.

4

Katharine Hepburn, Wallflower

Whenever there's a retrospective showing of Katharine Hepburn's films, I invariably find myself heading straight for *Alice Adams* again, telling myself the while that I really ought to be saving the time for *Quality Street*, a performance I scarcely remember. Why *Alice Adams*, as often as opportunity allows? Possibly because I think it the lady's own best work in films, possibly because I think it the best early film in which she appeared. Possibly. Certainly because it is the most enigmatic, devious, contrary, yet ultimately triumphant assertion of *self* that an extremely self-assertive woman has managed to arrive at in a long, busy, insistent career.

Consider what we're up against in coping with the film. There are two things wrong with it and, mysteriously, both are right. One of them wasn't necessarily wrong in the first place, it's just gone wrong since we got to know Hepburn better. This. In the adaptation of Booth Tarkington's novel, Miss Hepburn plays, as I suppose everyone knows, a lower-middle-class girl of better-than-that pretensions. Her pretensions, indeed, are horrendous because they are so palpably what they are: refinements fabricated out of whole cloth, airs and graces that never were appropriate on land or sea. She is pushy, she is willing to lie about her family's social standing, she is—to her knowing neighbors—the town joke, so much the town joke that when she goes to a local dance she is left entirely alone, a wallflower to wipe away the memory of all wallflowers before her. We see her standing there, pitifully trying to attract attention, utterly unattended.

And, looking at the sequence today, we don't believe a frame of it. The girl—no matter what else we may know about her—is so breathtakingly beautiful that the only conceivable next step is for a stag line to form instantly on her left, every male in the room fighting for position up front, and for her to dance, dance, dance all night. Are they idiots? we ask ourselves as we watch the local boys cut this ravishing creature dead.

Curiously, when *Alice Adams* was first released, in 1935, this preposterous inversion of all common sense seems to have bothered no one. The *New York Times* reviewer found the film at its most poignant during the sequence, speaking of Miss Hepburn as "an unwanted interloper whose pitiful finery is in sad contrast to the resplendent gowns of the other girls." Gowns! Do you realize that that man, instead of looking at Miss Hepburn, was looking at her *clothes*? And what young sporting blood, pray tell, ever danced with the best dress at a party?

Yet the scene held, no doubt for a reason. I suspect that audiences, even after Miss Hepburn had been three years in pictures and made seven earlier films, were able to evade her beauty, or in some way discount it, because they felt insecure with her, unsure of just who and what she was. I think they thought she might bite, and they were in fact afraid of her. I suspect that the fearless John Barrymore was afraid of her when he found himself overwhelmed by this gale of sound, this profile more undeflectable than his, in her first film, *A Bill of Divorcement*. Fortunately, he was playing a man mentally ill and so was able to account for his bafflement. Actually, he was fine in the role, and I'm joking in part; but only in part.

For Miss Hepburn came onto the screen as though she'd been spun from a UFO during a particularly powerful northeaster, an unfathomable force rather than a possible familiar. She didn't look like other people, she didn't talk like other people, and, what is more, she didn't care. Whoosh! Her self-confidence, verging on assault, wasn't based on anything very tangible at the time: a modest Broadway success, a lot of understudying. *She* was her self-confidence, and, given an open door, she simply charged through it, unstoppable, unassailable, not even bothering to lower her upper lip until she'd shot whole paragraphs past it. Declaration of independence.

So, when the scene in *Alice Adams* held, it held because she *told* it to, because the audience didn't dare not believe her. (Today we love her more, which means we are able to take a second, less cautious, look.) The other flaw in *Alice Adams* never was a flaw, though some counted it one at the time. The happy ending. Mr. Tarkington's novel had ended with her losing the young man she'd never really leveled with. Logical. If the film had ended that way, I think audiences would have torn RKO down, sound stage by sound stage. I confess I'd have helped. For the personality we'd been in thrall to, however imperious her behavior, *had* to be vulnerable somewhere. We couldn't see it, we just knew it. The more she grated on us the more we ached for what was hidden inside her. She had to have a man, for our sake, not for hers. She commanded the frames, we demanded the ending. The emotional line of the film led us to it; there would have been no complexity without.

Yet subsequently, as Miss Hepburn went on having both successes and failures, an uncertainty developed. If she was vulnerable, couldn't that be shown, possibly with tears? She tried that, crying a lot, in *Mary of Scotland*, and it didn't work. Belied the steel that was in her. But the steel, unrelieved, was becoming a problem, too: in *Holiday*, still beloved by many, critic Frank Nugent called her mannish and overly precise, concluding that her intensity was apt to be too much for "even so sanguinary a temperament as Cary Grant's." Her career shot up and down, erratically, and a group of less than prophetic exhibitors took out a trade-paper ad labeling her "box-office poison." The independence and the vulnerability still hadn't quite come into balance. The lady remained hard to *place*.

Also to lick. Off she went to New York, up she came with a big fat hit in Philip Barry's *The Philadelphia Story*, back to the coast to make a successful film of it. But, strangely, two more years would elapse before she had another film in release. Wouldn't even *hits* put her permanently on top?

The next one did, and the solution turned out to be simple. Cast with Spencer Tracy in *Woman of the Year* she found herself playing opposite a leading man even more independent than she. Eureka! 'Twas all that was needed. She could be as willful as she'd seemed to be from birth, he could knock her ears back when absolutely necessary, the twin strains in her temperament could surface together. Done and done.

Or so I read the securing of a career, after which all may not have been gravy but there's been caviar constantly on the table. No one has to place Miss Hepburn these days. She's the girl we didn't dance with, and don't we wish we had?

5

Window Candy

Anybody around here remember window candy?

Chances are you don't even know what it is, though a moment's reflection would probably clear everything up. I'm not at all certain that window candy was ever a purchasable commodity in very many places at any time, and I'm sure as sure can be that no one anywhere can lay hands on it now.

But it was once mountainously, deliciously, potluckily available. In my hometown at least. When my sister and I were very young and first trooping off to afternoons at the movies, we were always given a nickel apiece to buy whatever a nickel would buy in the way of incidental refreshment. This was of course common practice, and most thoughtless matinee-sports would simply go into Woolworth's and squander the precious coin on exactly five cents' worth of chocolate-covered peanuts, or whatever. Maybe a box of Cracker-Jack.

Not us. My sister and I had somehow or other hooked into the glucose underworld, we were among the furtive few in the know. Bypassing Woolworth's altogether, disdaining the handful of sourballs with which so many of our friends contented themselves, we headed straight for the finest homemade candy shop on the main stem, a confectionary curiously named The Ring-Ting. We had no intention of marching in the front door, past the glittering window display of multicolored bonbons and peppermints, not to mention the assorted chocolate creams. At the main counter our pitiful nickels would have bought us approximately three peppermints or one and one-half ounces of maple fudge.

But we did check the windows. Was the display a new one? Were the bonbons—then covered with a rich sugary icing, not the paraffin or perhaps plastic in use today—gleaming fresh? If the display looked particularly dazzling, indicating that the proprietors had laid out a new assortment within the past few days, we knew we were in clover, on the way to a feast.

And so around the corner, down the side block, into the alley, and up to the screen door that was unmistakably The Ring-Ting's back entry. Unmistakable because of the vanilla-drenched odors that drifted from the kitchens that were partitioned off from the salesroom, unmistakable—as we peered through holes in the screen door—because of the huge vats that bubbled with such promise on the stoves. (Homemade candies were actually made on the premises in those days, premises we'd have been happy to call home.)

We'd knock politely, a girl in something like a baker's smock would come pleasantly to the back door, we'd ask yearningly if they had any window candy today, she'd nod (heaven was near now), take our proffered nickels, and depart. A few minutes later she'd reappear with two enormous bags crammed to overflowing with nougats and penuche and caramels and chocolate creams in six or seven flavors, a treasure-trove that would hold us straight through the movie even if we saw the movie twice. Off we went, literally counting our blessings. I feel sorry for youngsters who've never had such a delightfully unwholesome experience.

What we now had in our proud possession, of course, was the stale candy that had been removed from last week's—or last month's—window display in order to make room for the new one. The peppermints, to be sure, were rather whitish around the edges instead of the solid pink or green they'd once been, and they'd hardened enough to satisfy a squirrel whose teeth needed sharpening. The chocolates, too, had paled, rather, and what had been creamy was chunky. I think only the peanut brittle had retained its original texture. What matter? You can't really see what you're eating in the dark, and we could lie to our dentists later. Volume was what counted, volume and a variety more infinite than Cleopatra's. (We didn't know anything about Cleopatra then, but we sure knew how to lick the system.)

In due time some busybodies—I think they were connected with the Board of Health—became aware of what was going on, and, pursuing their sworn duties as killjoys, put a stop to it all. A sad day, a very sad day; even the girl in the smock seemed to feel it as she shook her head ruefully and told us not to come down the alley anymore. I'm sure she hated having to throw all that splendid stuff into the trash can, which is no doubt what The Ring-Ting was at last required to do. I used to have nightmares about that, let me tell you. The waste!

I shouldn't be mourning joys that cannot be recovered—I suppose even the federal government finally got into the act, passing crazy pure food and drug laws that suppressed ecstasy throughout the nation—but the memory does come to mind every time I go to a movie nowadays and find myself shelling out eighty-five cents for an unprepossessing box of candy that's scarcely three-quarters full. (It's been explained to me that the box is full when it's packed but that the candies gradually settle down; I don't believe a word of it.) As one who has lived, I don't like coming to the end of my candy before we've got to the opening credits.

I see that I have inadvertently confessed something here. I still do buy candy when I go to the movies. Movies and candy go together. I'm not entirely sure why this is. Certainly I never think of picking up a slew of peppermints when I go to the theater, and that has nothing to do with my present ignoble function as a reviewer. I never did, not even when I was twelve. There were stock companies—as well as movies—in my hometown, and I can't remember ever taking such creature comforts along when I went to see the young—the very young—Ralph Bellamy play the Reverend Davidson in *Rain*. The situation just never called for it, that's all.

Perhaps we don't feel as free to munch in the theater for fear of disturbing the actors. (You can't disturb the actors in a movie, and you don't worry about disturbing the other patrons because most of them are munching right back; besides, the sound helps to drown out the conversation going on in the row behind you.) Perhaps movies are more agitating than the legitimate theater—all those exorcisms and towering infernos—and nervous people must keep their hands and teeth busy. Perhaps we mostly go to the movies in search of fun while we mostly go to the theater in search of truth, and truth doesn't respond well to the rustle of popcorn. I don't know.

I must speak only for myself. Plainly, one of us is retarded: me, or the movies. But then, you see, I have had this traumatic experience. For good or ill, in sickness or in health, I want my window candy back.

INDEX

A Note on the Type

The text of this book was set on the VIP in Century Schoolbook, a type face based on Century Expanded, which was designed in 1894 by Linn Boyd Benton (1844–1932). Benton cut Century Expanded in response to Theodore De Vinne's request for an attractive, easy-to-read type face to fit the narrow columns of his *Century Magazine*. Early in the nineteen hundreds Morris Fuller Benton updated and improved Century in several versions for his father's American Type Founders Company. Century remains the only American type face cut before 1910 still widely in use today.

Composed by Publishers Phototype Incorporated,
Carlstadt, New Jersey. Printed and bound by
The Haddon Craftsmen, Scranton, Pennsylvania.

Typography and binding design by Virginia Tan.